W9-CLC-943

Terror in Ireland

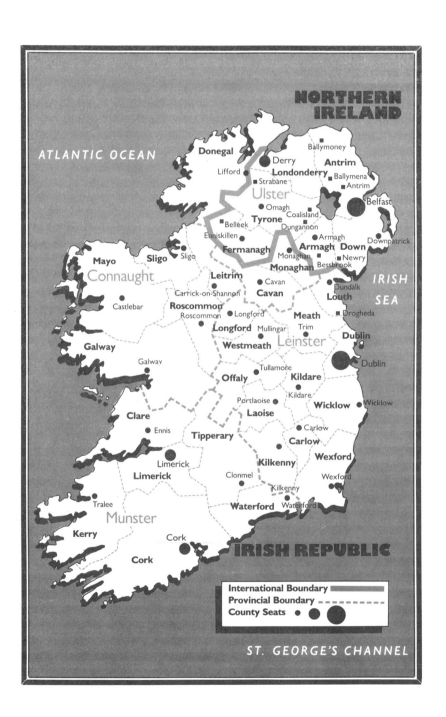

Terror in Ireland

The Heritage
of Hate

Edgar O'Ballance

PRESIDIO PRESS

Copyright © 1981 by Presidio Press

Published by Presidio Press,
31 Pamaron Way, Novato, CA 94947

Library of Congress Cataloging in Publication Data
O'Ballance, Edgar.
      Terror in Ireland.

      Bibliography: p. 277
      Includes index.
      1. Irish Republican Army--History.   2. Ireland--
History--20th century.   3. Northern Ireland--History.
4. Terrorism--Northern Ireland.   I. Title
DA959.012   941.5082   80-22049
ISBN 0-89141-100-3

Cover design by Jon Goodchild

Typeset by TypeCraft

Printed in the United States of America

Contents

Abbreviations

ASU	Active Service Unit (IRA)
BBC	British Broadcasting Corporation
CIGS	Chief of Imperial General Staff
Co	County, in Ireland
CO	Commanding Officer
CRA	Civil Rights Association
DUP	Democratic Unionist Party
EEC	European Economic Community
GOC	General Officer Commanding
IDF	Irish Defense Force (Eire)
INLA	Irish National Liberation Army
IRA	Irish Republican Army
IRB	Irish Republican Brotherhood
IRC	Irish Republican Clubs
IRSP	Irish Republican Socialist Party
MFR	Mobile Field Reconnaissance (unit) (British)
MP	Member of Parliament (Westminster or Stormont)
NAIF	National Assistance for Irish Freedom
NATO	North Atlantic Treaty Organization
NLF	National Liberation Front
Noraid	Irish Northern Aid Committee
OUP	Official Unionist Party
PD	People's Democracy
RAF	Royal Air Force (British)
RIC	Royal Irish Constabulary
RTE	Radio Telfis Eireann (Irish)
RUC	Royal Ulster Constabulary
SAS	Special Air Service Regiment (British)
SDLP	Social Democratic and Labor Party
UDA	Ulster Defense Association
UDI	Unilateral Declaration of Independence
UDR	Ulster Defense Regiment
UFF	Ulster Freedom Fighters
UN	United Nations
USC	Ulster Special Constabulary

UUAC	Ulster Unionist Action Council
UUUC	Ulster United Unionist Coalition
UVF	Ulster Volunteer Force
UWC	Ulster Workers Council
VUPP	Vanguard Unionist Progressive Party

1 The Heritage of Hate

"Hell or Connaught"
—Oliver Cromwell's depopulation policy in Ireland

THE 32,000-SQUARE-MILE island lying off Britain on the edge of the Atlantic Ocean, now known as Ireland, has a dark and painful history. About the year BC 200—some historians say two or three centuries earlier—the Celts began to arrive in Ireland, then known as Ierne, from Western Europe. Typified by dark hair and blue eyes, they were also known as Milesians, after Milesius, a legendary king of Spain, whose sons are traditionally said to have seized Ireland. Legend has it that the race came from Scythia, by way of Spain, to establish a kingdom at Tara.

The Celts established a pagan civilization of petty kingdoms, which seemed to be forever at war or in dispute with each other, cattle raiding being a primary source of contention. The elected kings were drawn from certain dominant families, and so a class of Irish royalty, or nobility, developed by intermarriage between ruling houses. As kings were frequently killed in battle or overthrown and replaced by others, this gives some substance to the claim of all Irishmen that they are descended from kings.

Christianity, according to tradition, was brought to Ireland by St. Patrick, but small groups of Christians were probably already living there before he started to proselytize. They would have been refugees from Britain who fled when the Romans withdrew their legions from England in AD 410. It seems there were, by AD 431, sufficient Christians in Ireland for the pope in Rome to appoint a bishop, called Palladius. Actually, however, it took about two hundred years to convert the Irish people completely, but it was a peaceful conversion that did not throw up any martyrs.

There were no towns in Ireland, and where monasteries sprang up, settlements formed adjacent to them. A monastic, rather than diocesan, hierarchy developed. Irish monks and priests were held in high regard in the British Isles as well as in Western Europe in those dark days of Christianity. Irish monks traveled as missionaries, seeking the "White Martyrdom" as far afield as Iceland, and were welcomed at the courts of King Alfred of Wessex and the Emperor Charlemagne.

To this Christian Irish country of many kingdoms, monasteries, and churches, towards the end of the eighth century, came the pagan Norsemen mainly Norwegians and Danes the Vikings, at first to raid and plunder. Later the Danes returned as traders and then as settlers. In 840 they founded the city of Dublin; many of the other Irish ports developed round natural harbors or inlets, such as Belfast, Cork, Derry, and Drogheda, were originally Danish settlements. The Danes were in continual conflict with the Irish kings, who were unable to eject them because they were too divided among themselves. However, many tales are told of how the Fianna, a famous band of Irish warriors, fought against the Norsemen.

After establishing himself as the High King of Ireland by gaining the allegiance of the provincial kings through war, marriage, and other means, Brian Boru raised an army that defeated the Danes in 1014 at the Battle of Clontarf. This broke the political power of the Danes, and their importance in Ireland declined.

A century and more later, in 1155, Pope Adrian IV (Nicholas Breakspear, the only Englishman to occupy the Throne of St. Peter in Rome) issued a papal bull decreeing the English monarch, Henry II, to be King of Ireland. The following year, Dermot MacMurrough, King of Leinster, was defeated in battle and driven from the country by Ruaidhari O'Connor, the High King. Dermot fled to England, where, invoking Pope Adrian's bull, he made his allegiance to Henry II in return for a promise of help to regain his throne. King Henry encouraged some of his Norman knights, then probably the best fighting men in the world, to go to Ireland.

The first was Robert Fitzstephen, whose three ships landed near Wexford in 1169, with "30 knights, 60 men-at-arms, and 300 archers," the latter being mainly Welshmen. He was joined the following day by Maurice de Prendergast, who had ten knights and some archers. Together, the two Norman leaders, their followers, and some hundred adherents of King Dermot advanced and took the town of Wexford, held by Norsemen. Other Norman knights followed, and their leader came to be the Earl of Pembroke, Richard de Clare, known as "Strongbow." As well as helping King Dermot regain his throne, the Normans began to seize land and carve out baronies for themselves. The High King of Ireland was unable to persuade his kings to unite to drive out the Norman invaders; and soon his petty kings, or chieftains, as they became known, were entering into alliances with the Normans for their own devious purposes.

Strongbow married a daughter of King Dermot and assumed the additional title of Earl of Leinster. As other Norman nobility intermarried with the Irish ruling families, a Norman-Irish aristocracy developed. In the spring of 1171, Strongbow, at the head of 200 knights and about 1,000 men-at-arms, with King Dermot and his armed followers, appeared before the city of Dublin and seized it. The Normans remained in Dublin, successfully defeating every Danish attempt to retake it.

Suddenly suspicious and jealous of the rise of a new, powerful, and independent baronage developing in Ireland, King Henry II visited that country in 1171–72, intending to bring them to heel. He arrived in October at Dublin with a fleet of ships and 4,000 soldiers. He gave that city a charter of incorporation and arranged for it to be colonized by men from Bristol, England. The Normans in Ireland had to pay homage to Henry. The Irish kings were invited to do the same, but very few did so: Henry's writ, or rather that of his Norman subjects, was distinctly limited in its reach. King Henry also tried to curb the independence of the Irish Church, but was less successful.

Ulster and the remoter parts of western Ireland were still free of Normans. In 1171 John de Courcy set out from the Dublin garrison with a small band of Norman warriors and marched northward into the Kingdom of Ulster, then consisting of the present counties of Antrim, Armagh, and Down. De Courcy defeated King Dunleavy and assumed the title of Earl of Ulster.

In 1210 King John of England took an army to Ireland to put down a rebellion, and he established his authority in areas under Norman control. Successive English monarchs generally paid little attention to Ireland, allowing the areas under Anglo-Norman control to be nominally governed by a viceroy in Dublin.

During the 14th century, Ireland was divided into three political regions. The first was that of the coastal towns and the areas around them, such as the "Pale" around Dublin, held by the Anglo-Normans and governed by the viceroy in Dublin. The second was the region held by the independent barons, while the third was the wilder, more remote and less fertile parts of the country, where the native Irish lived under chieftains. The independent barons resisted dominance by the viceroy in Dublin, while the Irish chieftains resented the unpopular feudal law that the Normans attempted to impose on them.

Irish factions still fought against each other, and in Ulster especially were the O'Neills and the O'Donnells at each other's throats. However, the tendency of the Normans to merge with the native Irish and to "become more Irish than the Irish themselves" was as appealing then as it is now, and this worried the English monarchs. In those days English parliaments were convened wherever the king decided was the most appropriate and were usually for a specific objective. In 1336 one was summoned at Kilkenny by the Duke of Clarence, son of Edward III, to enact the Statute of Kilkenny. This act forbade the English settlers to use the Irish language, adopt Irish names, or wear Irish apparel, and decreed that marriage of an English settler with an Irish woman was high treason. Men of Irish blood were forbidden to live or to speak Irish within walled towns.

Despite this statute, the old Anglo-Norman colony in Ireland had practically disappeared by the end of the 14th century, having been absorbed into the Irish nation mainly by intermarriage. Its place was taken by the Dublin-oriented English community, England by this time having developed into a strong, viable state. In 1395 Richard II of England went to Ireland and at Drogheda received the submission of the O'Neills, the O'Donnells, and other princes of Ulster and Leinster.

The first English monarch to declare himself King of Ireland was a Tudor, Henry VIII (reigned 1508–47), who began to devise ways of asserting his authority and breaking the power of the Irish aristocracy and chieftains. The Reformation in England and the breaking away of the English Church from the authority of Rome caused many in Ireland to feel that King Henry had forfeited his right to the realm he claimed under the papal bull of Pope Adrian IV. The English Reformation affected only the English ruling class in Ireland and did not touch the large majority Catholic population.

It was Henry VIII's daughter, Queen Elizabeth I (reigned 1588–1603), who first imposed English rule over the whole of Ireland. At war with Spain, she feared that Catholic Ireland might form a willing stepping-stone for a Catholic Spain from which to invade England. She was somewhat justified since a number of Anglo-Irish barons who had remained Catholic and some Irish chieftains were certainly involved in intrigue with the Spanish. The Earl of Essex, then one of the Queen's favorites, was sent with an army to conquer and colonize the country. Thus began four centuries of despoilation, oppression, and mass displacement of the Irish people by the English that formed the heritage of hate which still causes emotional resentment in even usually calm and moderate Irishmen everywhere today. Ireland also became the battleground for struggles for the Crown of England. Irishmen were ruthlessly recruited when required, trampled underfoot when in the way, and deported, or worse, when no longer wanted.

After the English Reformation there was a great feeling of animosity by the Protestant English against Roman Catholics and the non-Conformist sects. The colonization policy put into practice in Queen

Mary's reign (1516–58) involved displacing native Irish from their land and giving it to English or Scottish settlers. In an attempt to save the land for their people, a number of Irish chieftains in Connaught decided in 1585 to swear allegiance to the English Crown and to adopt feudal law. This meant the chieftains assumed personal ownership of the land under the tenant system, which was completely alien to the Irish communal ownership tradition (established according to Brehon Law).

In 1597 the two principal northern chieftains, Red Hugh O'Neill, Earl of Tirowen, and Hugh Roy O'Donnell, Earl of Tirconnel, rose in revolt. They mustered their kerns,* galloglasses, and followers and won initial victories over Essex's army. This encouraged other Irish chieftains also to rise in revolt, and insurrection quickly spread across Ulster, Connaught, and Leinster. In 1603 a small Spanish force landed at Kinsale, on the southern Irish coast, and the viceroy, Lord Mountjoy, marched southward with 12,000 soldiers to besiege it. The two Irish earls mustered their armies and moved to join the Spaniards, but Mountjoy defeated the combined Irish-Spanish force. Hugh Roy O'Donnell fled to Spain, and his brother Rory became Earl of Tirconnel on swearing allegiance to the English crown. Red Hugh O'Neill, who was wounded at the Battle of Kinsale, surrendered and was pardoned upon assuring the Crown of his future fealty. The Tudor conquest of Ireland was complete, and Queen Elizabeth posted English garrisons across the length and breadth of the country, enforced unpopular English law, and made Protestantism the state religion. Land was taken from the rebels and given to English soldiers and others.

The two Irish earls remained in Ireland, intriguing and plotting against King James I (reigned 1603–25). Suddenly, in 1607, they both left the country and never returned. The Irish were left leaderless. They were the last of the old native Irish aristocracy, and with their departure hopes of successful and continued resistance against English rule evaporated. This abrupt, unexpected, and unexplained action is known as the Flight of the Earls: one of the intriguing mysteries of history that perhaps one day may be solved.

If the 16th century had been a bad one for the native Irish, the 17th was to be even more disastrous. It brought confiscation of land, displacement of people, and mass deportation. It was the century of the heritage of hate, associated so vividly with Oliver Cromwell. As Ireland was progressively conquered, the policy of gradually dispossessing the native

---

*Being men-at-arms with pikes, swords, and battle-axes. Galloglasses (from the Gaelic *galloglach* meaning "foreign youth") were armed foot-soldiers.

Irish and giving their land to English and Scottish settlers was implemented. For example, in Ulster large sections of Co Antrim had been given over to the Scots, who were Catholic and spoke Gaelic; but they were later joined and overwhelmed by infusions of Protestant English settlers and Lowland Scots, who brought with them the traditions and beliefs of Calvin and Knox.

After the Flight of the Earls, the lands of the O'Neills and the O'Donnells were confiscated and given over to English Protestant gentry to be let out to tenants. The Irish inhabitants were to be expelled. This became known as the Ulster Plantation, which seriously began in 1610 with huge influxes of Scottish immigrants, all hungry for land. Previous invaders of Ireland had been aristocrats, or aspiring aristocrats, who wanted only to rule; but these new arrivals had come to work. They built towns, churches and schools: they had come to stay. Some sections of the land were granted to English cities or English merchant companies to be settled with English immigrants. The city and environs of Derry, for example, were granted to the city of London—hence the Protestant title of "Londonderry." Most of the native Irish were evicted from Ulster, but a few were allowed to remain as their labor was needed by the new tenant-farmers. Also, rather than leave the holdings vacant, a few were allowed to stay on as tenant-farmers.

The English Protestant rulers and landowners in Ireland acted in a particularly repressive manner against the Catholic religion, which they regarded as a subversive element in the land; they especially persecuted the priests. This led to the formation in 1641 of an organization known as the Defenders, led by Rory O'Moore, to protect and help fugitive priests. It provided them with an underground route to safety, usually to France, safe hideouts, and "priest-holes." The organization sent candidates to French seminaries to train for the priesthood (this being banned in Ireland), and assisted generally in keeping the Catholic religion alive.

Needless to say, the confiscation of land and displacement of people in Ulster bred seething resentment. In 1641 the Ulster Irish chieftains, led by Sir Phelim O'Neill, took advantage of the rising friction between Charles I, the Catholic King of England (reigned 1625–49), and his parliament, and rose in rebellion. A well coordinated campaign was launched against the English garrisons, and the colonists and many exiled Irishmen returned home to join in the fight.

So well did this Irish rebellion go that by May of the following year Irish leaders were able to convene their own parliament at Kilkenny. A Supreme Council was chosen, and an Irish state, known as the Irish Catholic Confederacy, was proclaimed, which still recognized Charles I as King of Ireland. The Irish Catholic Confederate Parliament raised taxes, issued its own coinage, and manufactured weapons and powder. An Irish army was organized on a provincial basis. In 1645 the Papal Nuncio arrived at Kilkenny, bringing arms for 6,000 men and £20,000, a huge sum of money for those days. The Irish Catholic Confederacy eventually dissolved in 1649, owing to both internal and external pressures and to the appearance of Oliver Cromwell on the scene.

Meanwhile, the civil war that had broken out in England between Charles I and his parliament spilled over into Ireland. King Charles wanted to be able to withdraw his troops from Ireland to fight in England for him, but Ireland was in a state of open rebellion; so he invited the Irish leaders to meet him in Oxford in October 1642. Unwilling to grant all the Irish demands, the king was unable to come to an agreement with them. However, they all seem to have parted on reasonably good terms, as the Irish Catholic Confederacy took to the battlefield in Ireland against parliamentary troops sent over to fight against the king.

King Charles lost out to the Parliamentarians and was executed in London in January 1649. The Puritan Ironsides and Parliamentarians were bent on vengeance against the rebellious Catholics in Ireland. Oliver Cromwell, who had formed and led the victorious New Model Army, landed in Ireland in August as lord lieutenant and commander in chief. Having the utmost contempt for the Irish race and a deep hatred of Catholics, he set about ruthlessly crushing the Irish people. He captured Drogheda on 10 September, where he massacred the defending garrison and many of the inhabitants, including women and children: over 3,500 fell to his sword. The few who escaped death at his hands were deported to the English colonies in the West Indies, mainly Barbados. Cromwell then moved on to seize Wexford, where he again slaughtered most of the garrison and deported hundreds of the townspeople and refugees in the town. He was determined to capture and execute all Irishmen who had been in any way involved in the Rebellion that had begun in 1641.

An ardent Puritan, Cromwell rigorously sought out the Catholic clergy and executed many priests. The Catholic religion was banned; the bishops were deported so that no more priests would be ordained. A special concentration camp was set up for Catholic priests on the barren island of Inishbofin, off Galway, where they were detained in squalid and inhospitable conditions until the restoration of the monarchy in England in 1660. In May 1650 Cromwell returned to England to become its lord protector, virtually a military dictator. He left his task of punishing the Irish people to his generals, one of whom was his younger son, Henry.

Ireland by now had suffered a decade of misery, famine, pestilence, and devastating warfare. London merchants who had advanced money to finance parliamentary campaigns in Ireland now wanted their pound of flesh in the form of land. Cromwell's generals obliged them by literally depopulating a greater part of the country and forcibly banishing the native Irish to Connaught and Co Clare on the west coast. The penalty for refusing to move was death, as it was for any bold or desperate enough to return. The expression "Hell or Connaught" is one that has remained on the lips of the Irish even until today to describe limited alternatives to a desperate situation.

Demobilized English officers and soldiers also demanded and were given their share of land. By the mid-1650s four-fifths of Ireland had been given over to English landlords; much of this was parceled out to English tenants, some of whom sublet again. Known as the Cromwellian Settlement of 1652–60, this was the genesis of the huge estates of the Anglo-Irish landed nobility and gentry of the 18th and 19th centuries; these classes came to be known as the Ascendancy. With all the best land taken, the native Irish were left with marginal farmland, bog, and bracken, which allowed them only a bare subsistence living, with potatoes as their main food staple. Ireland had no industries and few towns, and the sublettings had become too small to employ outside labor. Cromwell had reduced a potential warrior race to a beaten, submissive one.

On the restoration of the monarchy in England in 1660, these Cromwellian land confiscations were confirmed; very few dispossessed Irish landowners ever regained their property and holdings. Gradually the banished people trickled back from Connaught and Co Clare, but only to poverty, many being reduced to beggary. The Cromwellian Settlement accounts for the English surnames so common in Ireland. The English settlers soon become absorbed into the Irish nation, and their own national identity disappeared within a couple of generations. The most common name in Ireland today is not O'Brien or O'Connor, but Smith.

In 1641 the estimated population of Ireland was quoted as being 1,448,000; during the decade from 23 October 1641 to 22 October 1652 the same authority estimated that 504,000 Irish people were killed or had perished (as well as 112,000 English soldiers and colonists).* This meant that about one-third of the Irish nation had been wiped out. Another 100,000 Irish were transported to the British West Indies colonies, and some 40,000 Irish soldiers sought service in foreign armies. The settlers in

---

*John Petty, one of Cromwell's surveyors in Ireland, who published some of his writings in the 17th century.

Ulster were spared the worst excesses of Cromwell's generals, perhaps because of their non-Conformist beliefs.

After the Restoration a feeble spark of resistance and protest was kept alive by the roaming bands of Tories and Raparees who, although little more than scavenging groups of robbers, sallied forth from their sanctuaries in the hills and bogs to strike against the English garrisons that dotted the country and to pillage English settlers. Tory was the anglicized Gaelic word *toraidhe,* meaning "pursuer," and *raparee* meant "pillager." Tory was later adopted as a sobriquet by the British Conservative Party.

In England the "Glorious Revolution" of 1688 displaced King James II, the last British Catholic monarch; his son-in-law, the Dutch Protestant Prince William of Orange, with his consort, Mary, was crowned in his place. King James fled to Ireland, where he was accepted as King of Ireland; but when he claimed authority over the whole of the country, the Protestants and non-Conformists in Ulster, in the key towns of Derry and Enniskillen, rose in revolt against him, in support of King William. The Irish Catholics gave their support to King James.

In May 1689 the Protestant garrison in the walled city of Derry was suddenly besieged by an Irish army. Governor Lundy was on the point of surrendering when thirteen apprentice boys rushed forward and shut the main gates. Then followed a siege that lasted 105 days, in which the defenders rallied to the motto of "No Surrender" as they repulsed all attacks. Lundy was replaced by Governor Walker, under whom the garrison held out successfully. The siege was a severe one: the Irish had constructed a boom across the mouth of the River Foyle, on which Derry stood, which prevented ships bringing in supplies. On 1 August 1689 one of King William's ships broke through the boom, and the town was relieved and saved. Even today, "Lundyism" is one of the most devastating insults one Orange Protestant can hurl at another.

The prolonged siege of Derry had given King William time to bring troops to Ireland; eventually, on 1 July 1690, the opposing Catholic and Protestant armies faced each other across the River Boyne, in Co Meath. At first the Catholic army seemed to be winning, but James II panicked suddenly and fled the field, leaving King William as the victor. The next battle was at Aughrim, Co Galway, the following year; the Protestant army of about 18,000 men advanced from Athlone to attack and defeat the Jacobite Catholic army, which was over 25,000 strong.

Under the command of Patrick Sarsfield, the Irish armies fell back on Limerick, where they were invested by those of King William. The general commanding the French contingent on King James' side thought the defenses were too weak and the site unsuitable for a successful battle, so he withdrew to Galway. The siege of Limerick had actually begun in August 1690 but had been abandoned, to be recommenced in the spring of 1691. After a six weeks' siege, Sarsfield surrendered. He led his 10,000 Irish soldiers out of the city to embark for France. The surrender of Limerick in 1691 was the first movement in what became known as the Flight of the Wild Geese—that is, of exiled Irish soldiers who died abroad. The legend arises from the flocks of wild geese homing in from the sea to land on the rugged west coast of Ireland in the evening. Their melancholic honking is said to be the murmuring of uneasy souls of dead Irish soldier exiles on their way back to their native land.

In 1692 and 1693 severe penal laws that discriminated against Irish Catholics were passed in Ireland, now under firm Protestant control. Irish Catholics could not own property worth more than £5, carry a firearm, vote in elections, hold public office, or be educated. They were granted only short-term leases on land, which in practice came to mean frequent evictions. By this time the use of the Irish language had disappeared from the major part of the country, lingering only in Connaught and a few other remote western havens. Irish Catholics now owned only one-seventh of the land, and the poorer parts at that.

The failure of the English Reformation to extend to Ireland was the root of much of the trouble in the ensuing Anglo-Irish differences, mainly because the Irish Catholic Church sympathized with and became involved in Irish struggles for political rights. By the Act of Toleration, religion and politics were separated in England, at least in theory, but in Ireland they remained intertwined.

The 18th century was a sad one of emigration, not only of Irish Catholics but also of immigrant non-Conformists, mainly Presbyterians, who had become disillusioned and were being discriminated against by the ruling Protestants. They fled from Ireland to the New World. In Ulster keen competition for the limited number of farm tenancies caused the non-Conformist settlers to turn to trade and manufacturing. Although they were handicapped by restrictions—Irish industry was not allowed to compete with that of England—they did develop a flourishing linen industry. Between 1700 and 1730 over 200,000 non-Conformists left Ulster for America; by the time the United States' Declaration of Independence was signed in 1776, America had half a million settlers of Ulster Presbyterian stock, which since claims to have produced ten U.S. presidents.

During the American War of Independence, Britain became anxious about the hostile attitude of the Spanish and French, who were openly aiding the American colonists. The British feared Spanish or French troops might be landed in Ireland; and so, as British soldiers were desperately needed on other battlefields and had to be withdrawn, authority was given for the formation of the Volunteer Force for the home defense of Ireland. This Volunteer Force eventually reached a strength of over 80,000, but of this number about ninety percent were Protestants, and the other ten percent non-Conformists: Irish Catholics were still not allowed to carry arms. This Protestant Volunteer Force gained immense political influence and in 1782 compelled the British government to establish in Dublin an Irish parliament with a good measure of legislative power.

By the mid-18th century many of the huge landed estates, owned for the most part by absentee Protestant landlords, were left in the hands of land agents whose task was to squeeze as much money from them as possible for their masters. Nonpayment of almost impossibly high rents resulted in frequent evictions. The next stratagem of the rapacious land agents was to enclose common land that had by custom been available for the Irish peasants to graze their livestock and to dig for peat, or turf as it was colloquially known, which was dried for domestic fuel.

Beginning in 1761 groups of men met secretly at night to level the fences and ditches with which the land agents had enclosed common land. They became known as the Levellers; unlike the Tories and Raparees, who had always been on the run and who had all disappeared by this time, they were part of the community, carrying out their normal occupations by day. The idea quickly caught on, and soon other similar groups sprang up across the country. One was known as the Whiteboys because they wore white shirts so they could instantly recognize each other at night. Another group was the Rightboys, after the nickname of their leader, "Captain Right." These midnight raiding groups bound themselves together by oaths of secrecy. Similar secret combinations had been briefly active during the famines of 1741 and 1756 to prevent the removal of grain from Ireland for sale in England.

To the grievances of land enclosure and unreasonable rents was added the imposition of a tithe that had to be paid to the Protestant Church of Ireland. The Levellers and the other similar groups took to harassing the land agents by ruining crops, setting fire to barns and stacks, releasing livestock, and damaging the landlords' farm buildings. Occasionally kangaroo justice was meted out to certain land agents accused of particularly harsh or cruel conduct. The authorities regarded these nocturnal activities as popish-inspired and directed against the Protestant Ascendancy, which in turn used the military to take punitive action whenever possible.

Many of the large estates in Ulster also were owned by absentee Protestant landlords, and they too were subjected to their share of attention from

Leveller groups with such names as the Steelboys and the Oakboys. The only difference was that these groups were organized on a strictly sectarian basis. Toward the end of the 18th century, as Catholic and Protestant tenants were forced to compete against each other in a cutthroat manner, friction rose almost to the point of civil war; so instead of harassing the land agents, they began to harass each other. About 1785 the Protestants raised a nocturnal group called the Peep o'Day Boys, so called because they always attacked at dawn, on the initial pretense of searching for arms before burning down property. For their own protection and in retaliation, the Ulster Catholics raised a secret organization known as the Defenders to carry out reprisals. The Defenders spread quickly to many parts of Ireland.

On 21 September 1796 over twenty people were killed in a skirmish between the Peep o'Day Boys and the Defenders near Loughgall, Co Armagh. This gave birth to the Orange Order, a defensive organization to protect Protestants and their property from the Defenders. At first only Protestants were recruited into this secret society based on Biblical ritual similar to that in Free Masonry. The Orange Order pledged loyalty to the memory of King William III of Orange and to the primacy of the Protestant religion. Orange lodges quickly came into being in Ulster, and the following year some of them formed their own armed bands. The Orange Order decided to celebrate annually the apprentice boys' shutting the gates at Derry and the Battle of the Boyne by holding public ceremonial marches in the month of July. The first of these Orange Marches was held in 1797.

An Irish parliament sat in Dublin, but a desire for greater political power began to be felt by the Protestant Ascendancy, which wanted certain reform measures and perhaps also autonomy from Britain. The Protestant Volunteer Force, which had become far too independent and influential for the liking of the British government, had been replaced by a more complacent militia. In October 1791 Theobald Wolfe Tone, a Protestant Dublin lawyer, helped to found the Society of United Irishmen in Belfast. Originally it was a middle-class debating society, most of whose members had served in the now-disbanded Volunteer Force. At first all the members were Protestants, but later Catholics were admitted. One of the more prominent members, who had formed the Dublin branch of the United Irishmen, was Napper Tandy, now remembered in song.* Tandy had taken the Defenders' oath, was later betrayed, and fled abroad, first to America and then to France.

*"Oh I met with Napper Tandy and he shook me by the hand,
And he says how's poor oul' Ireland and how does she stand?
'Tis the most distressful country that ever yet was seen,
For they're hanging men and women for the wearing of the Green."

A split occurred in the ranks of the United Irishmen over policy. One faction wanted to use constitutional means to gain independence for Ireland, while the other faction, led by Wolfe Tone, insisted that revolutionary action was the only way to accomplish this aim. The United Irishmen were suppressed by the authorities in 1794 and went underground. A network of secret revolutionary cells developed, which alarmed the authorities governing Ireland from Dublin Castle. Informers were infiltrated into the ranks of the United Irishmen. Accused of treason in 1795, Wolfe Tone fled Ireland, first to America and then to France to seek military help. Britain and France had been at war with each other since 1793.

The United Irishmen organized a rebellion in 1798. Wolfe Tone, who had been given the rank of general by the French, embarked for Ireland but was captured, taken to Dublin, tried for treason, and sentenced to be executed. He committed suicide in his cell by cutting his throat on 19 November 1798. He is now revered by the Irish as their first revolutionary martyr, and there is an official annual pilgrimage to his grave in the Protestant Bodenstown churchyard at Clane, Co Kildare.

A small French force of about 1,000 troops did manage to land at Killala, Co Mayo, only to be defeated by British forces. The rebellion raised by the United Irishmen was initially successful but badly coordinated, and so was easily suppressed. The only major sectarian clash occurred in Wexford, where there was an uprising in which Protestant insurgents held the town for about a month. The main incident was the massacre at Wexford Bridge, where about one hundred Catholic citizens were piked—that is, killed by a pikeman—and their bodies thrown into the River Slaney. The leadership of the rebellion of 1798 had a distinctly Protestant character, and armed units of several Orange lodges took part, as did many Presbyterians, despite condemnation of it by their Ulster Presbyterian Synod. After the rebellion had been put down, over a score of Presbyterian ministers were either executed or deported. There was one pathetic sequel: the United Irishmen Robert Emmet returned to Ireland from France in 1803 and unsuccessfully tried to seize Dublin Castle to kidnap the viceroy. Emmet escaped, but was soon arrested and executed.

The Orange Order for a time after 1798 expanded rapidly to Dublin, into other parts of Ireland, and into England. It began to recruit non-Conformists and became violently anti-Catholic in character. The Protestant landowners and certain elements of the Ascendancy, which had given the Order a measure of initial support, were horrified by its conduct and exploits and withdrew from it. The Orange Order gradually fell into disrepute.

After the abortive rebellion of 1798, the British prime minister forced through the union of Ireland with England and Scotland by an act passed in 1801. The cross of St. Patrick was added to those of St. George and St. Andrew on the national flag, known officially as the Union Flag, but less formally as the Union Jack. The union was achieved by liberal bribery of land, titles, and money. The Irish parliament in Dublin was dissolved, and about one hundred Irish members of parliament were elected to sit in the British parliament at Westminster, London. A viceroy, who had to be a Protestant, was appointed to Dublin, and the country was virtually ruled from Whitehall in London, with directives carried out by senior civil servants in Dublin. The Act of Union was extremely unpopular in Ireland; only the Ulster Protestants and non-Conformists welcomed it.

In 1823 Daniel O'Connell, a Dublin Catholic politician who became known as the "Liberator" for his work in getting the penal laws against Catholics repealed, founded the Catholic Association, its object being to work for complete Catholic emancipation. The Catholic Association was proscribed in 1825. In 1828 O'Connell was elected to Westminster* but, being a Catholic, was debarred from taking his seat. He worked successfully by constitutional means, and when the last of the penal laws was repealed in 1835, he was able to take his seat in the British parliament, where he campaigned against the Act of Union. O'Connell was consistently opposed by Protestants, who saw their unique and dominant position being threatened and undermined by Catholics.

The next Irish revolutionary organization of note was the Young Ireland movement, founded in 1842, led by John Mitchell, and regarded by many as being the first Irish nationalist movement in the modern sense. Activist in character, it frequently clashed with Daniel O'Connell, who was a gradualist.

The next major disaster to befall Ireland was the Great Famine. During the Napoleonic wars, British governments had needed extra grain and encouraged the growing of it in Ireland, where it became an attractive cash crop to the landowners who grew it in quantity. As the grain was all exported to England to be sold at a huge profit, it did not benefit the Irish tenants, who were still forced to rely upon potatoes for their staple. Owing to potato blight in 1845, there was a partial crop failure that caused hunger and hardship amongst the Irish peasantry. Worse was to come the following year when there was a complete failure of the whole potato crop: the Irish peasants had nothing to eat. In 1847 there was a partial crop failure, and then in 1848 yet another complete failure.

---

*"Westminster" will be used throughout to denote the British parliament that sits at Westminster Palace, London.

The 1840s were hungry years in England too, and British prime ministers did not dare stop the import of grain from Ireland and release it to feed the starving Irish people, which would have done much to ameliorate their dreadful plight. Ulster was slightly less badly affected than the rest of the country by the potato blight: under tenants' rights agreements, the farmers had longer leases, protection against eviction as long as they paid the rent, and compensation when they left for any improvements made to the land; so they had some encouragement to improve their land. Short leases elsewhere in Ireland did not make for good husbandry.

In the Great Famine of Ireland over one million people died of starvation—some authorities insist it was two million—out of a population of about eight million. At least another two million were forced to emigrate, mostly to America, although numbers went to Canada, Australia, and other countries overseas. There was also a large-scale, but now much less publicized, Irish emigration into England, where thousands of men went to work as laborers. Most expanding English industrial cities in the 19th century had their adjacent "Irish towns." In short, in the Great Famine the population of Ireland was reduced by half. It was a disaster on the scale of the Black Death in England of 1348–49, which also reduced by half the population of that country, then estimated to be some six million.

Another result of the Famine was a large influx of people fleeing to the expanding city and port of Belfast in Ulster. Mostly Catholics settled in, or squatted, on the west side of the city, in what is now the Falls Road area, adjacent to what is now the Shankill district, where non-Conformist factory workers were huddled. This geographical proximity of antagonistic Catholic and non-Conformist communities competing bitterly with each other for a sparse living set the scene for sectarian riots, clashes, and disturbances that have continued spasmodically until this day.

2 Revolution and Failure

"We did it to make history."
> —The Invincibles who committed the Phoenix Park murders in 1882

THE IRISH REVOLUTIONARY spirit survived the Great Famine and the unsuccessful 1848 Rebellion. On St. Patrick's Day, 17 March 1858, the Irish Revolutionary Brotherhood was formed in Dublin. Later it changed its name to the Irish Republican Brotherhood (IRB). A secret society, it expanded rapidly and in March 1861 set up a front organization, the Brotherhood of St. Patrick, to advocate its nationalist views openly. Suspecting and disliking all secret societies, the Irish Catholic Church denounced both the IRB and the Brotherhood of St. Patrick. The IRB spread into the Irish communities in England and achieved its maximum strength of about 80,000 by 1864.

A "rising" was planned for 1865 but did not materialize; despite its numerical strength, the IRB had hardly any arms, lacked military expertise, and was riddled with police informers. The date of the rising was advanced to 1867, and more support was expected from the Irish in America.

By 1860 there were over 1.6 million people of Irish birth in the U.S., a figure that was increasing annually by 60,000 or more new immigrants from Ireland. Politically motivated groups were organized, often with the object of freeing Ireland from British rule. In New York, where there was a major concentration of Irish Americans, the Irish American Union appeared. In 1858 a New York branch of the Dublin-based Irish Republican Brotherhood was formed; it became known as the Fenian Brotherhood. Many of the Young Ireland members who had escaped from Ireland after the 1848 Rebellion joined. After the American Civil War, in which it is said that about twenty-five percent of the officers and soldiers on both sides were Irish, many Irish officers joined the Fenian Brotherhood, and their thoughts turned toward freeing Ireland by military means.

In 1866 one such Galway-born U.S. Civil War veteran, Col. Thomas

J. Kelly, became leader of the Brotherhood and managed to displace John Stephens, leader of the Dublin-based IRB. Colonel Kelly then assumed the direction of both organizations since the IRB was financed by the Irish Americans anyway. He planned the rising in Ireland to take place in 1867, in conjunction with a supporting terrorist campaign in England. In January that year Kelly landed in England and proclaimed a Provisional Irish Government (which he failed to persuade the U.S. government to recognize).

The Fenians began a campaign of bombing in England which caused damage and some loss of life. In one exploit a barrel of gunpowder was exploded outside the prison at Clerkenwell, London, to release two Fenian prisoners. It killed twelve people and injured over 120. There were also madcap schemes, one of which was to raid Chester Castle, a British military garrison, seize the arms, hijack a train, load the arms on to it, hijack the cross-channel Irish mail boat, and run the arms into Dublin. British authorities were alerted by informers in time to thwart this adventure.

Colonel Kelly's original date for his rising, 11 February 1867, passed without any action by the IRB in Ireland, which was by no means ready for rebellion. A new date, the night of 4–5 March, was then set. Poorly armed, ill coordinated, and badly led, Fenian groups rose in several places in Ireland, but in all instances the military and police had been forewarned of their actions by informers. Arrests and treason trials followed.

In September 1867 Colonel Kelly was arrested in England but was dramatically rescued in Manchester by three of his Fenians. In the process a policeman was killed. The three rescuers, Michael Larkin, William Allen, and Michael O'Brien, were captured, brought to trial, and despite their American nationality, were executed, gaining Irish revolutionary fame as the Manchester Martyrs.

In America the fate of the Fenian Brotherhood was no better than that of the IRB, being discredited by Kelly's failures.

The next Irish revolutionary group to emerge violently was that of the Invincibles, which projected itself onto the public scene on 6 May 1882, when two of its members stabbed to death Lord Cavendish, the chief secretary of Ireland, and his permanent under secretary, Thomas Henry Burke, in Phoenix Park, Dublin. Directed from London and Paris, the Invincibles were a secret assassination group of only about thirty members, including old Fenians. Their declared objective was to eliminate "British tyrants on Irish soil." Formed in 1881, the Invincibles had a short but hectic life of only about two years. Five were executed and others imprisoned. At their trial they said, "We did it to make history."

In the second half of the 19th century, Irish nationalism tended to be nurtured largely by the Protestant Anglo-Irish Ascendancy, who had little contact with, thought for, or anything in common with the Catholic Irish peasants. A sudden change of orientation occurred in 1875 when the National Irish Land League was formed. Designed to protect tenant farmers against abuses from land agents, and from eviction, its slogan was the "Three Fs—Fair rent, Fair tenures, and Free sale of produce." The Land League mounted a political "land war" on behalf of the tenants against absentee landlords and land agents. Although it was publicly disavowed, the Land League had a secret militant arm that operated at night, like the old Leveller groups, wreaking vengeance and destroying property and crops; several land agents were murdered, and many others were manhandled. These groups became known as Moonlighters, after the mythical character "Captain Moonlight" created to terrorize landlords and their officials.

In 1875 Charles Stewart Parnell, a Protestant landowner (whose maternal grandfather was an American admiral), was elected to Westminster and became the leader of a sizable group of members of parliament (MPs). In 1878 Parnell became the leader of the National Irish Land League. He divested himself of his estates and in 1880 initiated a "No Rent" manifesto. He also organized the boycotting of landlords and their land agents. At Tipperary, for example, where the landlord had taken a particularly hard line against his tenants, most of the shopkeepers moved out and built a new town, leaving the old one almost deserted and bereft of goods. The word "boycott" came from Capt. Charles Cunningham Boycott, the land agent for the Lord Erne's estates in Co Mayo, who came into particularly harsh conflict with the Land Leaguers. He was deprived of all communication and contact with local people, who were ordered to ignore him completely and not to supply him with anything at all.

In 1881 Parnell was imprisoned for his land war activities; but he was released the following year, when his National Irish Land League was proscribed. It was reconstituted in 1884 in a milder form as the National League.

In 1886 the British Liberal prime minister, William Ewart Gladstone, declared that it was his mission to pacify Ireland. That year he disestablished the Anglican Church of Ireland, which freed Irish Catholics from paying tithes, thus removing a source of considerable discontent. The Anglo-Irish Ascendancy was now hungry for more political power and wanted to be released from control by the Westminster Parliament. In 1870 a "Home Rule for Ireland" movement had been instigated by Isaac Butt, an Irish MP; at the general election of 1872, Butt's followers won more than half the hundred-odd Irish seats at Westminster. Later Parnell espoused the home rule issue which, together with his Land League activities, made him so popular that he became known as the "Uncrowned King of Ireland." He seemed to get on well with Gladstone, and at one time hopes were high of home rule for Ireland becoming a reality.

After the general election of 1885, Gladstone's Liberal Party needed the support of the Irish MPs, now led by Parnell, to govern. This was given on the condition a Home Rule for Ireland Bill would be pushed through parliament. Gladstone tried hard but was unsuccessful. The reasons for this failure, by a narrow margin, were that many Liberals were against it; the Phoenix Park murders and the activities of the Invincibles were fresh in everyone's mind. Randolph Churchill (father of Sir Winston Churchill), leader of the British Conservative Party, had gone to Ulster to rouse the Protestants and non-Conformists to demonstrate violently against home rule. This became known as his "Orange Card," which was a trump one. The slogan was "Ulster will fight, and Ulster will be right." The non-Catholics in Ulster feared they would be harshly discriminated against if they became a minority in an autonomous Catholic Ireland.

The intense feeling whipped up among the non-Catholic population in Ulster by Randolph Churchill and others resulted in a sudden revival and rehabilitation in 1885 of the Orange Order, mainly by non-Conformists. The Orange Order, which now had an element of militant trade unionism within its ranks, tried to shed its former roughneck reputation, hoping to become respectable and to attract more Protestants.

Parnell had a sudden disastrous fall from power in 1890, when it was revealed he had been involved in a domestic scandal that resulted in divorce proceedings. Although his party reelected him leader, a great deal of moral condemnation was marshaled against him. The Catholic primate of England and senior members of the Catholic hierarchy in both England and Ireland urged Gladstone to disassociate himself from Parnell, which he did. Abandoned, Parnell died in October 1891, a broken man. It is one of the fascinating mysteries of history whether Parnell used Gladstone, or Gladstone used Parnell. One suspects that it was a little of both, but in their own ways both men worked hard for home rule for Ireland; had they succeeded, much bloodshed and misery might have been averted.

When the 19th century drew to a close, Ireland had largely recovered from the effects of the Great Famine and was better off economically than it had been for centuries. On the political side, the penal laws against Catholics had all been repealed, and landlord-tenant problems were being slowly faced. Neither terrorist revolutionary activities nor constitutional methods used by the Anglo-Irish Ascendancy had achieved home rule. The non-Catholic population of Ulster was convinced it had won a significant victory.

Reinforcing the heritage of hate of the native Irish for the English, as the 20th century unfolded, three distinct political power blocs emerged, all mutually hostile. One was the "Orange Card" of the Protestants and non-Conformists in Ulster, who for convenience and clarity can now be collectively referred to as Protestants, or non-Catholics; the political distinction, if not the narrow religious one, merged in mutual self-interest. This power bloc, a majority in parts of Ulster, was rigidly in favor of continued union with Britain for both economic reasons and sheer survival of identity.

The second, based in Dublin, consisted of the relics of the old Anglo-Irish Ascendancy, mainly Protestant, with English names and ancestry, who were working for home rule by constitutional means, most having foresworn violence. They visualized an autonomous Ireland linked closely to the British Crown.

The third political bloc, as yet hardly articulate and not yet developed, was that of the native Irish republicans, who wanted Ireland to be completely severed from Britain. They were the activists of the secret Irish Republican Brotherhood, which was coming to life again, using Irish separatists and cultural movements as fronts and pawns in the struggle for independence. The differences between these three competing factions sharpened and widened during the first quarter of the new century.

In 1904 a network of politically orientated Unionist Clubs was established in towns throughout Ulster. The following year, the Ulster Unionist Council was formed to unite all Unionist associations and to provide a central authority to formulate non-Catholic political policy. It was concerned only with Ulster, as Unionists in the other three Irish provinces were represented by the Irish Unionist Alliance, while in London the Union Defense League had been formed.

The British Liberal Party again came to power at Westminster in 1910, but with only a small majority. Once again it sought the support of the Irish MPs, who were now led by John Redmond, the Catholic leader of the Irish National Party. His price was home rule for Ireland, a demand which prompted and provoked the Dublin-based Irish Transport and General Workers Union to demonstrate in favor of an independent Ireland, one of the first Irish republican manifestations of this sort.

The out-of-power British Conservative Party, the Tories, opposed the Home Rule Bill and enlisted Edward Carson, a Protestant Dublin lawyer who was the sitting MP for Dublin University, to organize and lead active Protestant Ulster dissent. Carson did this with amazing energy and style. For example, on one occasion, at an open air meeting, he persuaded some 80,000 people to sign, some with their own blood, the Ulster Solemn League and Covenant as a protest against home rule. In all, eventually 471,414 people signed this covenant.

Carson found an existing loophole in the law that permitted the training of civilians in support of the constitution, so he raised the Ulster Volunteer Force (UVF) in 1912 and began drilling it in a military manner. Carson and other prominent Ulster leaders were prepared to resist the imposition of home rule by force, if necessary, and secretly planned to establish a separatist government if it should ever materialize. Arms smuggling was organized to provide weapons for the UVF, and in April 1914 one large consignment of over 20,000 rifles was imported from Germany. This alarmed the British authorities, and measures were put into effect to prevent such an exploit being repeated.

Home Rule for Ireland, the declared policy of the Liberal Party, caused considerable unease within the British army officer corps. In the summer of 1914 fifty-eight British army officers stationed at the Curragh, the main British military complex in Ireland, resigned when they thought they might be ordered to use military force to impose home rule on the unwilling Ulster Protestants. Many British officers were of Protestant Ulster stock. The British war minister, John Seely, and the chief of the Imperial General Staff, Field Marshal Sir John French, also resigned, thus leaving Britain to enter World War I without either a war minister or a chief of staff.

Nevertheless, slowly and successfully, the Home Rule Bill passed through both houses of parliament, the Commons and the Lords, on 18 September 1914. The previous month, on 4 August, World War I had broken out, and there was hesitation about placing the bill on the Statute Book. Speaking for the Ulster Protestants, Edward Carson pledged full support for Britain in the war but only on the condition the Home Rule Bill was dropped. John Redmond, leader of the Irish MPs, agreed to pend the issue for the time being; so the royal assent required to convert the bill into an act of parliament was withheld. World War I had neatly solved the British prime minister's dilemma: had he attempted to enforce home rule on Ireland, insurrection from the Ulster Protestants would have been almost certain, while the loyalty to the government of many officers, both civil and military, would have been doubtful.

In 1902 the National Council, which had separatist aims, was formed; then in 1905 the Duncannon Clubs appeared with similar aspirations, the first club being established in Belfast. The Duncannon Clubs expanded rapidly and in 1906 merged with the Cumann na Gaelheal, a political separatist organization, to form the Sinn Fein League. In 1908 the Sinn Fein League absorbed the National Council. Sinn (pronounced Shinn) Fein is usually translated as "Ourselves Alone," or sometimes as "We Ourselves." The driving force behind these organizations and mergers was a journalist, Arthur Griffith, the leader of the Sinn Fein. In 1898 he established a newspaper, the *United Irishman*, and plunged into organizing a political revival with a purely Irish dimension. Griffith was not a republican but was certainly a separatist; his ideal solution was a "dual monarchy" of Ireland and England. The Sinn Fein, which expanded rapidly, was an overt political party, and all its meetings were open.

The secret Irish Republican Brotherhood had long been dormant, although it still survived and was in contact with its sister organization in America, the Clan na Gael, which had consistently provided funds for Irish revolutionary purposes. In 1907 Tom Clarke, an old Fenian who had been a longtime member of the IRB, returned from New York to Dublin. He had been imprisoned for some years in England for his Fenian exploits. Clarke began to revive and revitalize the IRB. Determined to work for a republican Ireland, the newly activated IRB infiltrated Irish republican and separatist societies, placing its key members in positions of importance with the object of manipulating and eventually using them in the ultimate struggle against the British government. In November 1910 the IRB launched its own newspaper, *Irish Freedom*, in Dublin.

It should be emphasized that, unlike the Sinn Fein League, the IRB remained a secret society about which little was known by the general public. IRB members did not advertise their membership and were seldom personally identified and labeled as such. One of the IRB executive committee's first decisions was to support, infiltrate, and secretly gain control of a volunteer force that was being raised to counter that of Edward Carson in Ulster.

By a decision made at a public meeting on 13 November 1913 at the Rotuna, Dublin, an organization known as the Irish Volunteers (sometimes referred to as the Irish National Volunteers) was formed. It was to be modeled on the UVF, trained as a military force, and eventually armed. The man selected to lead the Irish Volunteers was John (Eoin) MacNeill, who was elected president of its executive committee and nominated chief of staff. MacNeill was a professor of Archaic Gaelic at the National University of Ireland. He had no previous military training or experience and little political acumen. He was a good front man for the IRB. Most of the Irish revolutionary intellectuals had publicly foresworn violence and, as they did not generally attract any mass following, they were regarded by the Dublin authorities as being fairly harmless. However, three key IRB members—Patrick Pearse, John MacDermott and Edmund Kent (Eamonn Ceannt)—were placed on the executive committee.

Commanded by Col. Maurice Moore, the Irish Volunteers marched through the streets of Dublin in their light green uniforms. This did not unduly upset the Dublin Castle authorities either, as they thought it was merely a defensive gesture and counterdemonstration to the UVF activities in Ulster. It was thought the Irish Volunteers would not have been able to obtain any arms because of the stringent precautions introduced since the UVF exploit.

However, the Irish Volunteers did manage to obtain at least two small shipments of illegal arms, one of which caused an incident. A consignment of 1,500 German rifles and 49,000 rounds of ammunition was openly landed in broad daylight at Howth Harbor, near Dublin on 26 August 1914. The arrangements were made by Erskine Childers,* an Englishman who had espoused the Irish republican cause. Irish Volunteers were marching away with the rifles on their shoulders when British troops belatedly arrived on the scene. The Irish Volunteers quickly disappeared with their arms and ammunition; only twenty weapons were seized by the soldiers. A hostile, jeering crowd gathered and began throwing stones at the troops. Shots were fired, and three people were killed and thirty-eight injured.

Another volunteer body had been formed in Dublin in 1913, by James Connolly, an organizer of Irish labor and a trade union leader who wanted an Irish socialist republic. Originally it was a strong-arm group to give his demonstrators some protection during the series of industrial troubles that year. In 1914 Connolly turned this group into a volunteer military force, the Irish Citizen Army. Emulating the Irish Volunteers, Connolly dressed his members in dark green uniforms and marched them through the streets of Dublin. He even mounted mock attacks on government buildings. Connolly employed ex-regular noncommissioned officers who had served in the British army, and he also managed to buy some weapons illegally from British soldiers in the Dublin garrison.

One colorful character who joined the Irish Citizen Army was Countess Markievicz, nee Constance Gore-Booth, a member of the respectable upper class English family. In 1909 she had founded the Fianna Eireann, a revolutionary youth movement. The leadership of the Fianna Eireann was infiltrated by the secret IRB. Yet another organization in which the

---

*Childers had fought as a British officer in the Boer War and was the author of several books.

IRB showed great interest was the Cumann na mBan, the uniformed women's military volunteers, which had a nationalist character and was dedicated to supporting Sinn Fein objectives.

Under the leadership of John MacNeill, the Irish Volunteers expanded rapidly from about 13,000 in December 1913 to over 180,000 by August 1914. This caused John Redmond, leader of the Irish National Party at Westminster, to look at it enviously. He demanded and obtained a seat on its executive committee, and probably saw himself as a rival to Edward Carson and his UVF in Ulster in the conflict over the home rule issue. Redmond's membership in the Irish Volunteers gave that body more respectability in the eyes of the Dublin Castle authorities.

Shortly after the war began, the question arose in the British parliament of withdrawing British troops from Ireland to fight in France. John Redmond said that if this were done, his Irish Volunteers would defend Ireland. This was over-optimistically interpreted by the British to be an absolute declaration of Irish wholehearted support for the British war effort. This impression seemed to be confirmed when Redmond openly urged his Irish Volunteers to join the British army; over 150,000 of them eventually did so. In all, well over 200,000 Irishmen, excluding Ulster Protestants, volunteered and served in the British army. Later on in the war it was said that there were "more Irishmen fighting for England than against her."

Redmond's call to British arms had shattered the strength of the Irish Volunteers. He remained on the executive committee for a while longer, only to resign when he realized that those who remained formed a hardline revolutionary, anti-British core. He took with him many moderate Irish Volunteers and formed his own organization, the National Volunteers; but due to subversive action and intimidation instigated by the IRB, Redmond's National Volunteers never gained any popularity or mass support.

At a meeting on 9 September 1914 of the supreme council of the IRB, from which the smaller executive committee was selected, it was decided to plan a revolutionary uprising sometime during Britain's war with Germany. Arrangements to obtain military help and arms from Germany were to be made through the Clan na Gael in America.

When the supreme council of the IRB met again in September 1915, old members were pushed out and new ones brought in. Denis McCullough was appointed president, John MacDermott was reelected secretary, and Tom Clarke appointed treasurer; these three men formed the core of the all-powerful executive committee, and all three were prominent in the Irish Volunteers movement.

The IRB supreme council also agreed to appoint a small, select military council to carry out the detailed planning for the projected revolutionary uprising. This council consisted of Patrick Pearse, Joseph Plunkett, and Edmund Kent—all IRB members who were still on the executive committee of the now very much depleted Irish Volunteers. The IRB members were a very secretive, tight-lipped group, and neither the chief of staff, John MacNeill (who was not a member of the IRB), nor his staff officers knew of their activities. Indeed, it appears that even Denis McCullough, president of the supreme council of the IRB, was not always kept fully informed as to what exactly the military council was doing.

The following month, October, Tom Clarke and Sean MacDiarmada were brought onto the military council. In January 1916 James Connolly, leader of the Irish Citizen Army, was also coopted because it was thought that in his impetuous enthusiasm he might start a revolutionary uprising on his own before the IRB was ready, and so spoil its chances. Later, Thomas MacDonagh also became a member of this key planning group.

By January 1916 the military council preparations were nearly ready, with the date of the uprising to be in or about the last week in April, which was Easter week. Contact had been made with the German government, and although hopes of German troops being sent to fight in Ireland had been dashed (the German High Command did not think very highly of Irish rebel efficiency, or indeed of the Irish rebel cause), promises had been given to send a large consignment of arms in April. The arms were expected to be landed on the Kerry coast by night; they were to be distributed out to Irish Volunteer units in Limerick, Cork, and the southwest of Ireland.

These units would openly rise in insurrection and take over that area, while other Irish Volunteer units in the east, center, and west of Ireland would also mobilize to take what offensive action they could to draw off and confuse any British troops sent against them. The key to success was to be a *coup de main* in Dublin at the same time. The city was to be seized and made the seat of the provisional Irish government. Joseph Plunkett drew up the plan for this coup. The forces to be employed were the Irish Volunteers and the small Irish Citizen Army. It was arranged that these two forces in Dublin and the Irish Volunteers throughout the rest of the country would be mustered for a practice exercise on Easter Monday. Thus far the IRB military council had not confided in John MacNeill, or told him of the part he and his volunteers were to take. The secret IRB was comparatively small, probably less than 2,000 members.

The Irish Volunteers staged a massive march in Dublin on St. Patrick's Day, 17 March 1916, but the police stood by and watched. The Dublin Castle authorities considered this sort of demonstration to be a safety valve to counterbalance the much larger Orange Order demonstrations that had taken place in Ulster. The parade of the Irish Volunteers went off peacefully.

At a Dublin railway station two days later, however, relatives and friends seeing off soldiers of the Leinster Regiment, who were going to France, turned on and manhandled a jeering crowd of nationalists. On the 20th a group of Dubliners waving Union Jacks attacked an Irish Volunteers' hall; shots were fired, and the police had to be called. The authorities in Dublin Castle smiled to themselves, thinking that it was just the Irish letting off steam.

During World War I the British naval intelligence cracked the German code used for messages between their embassy in Washington and their foreign office in Berlin. One such intercepted message indicated that a German ship with arms on board had left Lubeck, Germany, on 12 April and was due in Irish waters by the 21st; the message added that a nationalist rising was planned for Easter Eve. This message was passed to the chief secretary at Dublin Castle, Augustine Burrell, who held executive power (the office of lord lieutenant, or viceroy, had become a nonexecutive one by this time). Burrell and others saw the message but took no action. The next day, 19 April, both the chief secretary and the commander-in-chief of British troops in Ireland left the country to spend the Easter weekend in England.

It was not until 19 April that John MacNeill, chief of staff of the Irish Volunteers, became aware that this force was due to take part in an uprising that weekend. Surprised and angry at being deceived, he told the executive committee and the military council that it was a foolhardy scheme, that it would have no chance of success, and that he was countermanding the orders he had given for what he thought was to be merely a weekend mobilization exercise. MacNeill was shown the forged Dublin Castle directive, told that a large consignment of German arms was arriving off the Kerry coast on the 21st, and was persuaded that preparations were so advanced that it would be impossible to cancel the operation without risking the destruction of the whole movement. MacNeill was also persuaded that it was his patriotic duty to lead the uprising.

Things now began to go wrong for the IRB military council. On 20 April the German ship *Libau* (disguised as Norwegian and renamed the *Aud*) was intercepted by British naval ships and escorted toward Cork.

Just outside Cork Harbor, the crew scuttled the vessel. The *Aud* had on board 20,000 obsolete Russian rifles and one million rounds of ammunition destined for the Irish revolutionaries.

The following day, Good Friday, Sir Roger Casement, who had been put ashore on the coast of Kerry from a German submarine in Tralee Bay, was captured. He had planned to arrive in Ireland to take a leading part in the uprising. Taken off to Dublin and then to London, he was convicted of treason and executed on 3 August. His remains were eventually taken to Ireland on 23 February 1965 and reburied in Glasnevin Cemetery, near Dublin. He is now honored as an Irish patriot and martyr.

Nonetheless, the IRB military council met on Easter Sunday, the 23rd, and decided that the uprising must go ahead as planned on the morrow. John MacNeill again protested the unsoundness of the operation but was overruled and pushed aside. James Connolly, leader of the Irish Citizen Army, agreed with the decision. The still protesting MacNeill had already managed to have a notice inserted in that morning's *Sunday Dispatch*, a Dublin newspaper, notifying all Irish Volunteers that the previously ordered Easter parade was now cancelled. This further confused the issue, and the IRB now had to inform all volunteers that they should after all parade on Easter Monday morning.

The Easter Rising began early on Easter Monday, 24 April 1916, when about 700 volunteers mustered in Dublin. One group marched to the general post office building on Sackville Street (later renamed O'Connell Street) in the center of Dublin, where the Proclamation of the Irish Republic* was read out by Patrick Pearse, commander in chief. It was signed by seven people, all Catholics: Pearse, James Connolly (described as the commandant general), Thomas Clarke, Sean MacDiarmada, Thomas MacDonagh, Joseph Plunkett, and Eamonn Ceannt (Edmund Kent). John MacNeill, the protesting chief of staff, was not involved at all. The general post office was fortified and a green flag, on which were emblazoned the words "Irish Republic," was hoisted over the building. An Irish tricolor of green, white, and orange was later added.

The role and backroom direction of the IRB can be judged from the second paragraph of the proclamation, which began, "Having organised and trained her manhood through the sacred revolutionary organisation, the Irish Republican Brotherhood, and through her open military organizations, the Irish Volunteers and the Irish Citizen Army . . ." This gave rise to the expression "Irish Republican Army," which came into casual

*See Appendix A

use, and to the claim by the IRB to be the legal government of Ireland. However, at this time the current colloquial expression for Irish nationists of all shades was the "Sinn Feiners"; the secret IRB remained unknown.

Organized into four battalions, the Irish Volunteers took over certain strategic points in the city that have since become famous names. The 1st Battalion, led by Commandant Edward Daly, took possession of the Four Courts, the complex of sturdy legal buildings on the bank of the River Liffey. The 2d Battalion, led by Commandant Thomas MacDonagh, occupied Jacobs Biscuit Factory on Bishop Street. The 3d Battalion, led by Commandant Eamonn de Valera, took over Bolands Flour Mill, while the 4th Battalion, led by Edmund Kent, took over the South Union, a large workhouse complex. The Irish Citizen Army, only about 200 strong, led by Michael Mallin with Countess Markievicz as the second-in-command, marched to St. Stephen's Green, a central park in Dublin. Elsewhere in Ireland there was confusion, hesitation, order, and counterorder, as some units of the Irish Volunteers mobilized and some did not; those that did were soon dealt with by British troops.

The small British garrison in Dublin was taken completely by surprise, but reinforcements were quickly rushed over from England. There was five days' fierce fighting, during which the British troops formed a cordon round the center of the city where the rebels were in position; they then compressed it inward to squeeze them into submission. On Saturday, the 29th, when almost the whole of the center of Dublin was in flames, Patrick Pearse realized that a military victory was out of the question, so he formally surrendered unconditionally.*

Gen. Sir John Maxwell had been sent over to Ireland with full powers to crush the rebellion, and he dealt harshly with the rebels. In the fighting 1,351 people had been killed, and 179 buildings were destroyed or gutted by fire; over 3,500 men and 79 women were arrested. There were over 160 courts-martial, at which 97 people were sentenced to death, 16 of whom were executed. One was James Connolly; having been wounded in the fighting, he had to be strapped to a chair to be shot, as he was unable to stand up unaided. The remainder were given prison sentences, while 1,836 people were deported to internment camps where they were held without trial. The signatories of the proclamation and certain other principal leaders were executed. There were two notable exceptions, one being Commandant de Valera, who had been born in New York; the British government was anxious to persuade the American government

*See Appendix B

to join in World War I against Germany and was susceptible to American opinion. The other was Countess Markievicz, spared because she was a woman.

During the Easter Rising the Irish republicans were shown little sympathy by the citizens of Dublin. Many of the "separation women" whose husbands or sons were fighting in the British army in France were openly hostile, as they feared that such insurrections might put their army allowances at risk. Crowds jeered as the prisoners were marched away to captivity through the streets of Dublin, guarded by British soldiers with fixed bayonets.

From a practical military point of view, the Easter Rising never had any real hope of success, mainly because the leaders and their organizations had no popular support, and there was no coincident mass rising in sympathy. Had MacNeill not tried to countermand his order, and had all 12,000 Irish Volunteers risen in rebellion, the slaughter would have been that much greater. Pressure from the Ulster Protestants made certain the British authorities would take immediate steps to crush the rebellion firmly. The chances of seizing and holding certain positions while they carried out negotiations with the British were completely unrealistic.

However, from the political point of view, the Easter Rising turned out to be a huge success, as defeats on the battlefield sometimes do, and was the turning point for Irish republican fortunes. The harsh manner in which the British quelled the Easter Rising and the severe punishments that followed aroused general Irish sympathy and caused it to veer toward the Irish republicans, especially to the Sinn Fein movement that remained overt.

3　The Tans and the IRA

"Early this morning I signed my death warrant."
　　　—Michael Collins, after signing the Anglo-Irish Treaty
　　　of 1921

IN DECEMBER 1916 David Lloyd George became prime minister of Britain, and he took a rather different view of the Irish situation than that of his predecessor. On 4 April 1917 America entered the war, and neither the American nor British governments wanted to rock the boat over the Irish problem. In fact, the previous year, President Woodrow Wilson had ignored Irish-American pressure to appeal to the British government for clemency for those being sentenced to death, imprisonment, or internment for their involvement in the Easter Rising. In May Lloyd George offered John Redmond, leader of the Irish National Party, immediate home rule; but as this offer was linked to conscription in Ireland, it was turned down. However, John Redmond did accept Lloyd George's suggestion for a convention for all Irish political parties. The idea fell through when neither the Sinn Fein nor the Ulster Unionists would agree. In March 1918 John Redmond died, and John Dillon succeeded him as leader of the Irish National Party. Redmond had always worked against the Sinn Fein movement and those who demanded an independent republican Ireland.

Wholesale arrests after the Easter Rising had momentarily paralyzed and debilitated the revolutionary Irish organizations, and it was some months before they began to recover. In 1917 Lloyd George began releasing the Irish political prisoners and those in internment. They returned home with the aura of revolutionary heroes and began to reform and revitalize their own groups.

There were now three main groupings, the first and largest being the Sinn Fein, still a legal political party, still led by the aging Arthur Griffith. A Sinn Fein convention was held at the Mansion House, Dublin, on 26 October 1917, and Eamonn de Valera was elected its president, Griffith standing aside. As the only surviving Dublin commandant of the Easter Rising, de Valera had immense revolutionary prestige.

The next political grouping was the framework of the Irish Volunteers who had been the shock troops of the Easter Rising. Most of them had rapidly gone underground; but on finding they had suddenly become popular and were also regarded as heroes, they began reappearing in large numbers. De Valera was also elected president of the Irish Volunteers, and plans were made to reorganize and expand them. At a later convention, a general headquarters staff was appointed, and the title changed to National Volunteers. Cathal Brugha (Charles Burgess) became chairman of the executive committee and chief of staff; Richard Mulcahy was his deputy. Other appointments included Michael Collins as director of organization and intelligence. The exhilarating atmosphere of high Irish revolutionary morale caused new recruits to flock in to join the National Volunteers; by mid-1918, their total strength exceeded 100,000. Military training was carried out almost openly, and arrangements were made to procure illegal arms. Because of this activity, several National Volunteer officers were arrested.

The third political force was the Irish Republican Brotherhood, which had provided the leadership and organization for the Easter Rising. The IRB too has been shattered, but when Cathal Brugha returned to Dublin in November 1916 he was able to organize an IRB convention. Thomas Ashe, another Easter Rising hero, was elected president of the Supreme Council. The widow of the executed Tom Clarke had passed on to him all the secret IRB documents, files, and papers her husband had possessed. Ashe was soon arrested and died in prison in August 1917 while on a hunger strike.

Considering itself to be the "government of the Republic of Ireland," the IRB decided to penetrate, with the ultimate aim of controlling, the new Sinn Fein Party. In the confusion as to which of all these political organizations and forces demanded allegiance, the IRB attracted the most loyalty, even from the many who were not initially hard-line republicans. Many of the National Volunteers, for example, were made to take a republican oath. It was during this uncertain period between 1919 and 1921, in the fighting against the British security forces, that the insurgents collectively and unofficially became known as the "IRA," the Irish Republican Army. To their opponents, the British, they were generally known as "Sinn Feiners" or "Shinners."

Michael Collins, a member of the IRB who had fought as an Irish National Volunteer officer in the Easter Rising, had been interned with many of his colleagues at a camp in Wales. This camp became something of an Irish revolutionary school in which Collins emerged as the dominant leader. A large man physically, an extrovert with a magnetic personality, he was a good organizer and possessed the hard streak of ruthlessness necessary to make a successful revolutionary leader. He was also intensely ambitious. Born near Cork in 1890, he had gone to London in 1905, where for ten years he worked at several clerical jobs. In 1909 he joined the IRB and was later appointed treasurer.

At the British general election of December 1918, the Sinn Fein candidates won 73 out of the 105 Irish constituencies for the Westminster Parliament; but as they decided upon a policy of abstentionism, none took their seats. (The Ulster Unionists won twenty-six seats, and the Irish National Party six.) Instead, the elected Sinn Fein candidates—of whom only twenty-seven could be mustered, the remainder being either in British custody or on the run—met briefly on 21 January 1919 at the Mansion House, Dublin, as the First Dail Eireann (Irish Assembly). The Supreme Council of the IRB officially handed over to the Dail all the powers it had assumed, which technically solved the uncertain loyalty problem. It later caused difficulties, however, for as only Sinn Fein members sat in the First Dail, elements of that party claimed that the IRB had passed on its assumed powers to the Sinn Fein party, and not directly to the Dail. The obvious choice for the office of president of the Dail, Eamonn de Valera, had been arrested in May 1918; so Cathal Brugha was elected instead. Two of the other absentees were Michael Collins and Henry Boland, who were in England planning to spring de Valera from jail.

The same day as the First Dail met, insurgent action recommenced against the British security forces with the ambushing of a vehicle loaded with explosives near the quarry at Soloheadbeg, Tipperary, and the killing of two escorting policemen of the Royal Irish Constabulary (RIC). The shots fired were regarded as the first shots of the Irish insurgent war against the British.

The Royal Irish Constabulary, which had been granted the prefix "Royal" for its good work in putting down the Fenian Rising of 1867, was about 10,000 strong and was dispersed in a network of barracks, police stations, and small police posts throughout Ireland (except Dublin, which was policed by the Dublin Metropolitan Police). All except a few senior officers in the RIC were Irishmen, who now faced a problem of conflicting loyalties, as Irish republican and popular pressure was put upon them to defect from their British paymasters. By April 1919 the RIC personnel were being ostracized by the people, and many of them retired.

On 3 February 1919 de Valera was sprung from Lincoln Prison in England. He returned to Ireland but had to remain underground. The following month Lloyd George began to release Irish prisoners and internees who had been under arrest since 1917. The second meeting of the

Dail took place in Dublin on 1 April 1919, and this time Eamonn de Valera was elected president. He formed a cabinet that included Cathal Brugha as war minister and Michael Collins as finance minister. The Dail was short of money, so Collins floated a £16 million Irish loan and in June 1919 de Valera went to America as "president of the Irish Republic" to raise money for this loan. These first two Dail meetings had not been taken too seriously by the Dublin Castle authorities, and it was not until after an incident on 7 September at Fermoy, Co Cork, in which Irish insurgents fired on some British soldiers marching to church, killing one and wounding four, that the Dublin Castle authorities proscribed the Dail Eireann.

On 22 December 1919 Prime Minister Lloyd George pushed the Partition Bill through the British parliament; it emerged as the Better Government of Ireland Act. It provided for two parliaments in Ireland—one in the south at Dublin, and the other in the north at Belfast—and a joint Council of Ireland to coordinate the two parts, which could proclaim a "Union" of Ireland with a single parliament. This was acceptable to the Ulster Unionists, but neither the Sinn Fein nor the IRB would look at it.

Meanwhile, Irish insurgency was developing into a wide scale war of ambushes and raids against the British security forces. In particular were RIC stations and small posts raided for weapons, with hope of intimidating the personnel into defecting. As director of organization and intelligence of the National Volunteers, Michael Collins used the IRB, the Cumann na mBan (the women's organization), and the Fianna Eireann (the revolutionary youth group) to gather intelligence for him, which ensured many successful exploits. In November 1919, for example, arms were seized in a daring raid on a British naval sloop in Bantry Bay, Cork; but on 19 December an attempt to kill Lord French, the lord lieutenant of Ireland, failed.

Collins also organized and rigidly controlled a small group of executioners, who at first were simply known as "The Squad." Their task was to kill selected people in the British administration and security forces, and also to mete out rough kangaroo justice to defectors, informers, and any who transgressed the unwritten IRA code. On 21 January 1920 Collins's squad killed the head of the Dublin Metropolitan Police Criminal Investigation Department; a reward of £10,000 was offered for Collins's capture, dead or alive. The Dublin Castle authorities operated an Intelligence and Secret Service Department that worked closely with the Criminal Investigation Department.

Ireland was being taken over by the gunmen. On 19 March 1920 Thomas MacCurtain, the lord mayor of Cork, was killed in his own home in front of his family by several gunmen who escaped and were never identified. The British authorities stated that MacCurtain, commandant of the IRA's 1st Cork Brigade, had been killed by his own side because he had not pursued the insurgent war with sufficient vigor. The IRA accused the British, alleging they had an assassination squad.

The insurgent war was placing a great manpower strain on the British security forces in Ireland despite the presence of 40,000 British troops. Intimidation had slowed down recruitment for the RIC to a stop. To fill this expanding police shortage, the British government recruited a body of temporary constables to be attached to the RIC. Recruited in England, they were mostly ex-soldiers who had been unable to settle down to civilian life after the war. When the first batch of them arrived in Ireland on 25 March 1920, there was a shortage of dark green RIC uniforms, so they were dressed in army khaki and black boots, black belts, and black berets. The Irish nicknamed them the Black and Tans, which had been the name of a famous Limerick pack of hounds. They were not subject to military law, nor to the jurisdiction of the local courts. Objecting in principle to such a temporary, untrained body being attached to a professional constabulary, the inspector-general and other senior officers of the RIC resigned. The Black and Tans, or the "Tans" as the local Irish called them, soon dominated the insurgent warfare scene, and they earned the undying hatred of the Irish people for their brutality and excesses.

As the manpower of the RIC drained away and the conduct of the Tans begain to disturb the British government, Winston Churchill came up with another idea: raise another temporary police body. This was called the Auxiliary Division, the Auxiliaries, or the "Auxes," as the Irish called them. The members were all former British officers who had served in the war and were graded as temporary cadets, having the status of an RIC sergeant. By the end of July 1920, over 500 had landed in Ireland. It was hoped that, being ex-officers, their behavior and conduct would be more restrained and humane than that of the Tans. At first it was, but discipline soon deteriorated.

The insurgent war was developing bitterly, and by the end of June over 80 soldiers and RIC personnel had been killed. During June and July over 500 members of the RIC resigned. On 17 June there was a police mutiny at Listowel, Co Kerry; a number of RIC men who were being posted to outlying stations refused to go, as they considered their assignments to be too dangerous. After this the RIC tended to remain grouped together in barracks and towns, more or less giving the countryside over to the Tans, the Auxiliaries, and the IRA. In the vicious warfare that developed, many bodies of Irishmen were found in ditches at daylight, sometimes mutilated. From March 1920 onward the struggle between the British security forces and the IRA became known to the Irish in retrospect as the "Tan War," as the Black and Tans played such a prominent and much publicized part in it. The Tans' depot was at the RIC barracks at Gormanston, Co Meath; by September that year, their strength had risen to over 2,000, while that of the RIC had declined to 8,000.

By 1920 the National Volunteers had been organized on an area basis by Michael Collins. A division usually covered a county, within which there were brigades, battalions, and companies, depending upon the size of the area and the number of volunteers available. The volunteers received no pay, and either had to keep themselves or live off the country. Many of them did not move far from home, and therefore knew their own areas intimately and were always available for night operations.

The IRA propaganda section, directed by Erskine Childers, inflated the actual strength of the National Volunteers and did not dispute the RIC's claims that it rose eventually to over 100,000; nor did they correct the estimate of the Dublin Castle authorities, which was double that figure. Michael Collins wrote later that the IRA's strength at this period "never exceeded 15,000 men, of whom only 3,000 were effective fighters." The British security forces' exaggerated claims were perhaps in some way made to excuse their lack of success in the field.

Collins had a habit of committing most things to paper to ensure that matters of details were accurate, perhaps a practice he had learned in his clerical days. A continual flow of directives, orders, and documents emanated from the IRA headquarters. This had its drawbacks—many vital documents were seized in police raids, often revealing such details as names of undercover agents and locations of arms caches.

In July 1920 Collins organized a mobile element of men who were on the run and could not live at home. This took the form of "Flying Columns," each of about thirty volunteers with bicycles. This gave them speed and mobility, and with good intelligence they were able to ambush or outwit the road-bound Tans, Auxes, and British soldiers. These IRA Flying Columns, technically called independent brigades, attacked isolated RIC posts and barracks until practically all of them were deserted. Without any effective RIC presence in the countryside, British authorities were deprived of instant intelligence of IRA activities.

The IRA began burning the big houses in the countryside where Anglo-Irish or English gentry lived in some style and comfort throughout Ireland. The 19th century, and even before, had been the heyday of the building of fine Georgian mansions in Ireland. The IRA, like most Irishmen, was rather ashamed of its Georgian period. It was alleged the owners of the mansions were passing on information about the IRA to the authorities in Dublin. This intimidation caused an exodus of this class of antiseparatists and antirepublicans. Soon the countryside was scarred by ugly, burned out, derelict shells of the big houses.

The Black and Tans felt it was their mission to repay the IRA insurgents in their own coin and to terrorize the peasantry into refusing to help them. Until the Tans put this policy into operation, however, the majority of the people, especially the middle-aged and elderly, had no brief for the revolutionaries. The conduct of the Black and Tans changed this attitude quickly. On 20 September 1920, for example, when one of their number was killed in a pub brawl, the Tans rioted and burned down a number of buildings in the center of Balbriggen, Co Dublin.

The unthinking and unfeeling British handling of the Irish insurgency and the activities of the Tans and Auxiliaries had profoundly disturbing effects on Irishmen overseas. One unfortunate repercussion was a mutiny in a British regiment serving in India, the 1st Battalion, The Connaught Rangers, which recruited in Ireland. News of what was happening in their home province unsettled the unit, and on 28 June 1920 about 200 soldiers refused to obey the orders of their officers. Only about ninety were actual mutineers, led by Pvt. James Daly, who openly affirmed support for the Sinn Fein. The mutiny was quickly subdued. Over sixty soldiers were tried by court-martial and sentenced to terms of imprisonment; Daly was executed. This and other Irish regiments on the British Army list were later disbanded.

Intimidation and open sympathy for the Sinn Fein movement and the IRA reduced justice to a farce in Ireland. Juries either gave perverse decisions or would not convict. This caused the introduction in August 1920 of the Restoration of Order Act, which set up military courts to try civilians for certain offenses. One of the first men to be tried under this act was Terence MacSwiney, lord mayor of Cork and commandant of the IRA's 1st Cork Brigade. Convicted, he was taken to Brixton Prison in England, where he commenced a hunger strike, dying in prison after seventy-five days. Another harassment to the British came from the militant Irish trade unions which in 1920 began a campaign of strikes and deliberate obstruction toward the British administration by refusing to handle British goods or transport British soldiers or policemen by trains, trams, or buses.

The British authorities began to execute Irish rebels. One execution that horrified the world was that of Kevin Barry, an eighteen-year-old student. On 1 November 1920 Barry was convicted of taking part in an IRA raid in which a British soldier was killed. Within the next three months, twenty-four other rebels were executed. In the Tan War the taking of hostages by both sides was commonplace; a number of RIC men, Tans, Auxiliaries, and even a few British soldiers were captured and some shot. In the first four months of 1921, according to RIC reports, the IRA executed seventy-three informers, one being a seventy-year-old woman.

The Irish Catholic Church took a neutral course in this Anglo-Irish struggle, with the priests, especially the older ones, urging restraint on the IRA. But as the war wore on, an increasing number of younger priests came out openly in sympathy with the insurgents, some giving active support.

On 6 June 1920 the British brigadier in command of the Cork Area and two officers were captured while on "fishing leave"; they later escaped. It had been tacitly assumed that certain sporting venues and pastimes were off limits to the IRA and the war. These included horse-racing, where friends and enemies mingled on racetracks. The British threatened to close down all racetracks if there were a terrorist incident on any of them; but there were none—the descendants of kings were too fond of the sport of kings.

November 21, 1920 became known as Bloody Sunday. Michael Collins brought his squad into action, killing eleven British and two RIC officers. In most cases the officers had been taken from their beds in the early morning and shot. Collins insisted they were all working for the Dublin Castle–based Intelligence and Secret Service Department, and so it was a necessary act of war, but there is some doubt about this. That afternoon the Black and Tans fired into the crowd attending a football match at Croke Park, Dublin, killing fourteen people and injuring over sixty. Evidence suggests that these two incidents were unrelated to each other, but the IRA and the Irish people would not be persuaded of that fact.

In the town and countryside the Tan War became one of reprisal and counterreprisal, the difference between murder and reprisal having been long since lost. The Tans and the IRA gave each other as bad as they got. Protests were made in England about the way the war was being conducted, and general officers began writing open letters to the press, condemning the terrorism and the tactics and urging the disbandment of the Black and Tans. A lively "Peace with Ireland" movement held protest meetings. The British military in Ireland were embarrassed and uneasy and already had insisted that dark green police uniforms of the RIC be hurriedly produced and issued to the Tans and Auxiliaries to replace the military-type ones, as the soldiers did not want to be associated with the odium they generated.

Eamonn de Valera returned to Ireland on 24 December 1920 from his visits to America, where he had raised three million dollars for the Irish loan, but he had not been able to persuade the American government to recognize his "Irish Republic." De Valera reassumed all his offices, and one of this first problems was that Michael Collins, who was fast jumping to stardom, was at loggerheads with Cathal Brugha, his military superior at the National Volunteer headquarters. Disturbed by Collins's obvious personal ambition, de Valera suggested that Collins, as finance minister, pay a visit to America to raise more funds; but Collins refused to be sent out of the country. A personality clash developed between de Valera and Collins. De Valera spent most of 1921 trying unsuccessfully to obtain recognition and support for his republican movement from the Irish Catholic hierarchy.

The insurgent war dragged on throughout the winter of 1920–21 with extra bitterness and ferocity. The IRA was accused of using dum dum bullets, which were soft metaled ones with the nose split; on entering the body they expanded, inflicting tearing wounds. Dum dum bullets were outlawed by the then Hague Convention on the Laws and Usages of War. Also, a secret underground war of assassination and counterassassination had developed in mid-1920 between Collins's squads and similar units organized and operated by Dublin Castle's Intelligence and Secret Service Department; during the second half of the year this accounted for over one hundred victims. The IRA offered a £50 reward for the killing of a Tan or an Auxiliary. Despite the large reward offered for Collins, he was able to live and work in Dublin, seeming to have a charmed life against assassination or capture.

On 9 February 1921, while searching for arms, the Auxiliaries looted a shop in Trim, Co Meath. The commandant of the Auxiliary Division, Brigadier Crozier, immediately investigated the matter and instantly dismissed twenty-one cadets; another five were remanded for trial. Two young Irishmen taken into custody that night by the Auxiliaries were found the next morning in a field near Drumcondra, a suburb of Dublin; one was dead and the other mortally wounded. A few days later, Brigadier Crozier's disciplinary decision was reversed on political instructions from London, and all twenty-six Auxiliary cadets were reinstated. On the 25th Brigadier Crozier resigned. These incidents and the controversy over them were fully reported in the British press, causing intense disgust in England and disquiet in government circles.

At the British general election on 24 May 1921, all the Sinn Fein candidates were reelected but again did not take their seats at Westminster. As a gesture of defiance, the IRA carried out one of its most spectacular exploits the following day by burning the Customs House in Dublin, the seat of British administration.

The British government was becoming anxious that the insurgent war might inflame and encourage Indian nationalists who also wanted independence for their country. Protracted negotiations between the British government and Eamonn de Valera began and continued until eventually, on 8 July, representatives of the British government and the Sinn Fein (which still included the IRB, the "Guardian of the Revolution") met at the Mansion House, Dublin. A truce to begin on 11 July 1921 was proposed and accepted.

Winston Churchill, then secretary of state for the colonies and chairman of the Cabinet Committee on Irish Affairs, and Field Marshal Sir Henry Wilson, chief of the Imperial General Staff, were against the truce; they both wanted another all-out campaign against the insurgents, which they were sure would crush them completely. The leadership of the secret IRB was also doubtful about accepting the truce, believing that a long truce would weaken dedication and discipline. Popular support in Ireland for their struggle for independence had grown as a result of the harsh treatment of the Easter Rising rebels, and then because of the brutality of the unleashed Black and Tans and Auxiliaries.

Nevertheless, on 6 December 1921, the Anglo-Irish Treaty was signed by a five-member Irish delegation led by Arthur Griffith, which included Michael Collins. Eamonn de Valera stayed behind in Dublin, aloof from the negotiations. Afterward, Collins said, "Early this morning I signed my death warrant." The outcome was an Irish Free State of twenty-six counties of Ireland, with its own independent government but linked to Britain by allegiance to the British Crown, as part of the British Commonwealth. The other six counties (of the thirty-two-county Ireland) had chosen to retain direct links with Westminster. The treaty did not recognize an Irish Republic, which the IRA had been ostensibly fighting for, nor did it make any mention of a united Ireland. In the Free State—the twenty-six counties—there were approximately 1,812,000 Catholics and 327,000 Protestants, while in Northern Ireland—the six counties—there were about 820,000 Protestants and 430,000 Catholics.

The Anglo-Irish Treaty was debated in the Dail in January 1922 and accepted by the narrow majority of sixty-four to fifty-seven. The members of the Dail were bitterly divided, those with republican aspirations accusing the others of selling them short by accepting something less than an independent Irish Republic of the whole country. De Valera, who was strongly against the treaty, was replaced by Arthur Griffith as president of the Dail. Griffith formed a cabinet in which Michael Collins was the finance minister and Cathal Brugha the war minister. Later, on 15 March 1922, de Valera formed a new political party, the League of the Republic (Cumann na Poblachta).

As the Free State came into being, those of the National Volunteers who accepted it became the Free State National Army. Michael Collins was appointed commander in chief. The National Volunteers were also divided on whether to accept the treaty. The hard-line IRA headquarters said that of the fourteen IRA divisions in the field, and five independent brigades, into which the National Volunteers had been organized by Michael Collins, only six divisions and two independent brigades opted for the treaty: all the others wanted to fight on. Solely inspired by the goal of an independent Irish Republic and now led by Rory O'Connor, the IRA refused to take orders from the new Free State army.

The British army began progressively to evacuate the Free State and to hand over their barracks and posts to the Free State army; but as the IRA was determined to gain possession of as many of them as possible, it became a mad scramble between the Free Staters and the IRA. Once in occupation, neither side would yield to the other. A state of hostile tension between them became acute, and by April there were virtually two armies snapping at each other's heels in the race to occupy military buildings, especially in Dublin.

The number of incidents between the Free Staters and the IRA increased in April 1922, and during the first week in May six men were killed and forty-nine wounded. But both sides hesitated to provoke a full-scale clash, or even make a deliberate attack on each other; each unsuccessfully sought a compromise. The reason for this hostile hesitation was the danger to the new Free State from the reactivated Ulster Volunteer Force, which demanded that the union with Britain be retained. Edward Carson and his UVF openly threatened to intervene in southern Ireland to help deal with the rebels.

On 18 June 1922, the IRA held a convention in Dublin (which was really run and organized by the IRB) at which it was stated that there were 112,650 volunteers in the Irish Republican Army, all opposed to any compromise with the Free State. This number was highly suspect and must have been mentioned for propaganda purposes; the true figure was probably in the region of 20,000 to 25,000. By a narrow majority it was decided not to renew the war with Britain—a decision influenced, not a little, by the impatient and aggressive attitude of the UVF.

On 22 June 1922 Field Marshall Sir Henry Wilson, the CIGS, an Irish-born Protestant, was killed in London by two IRA men who were subsequently arrested and executed. Both Arthur Griffith, president of the

Dail, and de Valera disassociated themselves from involvement in the assassination, which had occurred after the Anglo-Irish Treaty had been signed, during what was regarded as a truce period. Firm proof as to who ordered the killing has never been convincingly forthcoming. At the time it was generally believed that the execution of Field Marshall Wilson had been ordered by Michael Collins as a reminder to both Winston Churchill and David Lloyd George that they were both still on his "Death List," in case they were tempted to deliberately prolong negotiations for the British military withdrawal from the Free State. Field Marshall Wilson had opposed both the treaty and the truce.

Friction increased between the Free State government and the IRA. In June 1922 several IRA leaders were arrested in Dublin. In retaliation, the IRA kidnapped the deputy chief of staff of the Free State army. The British army handed over four artillery guns to the Free Staters who, under urging from the British government to put their own house in order quickly, mounted an attack on 28 June on the IRA headquarters at Four Courts. After a three-day siege, the IRA headquarters was bombarded into surrender. Then the Free State army attacked various other barracks in and around the city that had been occupied by the IRA; its artillery bombardments induced several of them to surrender. Despite the possession of these heavy weapons, the fighting in Dublin was not all one-sided, and Cathal Brugha, the war minister, was fatally wounded when he walked out from one of the barracks after surrendering to the IRA; he had been carrying a pistol in a holster.

Then under the influence of Rory O'Connor and Liam Mellowes, the IRA made a surprising and disastrous decision: it pulled out all its men from the Dublin area, where it was felt they were at a serious disadvantage under the Free State artillery. Under the command of Liam Lynch and Luke Dillon, the IRA moved southward, determined to hold a line from Waterford to Limerick and to hit back at the Free State army with Flying Columns. Although at that moment the IRA did not have any artillery, it was by no means beaten. The Free State army had less than 25,000 soldiers and limited artillery ammunition, while the IRA could muster as many, and perhaps more, men. The explanation for this seemingly poor military strategy was that the Free State government had a strong, determined, and energetic leadership under Michael Collins, while that of the IRA was weak and indecisive. The military leadership of the IRA pushed aside its civilian "Republican Government," of which Eamonn de Valera was the president, and took over the conduct of the war. Mediocre IRA personalities obtruded and pushed others aside regardless of their ability. President de Valera, for example, who as a commandant in the Easter Rising had acquitted himself extremely well in the military field, became nominally an assistant to Sean Moylan, the IRA director of operations. The IRA leadership was indifferent, it had no overall war plan, and seemed to be at a loss as to what to do next, retreating in a negative manner from Dublin, the potential center and seat of power.

The IRA made only one offensive in the civil war, and that was simply to push Flying Columns northward; but all were checked and had to withdraw again. In July 1922 the Free State army, now with about 60,000 men under its commander in chief, Michael Collins, struck back. Free Stater columns successfully drove the IRA from Waterford, and then Limerick, and then southward progressively from other towns. An amphibious operation enabled the Free Staters to seize Tralee, and on 10 August a similar type of operation drove the IRA from Cork. Everywhere the IRA had been driven from the towns in the Free State counties and had to take to the countryside and fall back on guerrilla warfare. In this first forty-three-day phase of the Irish Civil War, the Free State army admitted to over 600 casualties; the IRA must have suffered many more.

The Free State lost several prominent leaders, and on the day Cork was taken from the IRA, Arthur Griffith died. Liam Cosgrave replaced his as president of the Dail. A fortnight previously, Henry Boland, who had helped spring de Valera from jail in England, was fatally shot while trying to escape at Skerries, Co Dublin. He had been a member of the Supreme Council of the IRB and was a friend of Collins. On 15 August Michael Collins was ambushed and shot dead on the road between Bandon and Macroom, near Cork. Who gave the order for his execution, if indeed it was that, whether the killers were from the IRA side, or from Collins's own squads, or whether it was a chance ambush that caught a big fish, is not known for certain. Even today, tongues are silent. That Collins had many enemies, and that he had been a ruthless executioner with his assassination squads cannot be denied. Many were suspicious of the IRB and of Collins's leadership of that secret organization. Collins had accumulated a great deal of power: at the time of his death he was commander in chief of the Free State army, president of the Supreme Council of the IRB, finance minister in the Free State government, and a member of the Dail. Despite the savagery of the warfare in Ireland since 1916, Collins was generally felt to have been a moderating influence against excesses; certainly ruthless savagery became even more unbridled after his death.

In the British general election of October 1922, David Lloyd George's coalition government fell. His negotiations with the Sinn Feiners granting the Free State an independent government were extremely unpopular with the Conservative Party; but as much as anything else, he had been driven from office by the British people, who were saddened and sickened by his authorization and seeming support of the activities of the Black and Tans and the Auxiliary Division, and generally by the inhuman way in which the campaign against the Irish insurgents had been conducted.

Driven into the countryside, the IRA did not do nearly as well as it had expected, much to its surprise. This time it was faced with a determined enemy in the form of the new Free State army, many of whose soldiers had been former comrades but who had no scruples in firing on and killing fellow Irishmen. The war took an even more bitter turn in the autumn of 1922. In its October pastoral, the Catholic hierarchy in Ireland openly condemned the IRA and, worse still, refused the Sacraments to its members—an extremely serious matter for devout Catholics, which most IRA men were.

The Free State government adopted a hard line against the IRA and introduced military courts to try civilians for certain offenses without a jury. In November 1922 four IRA volunteers were executed on its orders; then, without even a facade of a trial, the Free State government ordered the execution of four senior IRA leaders who had been captured. They were Rory O'Connor, Liam Mellowes, Richard Barrett, and Joseph McKelvey, the IRA chief of staff. Then it summarily shot Erskine Childers, a member of the Dail, who had been captured with a pistol in his possession. Childers, the Englishman who had spent his youth in Ireland and become "more Irish than the Irish themselves," had been a member of the Irish team that negotiated with the British in 1921. He had always been suspected by Michael Collins of being in the pay of the British.

Free Staters captured Luke Dillon in January 1923, and then on 6 April, Liam Lynch was fatally wounded, which removed the two top IRA field commanders from the scene. In April there was a succession of arrests of other IRA leaders, some of whom had been betrayed by their own men. Frank Aiken became the IRA chief of staff. With the Catholic Church ranged against the IRA, people now hesitated to help IRA men and did so only through intimidation and example executions.

The IRA Executive Committee, and the general headquarters staff— that is, both the civilian and military members, several of whom held dual appointments—met in conference from 23–26 March 1923 to review their situation and determine future strategy. The members were divided: some were for suing for peace, others for continuing the struggle. On 23 April they again met. The situation had become even more desperate: the

IRA was down to less than 12,000 fighting men in the field; over 11,000 had been captured and were in Free State detention. The Free State army was preparing for a spring offensive. At this meeting Eamonn de Valera, still officially the president of the "Irish Republic" in the eyes of the IRB and its military arm, the IRA, came to the fore. The IRA was now short of men, arms, ammunition, money, and above all—the one essential for success in a guerrilla war—the popular support of the people. Additionally, in Catholic Ireland, they needed the support of the Church.

On 27 April President de Valera stated that he had been in touch with the president of the Dail, William Cosgrave, and had offered to surrender on the condition that the Free State government would guarantee the IRA a "political lease of life." Cosgrave replied that surrender must be unconditional and that he had no intention of giving the IRA a prolonged lease of life. On 13 and 14 May the IRA Executive Council and its military staff met and decided to lay down their arms and quietly go underground. On 24 May President de Valera issued his now famous order to the "Soldiers of the Republic, Legion of the Rearguard still in the field," instructing them to hide their weapons and cease resistance, as "military victory must be allowed to rest for the moment with those who have destroyed the Republic." He made no mention of surrender or cease-fire; no amnesty was offered and none was sought. He just said that the IRA would cease fighting, as "further sacrifices of life would now be in vain."

And so the Irish Civil War ended. The sad characteristic of this war which divided families was the cold-blooded killings—the shootings of hostages, including women, of informers, of defectors, and the many executions by both the Free State government and the IRA. This brought out the darker side of the Irish character that had not been generally seen before.

Meanwhile in the north, the Ulster Protestants had viewed with considerable anxiety and misgiving the activities in southern Ireland and the political handling of them by Prime Minister Lloyd George. The Ulster Volunteer Force had been revived after World War I as returning soldiers were demobilized and rejoined it; at the time of the Orange Marches in 1919, the Unionist leader James Craig threatened to march against the Irish rebels in the south. There was considerable Protestant resentment in Belfast against Catholic workers who had infiltrated into the shipyards, a longtime Protestant preserve, during the war when labor was scarce.

The Partition Act passed in December 1919 was accepted by the Ulster Unionists, although it was not quite what they had wanted. The predominantly Catholic counties of Cavan, Donegal, and Monoghan were hived off from the province of Ulster to go to the Free State. The remaining six counties of the province—Antrim, Armagh, Down, Fermanagh, Londonderry, and Tyrone—in which there was an overall Protestant majority, came under the new Northern Ireland government at Belfast. Preparations were made for a Northern Ireland Assembly, and twelve members representing constituencies in Northern Ireland were elected to sit in the British parliament at Westminster.

In June 1920 Catholics attacked Protestants in Derry in an attempt to take over the Old City area. Following the annual July Orange Marches, violence broke out in Belfast in which Catholics were expelled from their jobs and homes. At the height of the Tan War, the IRA claimed to have 8,000 resident members in Ulster, and that they took action against the British security forces; but these claims were exaggerated, as the IRA in Ulster was extremely selective in its targets and only rarely operated outside solid Catholic areas. With the threat of the mobilized Ulster Volunteer Force waiting aggressively in the background, the solid Protestant parts were too tough a nut for the IRA to try to crack.

Consequently, the Royal Irish Constabulary, which contained a much larger Protestant element than in the south, held together and was able to cope with the insurgent situation much better than in the remainder of Ireland, even in the hard Catholic areas. The Black and Tans and the Auxiliaries were not deployed in Northern Ireland. However, there was still a shortage of police manpower; to supplement the RIC, the Ulster Special Constabulary (USC) was raised in October 1920, being largely recruited form the UVF on a Protestant basis. The USC was in three sections: A Section was for full-time service, B Section for part-time service, and C Section for call-out in an emergency only.

Elections for the Northern Ireland Assembly were held on 19 May 1921 on a proportional representation basis; the Unionists won a two-thirds majority. Even though the Protestants were in a majority, this was increased by deliberate anomalies of plural votes for certain Protestant voters. The Sinn Fein also won six seats, three of which were allocated to Arthur Griffith, Eamonn de Valera, and Michael Collins; but, under the policy of abstentionism, none of them took them. The first prime minister of Northern Ireland was Sir James Craig, and the assembly was set up as a miniature model of the Westminster Parliament, the exception being there was no "official opposition." The several assembly committees all had Protestant chairmen and Protestant majorities. Ulster Unionists set about consolidating their gains. The first Northern Ireland Assembly was formally opened on 21 June 1921 by King George V, who objected to part of the prepared speech he was to read out. The offending passage was "Determination to crush the rebellion in the south-west of Ireland . . ."; it was omitted.

The Tan War spread to Northern Ireland in June 1921 with the Swatragh Ambush: an IRA unit of twenty men attacked a police barracks in Co Londonderry, killing one policeman. Tension increased and, roused by their Orange Marches, despite the official truce (21 July) and cease-fire, the Protestants instigated riots that caused fourteen deaths and over one hundred injuries in the month of July. In Belfast alone 161 Catholic homes were destroyed by fire. Other incidents followed. In February 1922 Catholics attacked trams in Belfast that were carrying Protestant workers to the dockyards, and this led to violent disturbances in which seven Catholics were killed.

For some time Michael Collins had been sending arms and ammunition to his IRA units in Ulster without informing Arthur Griffith's Free State government, and he also sent Free State army officers to organize activity against the RIC, the USC, and the Protestants generally. One of Collins's Active Service Units killed a Protestant member of the Northern Ireland Assembly in reprisal for the death of the seven Catholics in Belfast. In Northern Ireland it became a sectarian competition for murder and reprisal. During the Civil War in the south, IRA units moved towards the Northern Ireland border in some force, but they stopped short of clashing with the UVF. On 19 March 1922 IRA detachments had blown up a key bridge over the River Moyola and attacked the Maghera police station. On the 29th the so-called Collins-Craig Pact was made for a truce in Northern Ireland, but it did not last many days.

On 3 May the IRA attacked police stations at Bellaghy and Draperstown; on the 16th three policemen were killed at Ballyroan; on the 19th four men were shot dead at Desertmartin. On the 24th the IRA was declared an illegal organization, and over 500 Sinn Feiners were arrested and interned. On 1 June 1922 a curfew was introduced that covered the whole of Northern Ireland. In that month British troops ejected IRA units from the areas of Belleck and Pettigo, after which other IRA units hastily withdrew.

The Free State boycotted British and Northern Ireland goods; this boycott was taken up also in Derry, where there was a Catholic majority. Sir James Craig, the prime minister of Northern Ireland and leader of the Unionist Party, promised that if the boycott were lifted he would reinstate the 9,000 Catholic workers who had been ejected from Belfast after World War I. The boycott faded away, but Craig did not allow any of the Catholic workers to return: he was busy looking after strictly Protestant interests. On 1 June 1922 the old Royal Irish Constabulary, or such of it as remained in Northern Ireland, was formally disbanded; the Royal Ulster Constabulary (RUC) appeared in its place. Many of the A Specials were absorbed into the new RUC on a regular basis until 1924, when internment ended and these sections were disbanded, leaving just the B and C Specials in existence.

4 Dissension and Doubt

"This English agent sent fifty-two Irishmen to the British army in the last seven weeks."
—IRA card left on the body
of Adm. Sir Henry Somerville

CIVIL WARS ARE more bitter than most, and the winning side invariably indulges in a vicious witch-hunt. The Free State government was certainly no exception to this rule. The republicans—that is, the IRA-IRB—would not concede victory to their now hated opponents, the pro-treaty men, who were busily establishing the infant Free State. The IRA refused to accept the finality of defeat, and its members showed neither remorse nor penitence, only sullen, silent acquiescence. They had merely dumped their guns on orders, to await a more opportune moment to retrieve them. They spoke quietly to themselves of a second round.

On the other hand, the Free State government showed no magnanimity at all; arrests of IRA men continued, as did the relentless searches for arms. There were so many IRA men in detention at one stage that the government thought of borrowing the island of St. Helena from the British; then it considered using a large ship for the same purpose, but eventually discarded these ideas in favor of temporary detention camps to accommodate the overflow that could not be housed in existing prison buildings. In July 1923 the Free State government held 11,316 IRA prisoners. On 1 August it introduced the Public Safety Act, which gave it considerable powers of detention without trial.

During this period the republican IRA movement was held together by Sean Lemass, the defense minister in the "Republican Government," which claimed to be the legitimate one, and Frank Aiken, the chief of staff. There were many defections, especially of those seeking employment and by those who felt that the republican struggle had become futile. Little money was being received from the Clan na Gael, as that organization was confused by the Civil War situation and was in some doubt as to which side to give its support and money.

In the general election on 23 August 1923 the Sinn Fein Party, the legal political wing of the IRA, won forty-four seats, as against sixty-three gained by the Cumann na nGaedheal, the party formed by Liam Cosgrave in the spring of that year. Cosgrave was able to form a government and get on with the business of organizing the Free State without serious opposition: the Sinn Fein candidates elected to the Dail refused to take their seats. De Valera, although reelected, was in prison.

At a secret IRA meeting in October 1923, it was decided to strengthen and develop the republican political wing and to rebuild the IRA. The priority was to obtain the release of IRA detainees. A mass hunger strike was planned for October 1923, to begin in Mountjoy Prison, the main one in Dublin, and then to spread to Kilmainham Prison, also in Dublin, and then to the temporary detention camps. The IRA claimed that over 8,000 people took part in this hunger strike, but the solidarity did not last for many days, and only a handful continued with determination. On 20 November Commandant Denis Barry died while on hunger strike in prison; on the 22nd so did Capt. Andrew Sullivan. On the 23rd the IRA called off the mass hunger strike, believing it had failed in its purpose. Conversely, the Free State government thought the will of the IRA had been broken; the next day, they began releasing IRA detainees in small batches. The men went back to their homes, and the old territorially-based IRA units slowly began to reform.

The Free State army, which had settled down at a strength of about 60,000, was arming itself with captured IRA weapons, helped also by contributions from the British. In April 1922 Winston Churchill had to defend himself in parliament for giving the Free State government 4,000 rifles, 2,000 revolvers, and six machine guns, together with ammunition. The Free State army contained many discontented IRA men, the majority of whom had followed Michael Collins over to the pro-treaty side, largely in the belief that the Free State was but a necessary stepping-stone to the republic of all Ireland they had been fighting for. Discontent increased as they saw the Cosgrave government comfortably settling down to full acceptance of what had been gained from the treaty and taking no further action to turn it into a republic. On 6 March 1924 an ultimatum signed by Major General Tobin and Colonel Dalton of the Free State army, on behalf of the "IRA Organization," was sent to Liam Cosgrave demanding that steps be taken to establish a republic. Nine members of the Dail resigned in support of the ultimatum, a few Free State army officers deserted with their arms, and others refused to obey orders.

On the death of Michael Collins, or even before, the secret IRB began losing influence, being divided over the acceptance of the treaty. Many members turned away from the idea of a republic. After its defeat in the Civil War, the IRB was generally discredited and was extremely unpopular. However, after de Valera's "dumping of arms" order, it was reconstituted. The Supreme Council confirmed that its main purpose was to work for a republic, and that there could be no modification of this aim. Its strategy was to provoke a British reprisal attack on the Free State, and so reopen the war with Britain, which it felt it could ultimately win. The IRB continued with its old tactic of placing its senior members in key positions not only in the Sinn Fein movement and the IRA, but also in the Free State service. Gen. Richard Mulcahy, for example, became the defense minister in the Free State government, while Gen. Eoin O'Duffy became the commissioner of the Garda Siochana, the Free State national police force. The Garda Siochana replaced the old Royal Irish Constabulary and the Dublin Metropolitan Police, which had been dissolved. It was a bold experiment, basically an unarmed police force in a state seething with bitter animosity, littered with secret caches of arms, and inhabited by many men who had old scores to settle.

The task of dealing with the "IRA Organization" ultimatum and quelling the army mutiny fell to Kevin O'Higgins, vice president of the Dail and minister of justice. He immediately called in General O'Duffy and appointed him commander in chief of the Free State armed forces. His brief was to discharge the mutineers and other hard-line IRA activists, and to remove politics completely from the army, on the British pattern. O'Higgins, well known for his dislike and suspicion of the IRB, somehow overlooked, deliberately or otherwise, the fact that O'Duffy was not only a member of the IRB but one of its top leaders. A flamboyant and strong character, O'Duffy was perhaps dazzled by titles, had a thirst for power, and so was subverted. He took over the Free State army and swept it clean of politics. The IRB poacher had turned Free State gamekeeper; O'Duffy resigned from the IRB.

Kevin O'Higgins handled matters so well when negotiations and backstage talks began that on 11 March the "IRA Organization" withdrew its ultimatum. There were just two major incidents in this "army mutiny": on 16 March Free State soldiers raided Devlin's Pub in Parnell Street, Dublin, and in a shoot-out captured ten prominent mutineers. This operation had been authorized by the Free State National Army Council, chaired by Gen. Richard Mulcahy, the defense minister. As he was pursuing a policy of "no violence" while eradicating politics from the army, but was simply weeding out and discharging politically active officers and soldiers, O'Higgins was furious. He complained to Liam Cosgrave that the raid had been unauthorized, and that he had not known of it. On the 19th General Mulcahy had to resign from the cabinet.

The second incident occurred on 22 March 1924 when four men dressed in Free State army uniforms fired on passengers alighting from a ferry-boat from the Spike Island Treaty Port* at Cobh, near Cork. One British officer and five civilians were injured, as were eighteen British soldiers, one fatally. The assailants were never identified or brought to justice. The object had been to provoke a British reprisal, but the incident was settled peacefully. The British government accepted an apology and compensation from the Free State government and assurances as to the future safety of its servicemen at the Treaty Ports. This attack demonstrated the futility of any IRB hopes of cooperation with the Free State government to reopen the war with Britain. Much about this Free State army mutiny is still to be revealed. The Free State government did appoint a commission of enquiry but decided not to publish its findings or the evidence given.

After the army mutiny and the political cleansing of the armed services by General O'Duffy, Minister of Justice Kevin O'Higgins began releasing IRA detainees in larger batches, so that by 1 July only 209 remained in prison. De Valera was released on the 16th and resumed his position as president of the Sinn Fein movement. At its annual convention in Dublin in November 1924, it was confirmed that Sinn Fein members elected to the Dail would not take their seats; but signs of a divergence of opinion on this issue became apparent. De Valera wanted to campaign for the removal of the oath of allegiance to the British Crown required of every member of the Dail. A few others favored taking their seats in the Dail, if it were possible. This upset the hard-line republicans who regarded the Dail as a traitorous assembly. Claiming legality from the Second Dail, de Valera considered himself to be president of the "Dail of the Republic" and his Sinn Fein cabinet to be the rightful Irish government. However, the solid leadership core of the IRA for several months consisted of three men—Sean Lemass, the "Republican Defense Minister," George Gilmore, a member of the Sinn Fein cabinet, and Frank Aiken, the IRA chief of staff. De Valera hovered in the background, making only vague statements. In May 1925 David Fitzgerald revived the northern group of IRA units, and Jim Killeen the midland one; but the watching O'Higgins pounced quickly, and both men were arrested. Although many had dropped out for various reasons, a small group of hard-line republican activists worked to revitalize the IRA.

*One of the conditions of the Anglo-Irish Treaty was that Britain was allowed naval bases at three Irish ports. The Treaty Ports, as they became known, were at Spike Island and Berehaven on the south coast near Cork (required to refuel and support British warships in the Atlantic Ocean in time of war), and on Lough Swilly, Co Donegal, on the west coast (to cover the approaches to Merseyside and the Clyde).

A few days before an IRA convention was due to be held at Dalkey, near Dublin, nineteen of the leaders were arrested. Despite the enforced absence of so many senior members, the convention was held as planned on 14 November 1925. A new constitution was adopted, and the Executive Committee was reduced to twelve members, of whom seven were elected to the Army Council. Andrew Cooney was appointed chief of staff. It was agreed that the IRA would prepare for an armed revolution to take place in five years' time.

The issue of whether elected Sinn Fein members should take their seats in the Dail was raised, only to be rejected—abstentionism was to remain. Andrew Cooney was briefed to lead the IRA away from thoughts of constitutional approaches and to concentrate it upon future armed insurrection. The Cumann na mBan, at its annual convention, had voted overwhelmingly against allowing Sinn Fein members to enter the Dail.

Michael Price, commanding officer of the IRA's Dublin Brigade, was ordered to spring the recently arrested nineteen IRA men who were being held in Mountjoy Prison. With the aid of George Gilmore and one other member of the IRA, dressed in Garda Siochana uniforms, the three managed this by means of a trick.* Although on the run, much of the leadership of the IRA was again free.

The dispute deepened within the Sinn Fein movement over whether its elected members should enter the Dail. De Valera was openly campaigning for the removal of the oath of allegiance. On 11 April 1926 he and others resigned from the Sinn Fein. On the 16th he formed his own party, the Fianna Fail, usually translated as "Men of Destiny." The Fianna Fail Party considered the oath of allegiance to be the only bar to members taking their seats in the Dail. This political split further confused the Clan na Gael, and resulted in a lessening of funds from America. The IRA leadership did make attempts to reconcile the Sinn Fein and the Fianna Fail, but none were successful.

While Andrew Cooney was away in America trying to persuade the Clan na Gael to continue its support, Seamus Twomey was appointed acting chief of staff. He was a good organizer. By the time Cooney returned in October, he had raised the strength of the IRA to about 20,000 volunteers, tightened up the countrywide organization, imposed discipline, and instituted a program of training. Twomey also drew up plans for a number of raids on Garda Siochana police stations to obtain weapons, of which the IRA was extremely short. These began on 12

---

*According to J. Bowyer Bell

November, but only about twelve took place; two Garda officers were killed. The Free State authorities made many arrests.

In January 1927 Dan Breen took his seat in the Dail on a Sinn Fein ticket and accepted the oath of allegiance, which Liam Cosgrave had no intention of relaxing for the benefit of his opponents in either the Sinn Fein or the Fianna Fail. In the general election for a 153-seat Dail, de Valera's Fianna Fail won 44 seats, and Cosgrave's Cumann na nGaedheal gained 47. On 12 August 1927, by means of a compromise with his conscience and a trick, de Valera led his members in to take their seats in the Dail. Cosgrave was unable to form a government, and another election had to be held. Liam Cosgrave's party gained a majority; so de Valera and his Fianna Fail Party had to be content to be in opposition for the next five years. The Sinn Fein Party felt that both de Valera and the IRA had abandoned it.

Meanwhile, on 10 July 1927, Kevin O'Higgins, minister of justice in the Free State government, was shot and killed on his way to church at Blackrock, near Dublin, by four unidentified men. The IRA denied any implication in this murder. Odium had continually clung to O'Higgins from Civil War days; he was blamed (not entirely fairly, as such decisions were joint cabinet ones) for the death of the "77 Martyrs"—the IRA men executed by the Free State government—and especially for the reprisal execution of the "Four Hostages," who included Rory O'Connor, the IRA leader at the Battle of the Four Courts. Some suspicion rested upon certain of the army mutineers of 1924 but nothing was proved.

At the IRA convention of November 1927, the militant Seamus Twomey was confirmed in the post of chief of staff; Cooney wanted to resign. Even though the republican movement had splintered, the IRA had managed to pull itself together and was becoming a viable organization again. The countrywide network of IRA units had been knit into a revolutionary underground force dedicated to a "second round." Contacts and good relations had been reestablished with the U.S.-based Clan na Gael, which resulted in the resumed flow of money and also some arms. IRA volunteers met and paraded secretly, and as arms were received they were placed in secret dumps.

In June 1929 a new organization—the Workers Defense Corps—appeared, its members drawn from trade unions and the IRA. At its first convention, held in July, a number of left-wing IRA men appeared on its platform preaching socialism. The Workers Defense Corps was subsequently renamed the Irish Labor Defense League and was the first real venture of the Dublin-based IRA into socialist politics. The "Red Scare" really began in the Free State in March 1930, when the Workers Revolutionary Party was formed, the first of a spate of similar left-wing or communist parties that appeared in this year. IRA men were included in their membership, and the sudden increasing trend towards extreme socialism in the IRA caused the vision of a second round against the British to fade in spite of the fact that the military element of the IRA remained dedicated and active, although somewhat bewildered by the waves of socialism that were lapping against several countries.

Eventually both the Free State government and the Irish Catholic Church became seriously alarmed by the prospect of a socialist revolutionary movement that might threaten the very roots of their establishments. In October 1931 the government banned several political organizations. There was a general election early in 1932, in which the Fianna Fail gained seventy-two seats in the Dail, giving it a clear majority; de Valera formed a government. The republicans, although they differed with him, as he had deserted them, rather expected de Valera to release the IRA prisoners and purge the government service, the armed forces, and the police of pro-treaty men. But it did not work out quite like that.

Once in power de Valera played off the IRA and other republicans against the pro-treaty factions, broadening his own power base at their expense. He did take the IRA from the proscribed list and released IRA men sentenced by the military tribunals. On 22 February 1933 de Valera dismissed General O'Duffy from his post as commissioner of the Garda Siochana and appointed Col. Eamonn Broy in his place, with instructions to hunt down and arrest hard-line, active IRA men. For zealous work in this respect, the Police Special Branch in Dublin, consisting of former IRA men, became known as "Broy's Harriers."

There were also IRA killings in the Free State. For example, on 24 March 1936, Adm. Sir Henry Somerville, a retired English naval officer living in Ireland, was killed by unidentified gunmen at his home at Castletownshend, Skibbereen, Co Cork. His offense, in IRA eyes, was giving references as to good character for local lads who wanted to join the British armed forces. A card left on his body read, "This English agent sent fifty-two Irishmen to the British army in the last seven weeks." The following month, on 27 April, an alleged informer named as John Egan was shot dead by gunmen in Dungarven, Co Waterford.

On 21 May 1936 IRA Chief of Staff Seamus Twomey was arrested, which with the arrest of Jim Killeen in Belfast meant the IRA was deprived of its two top leaders. De Valera was pressing down hard on the IRA, and on 18 June 1936 again declared it to be an illegal organization in the

Free State. Sean MacBride became acting chief of staff until Tom Barry was appointed at the IRA convention later that year. MacBride became director of intelligence, but a personality clash occurred between him and Paedar O'Flaherty, the adjutant general, and O'Flaherty refused to take orders from the IRA Council.

Sean Russell, director of munitions, was one of the militants who had consistently urged that the IRA concentrate solely upon preparation for the "second round." He put forward a plan to operate a campaign of bombing in England as a preliminary step. On the other hand Tom Barry had wanted a war in Northern Ireland and did not like the idea of terrorism in England. The two men clashed. Barry brought Russell before an IRA court-martial, charged with misappropriation of IRA funds. Russell was convicted and lost his directorship and place on the Executive Committee. He then went off to America to try to persuade the Clan na Gael to back his ideas. The Clan na Gael was generally in favor of a strong militant line for the IRA but did not want to be forced into openly taking sides, fearing that would only deepen the split. In the meantime Paedar O'Flaherty, who wanted to start a terrorist campaign in England, went to that country without permission of the IRA military council and made several changes of appointments in the IRA there.

On 14 December 1937 Seamus Twomey was released from prison and reassumed his post as chief of staff. He found that IRA membership had fallen from the probable maximum of over 25,000 on-call volunteers in the early 1930s, all spoiling for a fight on any and every occasion, to less than half that number. He also found the IRA divided over future policy and weakened by leadership quarrels. On the credit side, he found that the basic network of IRA units and cells that spread throughout the Free State and into Northern Ireland, England, and Scotland was basically intact.

A fortnight after Twomey's release from prison, de Valera broke the link with the British Crown and so achieved by brash constitutional means what the squabbling republicans had not been able to accomplish by violence. De Valera also introduced a new constitution that changed the Irish Free State into "Eire"; his own designation changed from President of the Executive Council of the Dail to Taoiseach (leader), or prime minister. He followed this in April 1938 by making an agreement with Britain that brought to an end the economic war between the two countries and persuaded the British government to renounce its rights to the Treaty Ports. Since coming to power in 1932, de Valera had also encouraged the use of the Irish language, making proficiency in it a condition for entry into government service.

5 The S Plan

"For every man we have, the enemy has ten thousand men. Operations must therefore be so foolproof and so certain in action as to afford a 10,000-to-1 margin of safety, i.e., freedom from detection or capture."
—from the IRA S Plan of 1938

AT THE IRA convention of April 1938 there was strong lobbying on behalf of Sean Russell, the expelled director of munitions, and for his idea of a bombing campaign in England. The old leadership did not seem to have any positive alternative views, or any views at all except to condemn those put forward by Russell's proponents. Tom Barry, the former chief of staff, again put forward his idea for a terrorist campaign in Northern Ireland against British units stationed there but did not manage to muster sufficient support for it to be carried. As had become customary, the convention voted in a new Executive Committee, the majority of whom were supporters of Russell and his plan. The new IRA Council, solidly in his favor, reinstated him and appointed him chief of staff in place of Twomey. Some protest was made against appointing a dismissed volunteer to the key position in the IRA.

There was a sort out: some prominent IRA men resigned, others just faded into the background, others were asked to resign, and yet others were dismissed. One of those who resigned was Sean MacBride, who established a legal practice in Dublin and later defended a number of IRA men before the courts. Russell selected for his GHQ staff pure militants who had little time for politics, social causes, or anything that was a deviation from the military aim and role of the IRA.

In May 1938 the IRA Council formally adopted Russell's project for a bombing campaign in England. His visit to the U.S. had been successful, and the Clan na Gael had promised funds to back this operation. Russell himself was of the firm opinion that Prime Minister de Valera would tacitly approve such a campaign, and that the IRA would be able to count on a safe sanctuary in Eire. He began to search out and reenlist old IRA men experienced in handling explosives, one of whom was Seamus O'Donovan, who had been director of munitions in the Civil War but who had resigned from the IRA on his release from prison in 1924.

O'Donovan produced the famous S Plan for widespread, organized bombing and sabotage in England. It was an ambitious plan, well beyond the capabilities of the IRA, but it was eagerly and enthusiastically approved by the IRA Council. The S Plan laid down general principles to be followed and gave guidance on organization, selection of targets, and preparation. It was divided into two sections—Propaganda and Action. The action section was in two parts, that of direct action and that of political action. Targets for sabotage included not only military installations, but aircraft factories and other key industries at a time when Britain was rearming for World War II; and public services such as railways, postal and telephone services. Commerce, banking, and shipping were included, and each was discussed in detail. Propaganda action included issuing press statements, proclamations, and communiques.

Explosives and other necessary materials were slowly accumulated, and classes of instruction were held. Preparations in England included establishing safe-houses and "sleepers," and activating and harnessing the several Irish Republican Clubs and organizations and the small IRA units. Training in the handling and use of explosives was a period of trial and error, in which there were a number of accidents due to ignorance, inexperience, and faulty material.

As soon as the first sabotage teams were ready it was decided to have a trial operation in Northern Ireland, where the IRA leadership had continually and solidly supported Russell's plan. The first exploit was to blow up the customs posts at Claudy and Strabane, on the border with Co Donegal, on the night of 28 November 1938; but during the day, in a cottage near the border, the bombs exploded prematurely and killed three IRA men. This alerted the Royal Ulster Constabulary, which made a few arrests but waited for a month before swooping to make mass arrests in the hope of completely disrupting the IRA framework in Northern Ireland. However, as Russell had weeded out and replaced men who disagreed with his policy, the RUC arrested many who were no longer active and missed many of the new volunteers who were not known to the police.

Russell wanted legal authority to declare war on England in the name of the IRA, so he persuaded the few surviving members of the Second Dail (which dedicated republicans still regarded as the legal government of the "Republic of Ireland") to formally hand over their powers to the IRA to make it the legal government. A document was produced and signed by all concerned; it became known as the IRA-Dail Treaty and was taken seriously by many republicans. Apart from giving legality to the activities of the IRA members, it salved their consciences, as the Catholic Church had a narrow, strict interpretation of what were "just" wars. The IRA men wanted this approbation as the legal sanction to kill, without which they were considered to be criminals and gangsters. The first announcement of the IRA-Dail Treaty, which was signed at 16 Rathmines Grove, Dublin,* was made in 8 December 1938 issue of the *Wolfe Tone Weekly.*

The IRA Council, now considering itself to be the legal government of the "Republic of Ireland," decided to declare war on Britain. On 12 January 1938 an IRA ultimatum signed by Patrick Flemming as secretary of the IRA Council, and other members, was delivered to Lord Halifax, the British foreign secretary, demanding the withdrawal of British armed forces from Northern Ireland, setting a three-day time limit for agreement to comply, and outlining other conditions. Little or no notice was taken of this letter by the British Foreign Office. In accordance with instructions outlined in the S Plan on the 15th, when the time limit expired, copies of an IRA proclamation of declaration of war on Britain were posted in prominent places throughout Eire, Northern Ireland, and some of the major cities in England, asking for support. Little or no notice was taken of this either.

The following day major explosions occurred in England at electrical installations and power stations in London, Manchester, Birmingham, and Northumberland; the next day there were more. Then, as planned, there was a lull for eighteen days; British police arrested IRA men and suspects.

The next phase began on 4 February, when there were explosions at underground stations and Left-Luggage offices in London and in Coventry. On the 6th a bomb exploded outside the wall of Walton Prison, Liverpool. Then followed another deliberate pause until the last three days of March, when there were a series of explosions in London, Birmingham, Coventry, and Liverpool, after which there was another deliberate lull.

By this time a copy of O'Donovan's S Plan had been obtained by the British police, who were taking the IRA campaign seriously. A copy was passed to Prime Minister de Valera in Dublin, who had just persuaded British Prime Minister Neville Chamberlain to relinquish the Treaty Ports. De Valera thought Chamberlain to be a weak statesman, and he was hoping to persuade him to abolish the border between Eire and Northern Ireland, which would have achieved a united Ireland by constitutional

---

*According to J. Bowyer Bell

means. De Valera was extremely angry with the IRA for upsetting his antipartition campaign and disrupting negotiations. Far from allowing the IRA to use Eire as a safe haven from which to operate into England, he at once instituted tough anti-IRA legislation.

World War II was fast approaching, and the German government showed a vague interest in the IRA and its bombing campaign in England; they sent their agent Oskar Pfaus* to Dublin to make contact. As always the Germans were extremely ill-informed about the IRA, and Pfaus was told initially to contact General O'Duffy, one of the IRA's main opponents. However, Pfaus eventually made contact with Seamus Twomey, no longer an active IRA member, who put him in touch with Sean Russell. By this time Russell was running short of money for his bombing campaign in England, as funds from the Clan na Gael had not come up to expectations. The IRA was also short of arms and explosives so O'Donovan was sent to Germany to see what he could obtain.

As there seemed to be little hope of any immediate financial help from Germany, Sean Russell decided in April 1939 to visit the U.S. on a fund-raising tour and to persuade the Clan na Gael to be more generous. While he was away he deputed Stephen Hayes, the adjutant general, to be acting chief of staff. Russell did not do well in America, and in June was arrested and kept in detention while the British King George VI and Queen Elizabeth were making an official state visit to the U.S. The Irish lobby pressured the authorities to release Russell, and over fifty members of the U.S. House of Representatives refused to meet the British monarch.

Meanwhile in England the campaign was going according to plan, although several IRA men had been arrested. On 5 May 1939 tear-gas bombs exploded in cinemas in Liverpool; there were other explosions in both London and Coventry. Then, after a fortnight, on the 19th, delayed-action incendiary devices started fires in a number of hotels across England. On the 29th magnesium bombs exploded in a Birmingham cinema; two days later similar incidents occurred in London.

In 1939 preparations for defense against anticipated air raids in case of war were obvious in Britain, including Northern Ireland. Air raid wardens were being recruited and trained; gas masks, as they became available, were issued to the people. The IRA Northern Command headquarters in Belfast had a secret radio transmitter, linked to the Dublin headquarters, over which instructions were passed. On 31 May, on receipt of orders from the Dublin GHQ, IRA men persuaded the Catholic communities in Belfast to pile their gas masks in heaps on the roadways and set fire to

*According to J. Bowyer Bell

them. This acute form of civil disobedience horrified the loyal Northern Ireland Protestants, who took the Nazi threat extremely seriously.

The terrorist campaign continued in England, with lengthy pauses between spates of explosions. On 24 July 1939 the British home secretary stated in parliament that there had been 127 terrorist outrages in England, in which one person had died and fifty-five had been injured. He added that sixty-five people had been arrested and convicted in connection with them. On the 29th the Prevention of Violence Act was passed, aimed at control of Irish persons coming into England, their deportation, their registration while in Britain, and the detention of those suspected of committing acts of terrorism. On 5 August the first expulsion orders were executed.

On 25 August an explosion—the largest so far—occurred in Broadgate, Coventry, killing five people and injuring sixty. The device was being taken on a bicycle to be positioned when the IRA man taking it suddenly realized that it was about to explode. He hastily parked his bicycle, with the device on it, in Broadgate, and escaped, reaching Eire safely that night. Several people were arrested by the British police in connection with the "Coventry Bombing," including Peter Barnes and James McCormack (alias Richards), who were brought to trial, convicted, and executed on 7 February 1940.

In Eire there were extensive police searches and many IRA men were arrested. On the 25th a military tribunal (technically a Special Criminal Court) of five military officers was established in Dublin to conduct trials without jury. It was given considerable powers, including that of imposing imprisonment for refusing to answer questions. World War II broke out on 3 September 1939, and this changed attitudes and reactions. Prime Minister de Valera immediately declared Irish neutrality; he did not want anything to tempt Britain to invade Eire. About eighty IRA men were interned; they were joined by others arrested during the course of the war and remained in internment throughout its duration.

World War II brought about a change of policy within the Clan na Gael, now led by Joseph Garrity, who had visited Eire in July 1939. The Clan agreed that nothing should be done to endanger the neutrality of Eire, and all funds for the IRA abruptly ceased. The S Plan had been tailored to match promised funds from America; without American money there was no S Plan. Seamus O'Donovan, who had returned empty-handed once, was again sent to Germany to see what could be obtained from that country.

The planned IRA terrorist campaign in wartime England ran into the difficulties of a suddenly imposed system of internal security, wherein everyone was issued an identity card, conditioned to watch for espionage, warned against careless talk and asking sensitive questions, and urged to report any suspicious incidents immediately. There was a good but discreet working arrangement between the Eire Garda Siochana Special Branch and the British Scotland Yard Special Branch. IRA suspects were arrested almost as soon as they stepped ashore in England, arms caches were quickly discovered, and safe-houses identified and watched.

In Britain the tight wartime security and general alertness for enemy spies stifled IRA activity and movement. A few other bombing incidents occurred by teams left in the field who felt they must strike some sort of blow, but they became less frequent; the last one took place on 6 February 1940—the day before the "Coventry Bombers" were executed.

Prime Minister de Valera laid a very heavy hand on the IRA in Eire. A police raid on 9 September 1939 caught most of the IRA Council and military staff; only the acting chief of staff, Stephen Hayes, and one other managed to escape. More arrests followed, but like the Royal Ulster Constabulary in Northern Ireland, the Garda did not know the new men. Hayes tried to hold the IRA together and to reform a GHQ; but owing to keen police surveillance, lack of funds, and fewer safe-houses, he had a difficult time.

Stephen Hayes now pinned his hopes on help from Germany; but when O'Donovan returned to Eire in October, he brought unpalatable German advice. The Germans recommended the IRA to come to terms with Prime Minister de Valera, who already held over one hundred IRA men in his prisons. Most IRA prisoners were held in Mountjoy Prison, Dublin; in an escape attempt there on 22 October, an explosion intended to blow a large gap in the outer wall failed to blast one of sufficient width, and so none escaped. Soon many IRA men were on a hunger strike, a traditional Irish protest. One of these was Patrick McGrath, an Easter Rising hero; the Eire government was deeply concerned as to what the repercussions might be if he died. The survivors of the Easter Rising of 1916 were by their very existence regarded with awe as folk heroes. On the 9th McGrath was freed, on the forty-third day of his hunger strike.

The IRA had some arms but almost no ammunition, so Hayes authorized a daring raid on the Magazine Fort in Phoenix Park, Dublin, where the major part of Eire's army ammunition was stored. The huge Phoenix Park was closed at night to the public. On the evening of 23 December 1939, the small guard on the Magazine Fort was tricked into opening the gate, and the soldiers were tied up. Trucks were brought in, and almost all the ammunition stored there—amounting to 1,084,000 rounds of varying types—was quickly loaded onto them and driven away. Belatedly, the alarm was raised.

The audacity of this raid touched the Eire army on a raw nerve as it was held up to ridicule by the public; perhaps this as much as anything hardened its attitude towards the IRA. At once a massive army and police search was mounted that lasted for about a week. Roadblocks were erected all over the country; traffic halted for hours in Dublin and other cities while all vehicles were searched. The IRA problem was how to dispose of such a massive amount of ammunition, which far exceeded anticipation; although plans had been made to hide small amounts in various places, the sheer volume was too much for the caches to absorb. This made the task of finding it comparatively easy, and by 1 January 1940, over 850,000 rounds had been recovered. One large consignment was discovered in Northern Ireland by the RUC and returned to the Eire government. After the Magazine Fort raid, in January, the Eire government passed the Emergency Powers Act; once again the Curragh Internment Camp was opened.

Sean McCaughey had been released from prison in December 1939 and was appointed commanding officer of the IRA Northern Ireland Command. IRA strength in the province since World War II began had shrunk from about 500 down to less than 300. Generally, there was little scope for IRA activity because of tight wartime restrictions. The B-Specials and the newly established military part-time Home Guard patrolled during the hours of darkness, alert for the infiltration of enemy agents and any subversive activity. The Eire government formed a part-time Irish Defense Force, a sort of Home Guard, to protect key installations and to watch for invasion along the seacoasts. This eventually rose to a strength of over 250,000 and absorbed much of the nation's active manpower. The IDF also formed a tight surveillance screen over the IRA and its activities.

A number of shoot-outs occurred between the Garda and the IRA in the course of the year. One was on 2 January 1940, when a policeman was shot and killed while arresting Thomas MacCurtain, the son of the former lord mayor of Cork killed in the Tan War. Another policeman was killed and two wounded in another shoot-out on 17 August, which resulted in Patrick McGrath and Thomas Hearte, both IRA members, being executed at Mountjoy Prison on 6 September. Among IRA personnel arrested in 1940 was the sixteen-year-old Brenden Behan, who later achieved literary fame.

The IRA leadership suffered a severe blow on 17 February when the Garda raided a meeting of IRA leaders in Dublin and arrested a number of them. Once again, Stephen Hayes escaped, which meant that he was practically the only senior IRA member at large in Eire. He promoted his own men to fill the vacancies. Hayes made unsuccessful attempts to regain contact with Germany through Belgium, that country being neutral before May 1940, when it was invaded by the Germans. Suddenly, on 5 May, the German agent Herman Goertz was parachuted into Eire, avoided detection, and made contact with the IRA. The link was once again established, and the German agent was sheltered in safe-houses provided by the Cumann na mBan. The Eire authorities were alerted to the IRA-German liaison. Throughout the war the German ambassador in Dublin did his best to discourage German contacts with the IRA.

According to evidence later produced and substantiated, it seems that IRA prisoners and internees in Eire were given a rough time by prison staffs, with, one suspects, tacit government approval. Their rations were small, their food badly cooked, and they were in unheated cells or wooden huts in winter. If they refused food or prison clothing, they were left in solitary confinement for days on end. Censorship was now in force in Eire to maintain neutrality, and the Irish public did not know how miserable conditions were for IRA prisoners. It was also alleged that IRA men were occasionally beaten up by the prison staff and by soldiers brought in to guard the Curragh Internment Camp. Hunger strikes were frequent, and on 16 April 1940 Tony D'Arcy died while on one; on the 19th, so did John McNeela.

On 14 December 1940 IRA internees set fire to some of their wooden huts at the Curragh Internment Camp; on the 16th soldiers fired on IRA men, killing one and wounding others. The IRA alleged this act was deliberate, but no action was taken against the soldiers, as the authorities regarded the incident as an attempted mass break-out. The IRA internees came to be bitterly divided among themselves in the Curragh Internment Camp. As the prisons in Northern Ireland were filled with IRA men, a "prison ship" was brought into service to house them.

In the meantime, Sean Russell, the IRA chief of staff, had failed in his attempts to return to Eire. The Clan na Gael did not want anything to compromise Eire's neutrality, and would have nothing to do with him in this respect. Instead, Russell went to Germany, arriving in Berlin on 1 May 1940, to see what support he could obtain for the IRA. The Germans were not helpful at all, but eventually agreed to send Russell back to Eire by submarine, a project they named Operation Dove. In August 1940, a U-boat left Germany with Russell on board, but he was taken ill and died on the 14th of a burst stomach ulcer. He was buried at sea. News of Russell's death did not reach the IRA in Dublin until November 1940.

Wild and exaggerated rumors abounded of what had happened to him and how he died.

The IRA was now in a perilous state, and throughout the winter of 1940-41, Stephen Hayes, now the chief of staff, did his best to prevent it disintegrating completely. Senior members were either interned or on the run, while others had disappeared. No one seemed to know exactly who was on the Executive Committee or the IRA Council, where they were, or whether they were still active. Owing to the lack of this essential information, the IRA in Eire — or such of it as remained cohesive and contactable came directly under the personal control of Hayes.

On the international front, Prime Minister de Valera remained determined that his Irish neutrality would not be compromised, and he maintained full diplomatic relations with both Germany and Britain; but his military intelligence branch was given the task of hunting down any German agents operating in Eire. Of the handful of German agents parachuted into Eire (some with instructions to contact the IRA), all but Herman Goertz had been arrested. However, de Valera did lean toward the British in that he did nothing to prevent Irishmen from enlisting in the British armed forces, which over 200,000 did; they were allowed to return home on leave in plain clothes. He also allowed the RAF to overfly Eire; and rescued RAF pilots brought down in Eire were not detained, but sent back to Britain.

The British government had not imposed conscription in Northern Ireland, as the IRA had hoped, which would have aggravated the Catholic population and also presented subversive opportunities. Under Sean McCaughey the IRA in that province was much better organized. The Catholic population, especially in Belfast, was occasionally aroused to subversive action. When the first German air raids hit Belfast in 1941, the IRA instigated Catholics to light bonfires in the Falls Road area to guide German bomber aircraft to their targets and to light up the area so that German pilots could check their positions. As in the whole of Britain, in Northern Ireland there was a strict blackout in the hours of darkness. There were no street lights, vehicles had masked headlights with only a dim slit of light showing through, and windows of all houses and buildings where internal lights were used had to have special blackout screens or drapes. In fact, a curfew had to be imposed on the Falls Road area from October 1941 until January 1943.

Alarmed and puzzled at what was happening at the IRA headquarters in Dublin — or rather, the lack of information about what was going on — Sean McCaughey, commanding officer of the IRA Northern Command, went to Dublin to see Stephen Hayes. When he saw the vacuum and the chaos, he pressured Hayes into appointing him adjutant-general; for a while McCaughey held both appointments, retaining command of the IRA in the north. He began to suspect that many of the IRA failures and arrests had been the work of an informer, and moreover, an informer of high rank. His suspicion fell on Stephen Hayes.

Using his new authority as adjutant general, McCaughey carried out certain investigations which he felt confirmed his suspicions. On 30 June 1941, he and a few other IRA men from the north seized Hayes and held him prisoner. By threats and beatings, they forced confessions from him that he was the informer who had passed information on to the Garda. In particular, his captors accused him of revealing the locations of certain safe-houses at which IRA leaders had been arrested. On one occasion Hayes attempted to escape, but was prevented and again beaten.

Two former chiefs of staff, Andrew Cooney and Seamus Twomey, both now retired from the IRA, were consulted by McCaughey, and on 23 July 1941 Stephen Hayes was arraigned before an IRA court-martial. The evidence produced was mainly the "confessions" Hayes had been forced to write. He was found guilty and sentenced to be shot. However, none of the confessions had been signed, so McCaughey persuaded Hayes to rewrite them at length with fuller details. Slowly, Hayes rewrote his confession, which he completed and signed 28 August. Later, Hayes said it was a complete fabrication, and that he had taken his time in writing it out in order to stay alive as long as possible. In the meantime, he was kept bound to a chair under constant armed guard in a safe-house in Dublin. On 30 August McCaughey was arrested in Dublin. An emergency meeting was held by the IRA Council and a Northerner, Pearse Kelly, was appointed chief of staff.

On 8 September 1941 Hayes managed to escape; he immediately went to a Garda station to tell his story. The Garda quickly arrested the men responsible for kidnapping and holding Hayes. Hayes's lengthy confession was salvaged by the IRA, to be later edited and then selectively distributed to certain people. It was dated 10 September—two days after Hayes had escaped.

Sean McCaughey was put on trial, and evidence was given against him by Stephen Hayes, who was also put on trial. Both were convicted of several offenses. McCaughey was sentenced to be executed, but this was commuted to imprisonment. He eventually died while on hunger strike in prison, on 1 May 1946, after thirty-one days without food; he had been demanding an unconditional release. Stephen Hayes was sentenced to imprisonment; he was released in 1945, having been kept apart from other IRA prisoners for his own safety.

Most IRA men and many others doubted the accuracy of any of the

Hayes confessions, which when examined in detail showed considerable discrepancies. Hayes had commanded the IRA from April 1939 until July 1941, a period of failure and despondency, and he was judged in that context as a poor leader who had made poor decisions. The actions that made the IRA as a whole turn against Hayes were that after his escape from the custody of the IRA guards, he gave the Garda information, recognized the Dublin court, and gave evidence before it.

The new IRA chief of staff, Pearse Kelly, was arrested in November 1941; his place was taken by Sean Harrington, who was arrested in December; and his place was taken by Sean McCool, who was arrested in March 1942, when Sean McNamee became chief of staff.

On 26 January 1942, the first American troops landed in Northern Ireland; at an IRA conference in Dublin the following month, the significance of this was considered. It was decided that terrorist activity in the province should continue to be directed against British installations, but that great care should be taken not to involve any U.S. military personnel. It was confirmed also that no violence should be used in the south, or any IRA activity at all, in order not to antagonize the Dublin government, in the hope that the IRA would be left alone in Eire, which could then become a secure base from which to operate into Northern Ireland.

The IRA in Northern Ireland now had about 300 activists in Belfast, in four companies, and about another 100 men scattered across the province.* The IRA Northern Command had an unusual unit known as the Special Operations Group, which contained a few Protestants from the Irish Union. The Irish Union, which had been organized by Denis Ireland, was a nonviolent political organization seeking to persuade Protestants of the advantages of a united Ireland. Several Northern Ireland Protestants had joined the IRA through this group, one of whom was John Graham, who eventually became director of intelligence at IRA headquarters. Graham also started and edited a newspaper, the *Republican News.*

In Northern Ireland on 3 April 1942, in Dungannon, two IRA men evaded arrest by shooting at and wounding two RUC policemen before escaping over the border into Eire. Two days later, in Dublin, there was a shoot-out when members of the Garda Special Branch cornered three IRA men. One of the IRA men drew his revolver to fire at the police, but hesitated. The revolver was then hastily snatched by one of his companions—Brenden Behan, just released from a Borstal institution.† Behan

---

*RUC sources
†Borstal was a type of prison for young offenders. Note his play "Borstal Boy."

shot at the police, and then escaped, but was arrested soon after and sentenced to a term of imprisonment.

In the north, Hugh McAteer, who had been appointed commanding officer of the IRA's Northern Command, decided to cause a diversion to distract the attention of the RUC, so that republicans could commemorate the anniversary of the Easter Rising. For this purpose, on the 5th, the same day as the Dublin shoot-out, a six-man Active Service Unit led by Tom Williams fired on a RUC patrol in Belfast. The RUC men fired back, and the IRA unit took refuge in a house on Cawnpore Street. A gun-battle ensued in which one RUC policeman was killed and the six IRA men captured. Although there was no direct evidence that Tom Williams had fired the shot that killed the policeman, as the leader he was held responsible in law. He was tried, convicted, and executed. A few days later, Tom Morris, another IRA man, was stopped by a RUC policeman at Strabane on the border; Morris shot and wounded him. Although he escaped, Morris was soon arrested. The new IRA policy was to shoot to escape arrest, if such action were possible.

Because of the number of arrests that were being made of key personnel, deputies were nominated for the senior posts; they would automatically take over should the holder of the appointment be suddenly arrested or killed. On 23 May 1942, Sean McNamee, the IRA chief of staff, was arrested; as planned, his nominated deputy, Hugh McAteer, automatically became the chief of staff. McAteer still retained his position as commanding officer of the Northern Command.

The accent remained on IRA activity in Northern Ireland but quiet acquiescence in Eire. Arms and ammunition were taken from secret dumps in Eire and moved to others close to the Northern Ireland border. On 30 August 1942 a truck loaded with arms and ammunition was taken over the border into Northern Ireland to McCaffery's Farm, at Hannastown, and put into a barn. The two IRA men with the consignment, Gerard O'Callaghan and Vincent McDowell, were checking the arms and ammunition when a group of RUC policemen burst in. O'Callaghan was shot and killed, McDowell was arrested, and the arms were seized by the RUC.

A fortnight later, a large van carrying about twenty armed IRA men crossed the border into Northern Ireland near Cullaville, not far from Newry. The van was detected by four RUC men, and a gun-battle flared up in which one policeman and one IRA man were wounded. Outnumbered, the other three policemen were captured; but as the alarm had been raised by this time, they were released. The van and the IRA raiders hastily disappeared back across the border into Eire. The fact that the IRA was launching armed raids into the province upset the Dublin government, which had been under the impression it had been completely crushed.

Hugh McAteer, who had remained in Belfast, was arrested in September 1942. In a shoot-out the same month in Belfast between the IRA and the RUC, John Graham, the Protestant editor of the *Republican News*, was also arrested. His newspaper had claimed that the IRA mounted sixty attacks in Northern Ireland in the months of August, September, and October 1942. On 15 January 1943 Hugh McAteer and three others escaped from Crumlin Road Prison, Belfast. Although this dramatic escape—the first from this prison for years—gave the flagging IRA a little prestige, it had the converse effect of causing the RUC to redouble its efforts to suppress all IRA activities in Northern Ireland. In March 1943 there was an even more spectacular jailbreak in Northern Ireland, from Derry Prison; twenty-one IRA men escaped by tunnelling their way underground to beyond the prison's outer walls.

On 9 September 1942, at Ballyboden, Rathfarnham, Co Dublin, Sergeant O'Brien of the Garda Special Branch, was shot dead near his own front door. It was a vengeance killing, as O'Brien had been one of the most zealous, active, and most hated by the IRA of "Broy's Harriers." Maurice O'Neill was arrested, convicted of this murder, and executed on 12 November.

Hugh McAteer was again arrested in October 1943 and Charles Kerins became the IRA chief of staff. Kerins had little to take over as practically all the senior IRA men were in prison, interned, or in hiding; and the local IRA units had hardly any communication with their GHQ for reasons of individual security. There was no Executive Committee, no IRA Council, just a chief of staff without a GHQ staff, almost alone without any units or volunteers to command. On 15 June 1944 Kerins was arrested, tried, and convicted of the murder of Sergeant O'Brien. He was executed at Mountjoy Prison, Dublin.

As there was no IRA Council in being, no successor could be appointed: Charles Kerins had been the last remnant of the old IRA leadership. Gerald Boland, minister of justice in the Eire government, later boasted that "The IRA is dead," and that he had killed it in 1945. He was almost right. The IRA was a headless body that barely twitched. From the time of Kerins's arrest in June 1944 until the end of World War II in Europe in May 1945, there was no IRA activity of any consequence in either Eire or Northern Ireland. At the end of the war, over 1,000 IRA men were in the Curragh

Internment Camp; but they were bitterly divided amongst themselves, separating into hostile factions. Morale was bad, and treatment of the IRA men in prisons and internment camps had become worse. Apart from their own families and close circle of personal friends, the IRA internees were forgotten men, and the old IRA heroes were yesterday's men. The IRA was almost dead.

6 The IRA Phoenix Rises Again

"If a revolutionary movement is not active, it dies."
—Sean MacStiofean, chief of staff,
Provisional IRA, 1970–72

AFTER WORLD WAR II IRA prisoners and internees were only slowly released, and neither the government of Eire nor that of Northern Ireland showed any signs of magnanimity, nor was there any hint of an amnesty. Only two small batches of IRA internees, obviously carefully selected, had been released from the Curragh Internment Camp, one in 1943 and the other in 1944. They were mostly silent, disillusioned men who had lost hope of winning the battle the IRA way; most of them quietly returned to their homes to sink back in anonymity. A few managed to emigrate to the U.S., although wartime regulations in both countries made this difficult. Only a handful remained dedicated to the IRA ideal and secretly rejoined their old local units. A few were even instrumental in reforming old units that had disintegrated. As there was no active top leadership and therefore no central guidance, the IRA men met just to keep in contact and to hope for better IRA times. Such local IRA units as existed became old comrades' "talking shops."

During 1945 a few senior leaders began to reappear, taking steps to bring together again such members of the 1938 Executive Committee of the days of Sean Russell and the S Plan as had survived. This ad hoc but legal Executive Committee met in March 1945, stimulating a revival in Dublin. Patrick Flemming, the only available member of the IRA Council, was appointed chief of staff.

The Eire government did not want an IRA revival: it thought it had suppressed the IRA to extinction. The Special Branch of the Garda Siochana was instructed to track down and arrest any IRA leaders. The Special Branch had an almost immediate success in January 1946 when it burst in on a meeting of IRA leaders at the Ardee Bar in Dublin. Twelve were arrested, shattering the reforming IRA Council, the GHQ, and the

Dublin Brigade. Few in the IRA trusted their own GHQ after the Hayes Affair. This distrust was being slowly, very slowly, overcome but after these Special Branch arrests, obviously the work of an informer, distrust again mounted sharply.

Tony Magan, a senior IRA officer, was released from the Curragh Internment Camp in December 1946; he set to work to gather together and reactivate the shattered Executive Committee. They met in March 1947 and appointed an IRA Council. Liam McGuiness, commanding officer of the Dublin Brigade, was appointed chief of staff.

In July 1946 the Clan na Pobrachta (Republican Party) was formed by Sean MacBride, James Killeen, and Michael Fitzpatrick, two former chiefs of staff and an adjutant general, respectively. Its founder-members were tired of the old policy of constitutional abstentionism and wanted a voice in the Dail. On this issue it clashed with both the Sinn Fein and the IRA, both of which still adhered rigidly to the old principle. The Clan na Pobrachta gathered strength and won two seats in the Dail at local bye-elections in the autumn of 1947.

A general election was held in Eire in 1948, in which Eamonn de Valera's Fianna Fail Party did not obtain sufficient seats to govern without being in a coalition. No other Irish party would agree to work with de Valera, whose popularity was low at this moment. In fact, four political parties with little or nothing in common with each other combined into a coalition with the express purpose of freezing de Valera out of power. They were the Fine Gael Party led by Sean Costello, the Labor Party, the Clan na Talhmann (Farmers' Party), and Sean MacBride's Clan na Pobrachta, which held six seats. Sean Costello became the prime minister, and Sean MacBride, the minister of external affairs.

During the course of 1948 there was a gradual relaxation in Eire of the strict measures against the IRA, and by the end of the year the military tribunal had ceased to sit. All the IRA men had been released from the Curragh Internment Camp, and political prisoners were also being freed, although it was not until 1949 that all sections of the Special Powers Act were suspended, and convicted IRA men also released before they had completed their prison sentences. On 7 November 1948 Prime Minister Sean Costello introduced into the Dail a bill to repeal the External Relations Act of 1936, which still linked Eire to the British Crown. He said that the bill "will end, and end forever, in a simple unequivocal way, the country's long and tragic association with the British Crown." The bill was passed unanimously, and the Republic of Ireland Act came into force on 21 January 1949—the thirtieth anniversary of the Declaration of the Irish Republic by the First Dail in 1919. It was Sean Costello, and not Eamonn de Valera, who had constitutionally brought about the *de facto* Republic of Ireland.

In answer to a question in the Dail by Eamonn de Valera, leader of the opposing Fianna Fail, the prime minister replied that the name of the country in the English language was to be the "Republic of Ireland," and in Irish to be "Poblacht na mEireann." The official language was Gaelic, with English as the second language. As a republic, Ireland then automatically withdrew from the British Commonwealth of Nations, of which it had been a member since 1921, but retained certain nonpolitical links with Britain, such as trade agreements. No passports were required of either British or Irish citizens to visit each other's country.

At the IRA convention in September 1949, the decision was taken to prepare for a campaign of terrorism in Northern Ireland and to abstain completely from any activity in Eire. Tony Magan was appointed chief of staff. Magan was a silent, unconfiding man and a strict disciplinarian; his idea was to build a properly structured IRA that would be respectable and responsible, and would be accepted by the Irish people as such. Magan deplored the gangsterism that had occurred in the past and was tending to become inherent. He was fully aware that such criminal activities alienated not only the people, but also the government and the Catholic Church.

Magan insisted that all IRA members live blameless lives and dismissed those with criminal convictions. He disliked the left-wing socialism that had steadily seeped into the IRA since the 1930s, and rigidly enforced the IRA rule that members must not belong to the Communist Party. Magan viewed MacBride's Clan na Pobrachta with distaste. After some years of suppression, the *United Irishman* had reappeared as a monthly periodical in May 1948, and so the IRA once again had a legal voice, which Magan controlled and used to mold an ascetic, almost Cromwellian "New Model IRA."

To replenish its armory in preparation for the Northern Campaign, the IRA decided to embark upon a series of raids on British military establishments in both England and Northern Ireland. The first of these was on 3 June 1951 by a small IRA unit from Derry, on Ebrington Barracks, near Derry, which was then a joint Royal Navy–RAF antisubmarine school known as HMS *Eagle.* It was a silent, surreptitious theft of twenty rifles, twenty sten guns, two bren guns, six machine guns, and some ammunition. The sten gun was a small 9mm caliber personal automatic weapon in wide use with the British forces during World War II, while the bren gun was a light automatic weapon of .303 caliber, fired from a bipod.

The success of this raid stimulated the IRA and boosted its morale. Magan immediately formed a military committee, which was given the specific task of producing an overall plan for the Northern Campaign — a sort of new S Plan being envisaged with Northern Ireland as the target, instead of England. The three main personalities on this new military committee were Tony Magan, as chief of staff; Thomas MacCurtain, who had just been released from prison; and an older man, Patrick Logan, who had been the absentee Sinn Fein member of parliament for South Armagh, at Stormont. The plan for the Northern Campaign was eventually produced in outline and accepted by the IRA Council. The first stage was to continue to raid British military establishments in both England and Northern Ireland for arms and ammunition.

In October 1951 Liam Kelly, the IRA commanding officer in Co Tyrone, Northern Ireland, was dismissed from the IRA by Tony Magan for planning an action without GHQ consent. Piqued, and chafing at seeming GHQ inaction, Kelly founded a political party of his own, the Saor Uladh (Free Ulster), and also a military arm to it, the Fianna Uladh (Ulster Warriors). All the IRA men in his former command defected and joined him. Initially, the Saor Uladh recognized the governments at Stormont and Dublin, which brought Kelly into direct conflict with both the Sinn Fein and the IRA. Being popular and energetic, Kelly had developed a strong power base in Co Tyrone, and the weak GHQ in Dublin was in no position to take punitive action against him. An unspoken agreement developed to live and let live for the time being.

In the 1953 elections for Stormont, Liam Kelly was elected for the mid-Tyrone seat; but he was convicted of making seditious speeches both before and after the election, sentenced to imprisonment, and so automatically debarred from taking his seat. In June 1954 Kelly nevertheless was elected senator in the Upper House of the Republic of Ireland.

Kelly was released from prison in August 1954, and he concentrated upon his Saor Uladh organization. His Fianna Uladh had faded out and the one party encompassed both political and military roles. Realizing how unpopular recognition of the Dublin and Belfast governments was with the republican Irish, he included abstentionism in his Saor Uladh program, even though he retained his position as an Irish senator. Disdainful of IRA disapproval, the Saor Uladh carried out a few selected terrorist exploits in Northern Ireland on a completely independent basis. Kelly had made fruitful contact with the Clan na Gael in America and received arms and money.

The seeming inactivity of the IRA in Northern Ireland caused restless discontent. Splinter groups began to appear. One of these in Dublin in the early 1950s adopted the old title of the Irish Republican Brotherhood. Another was known as the Arm na Saoirse (Freedom Army) which, after some argument, was reabsorbed into the IRA. Yet another was the Irish National Brotherhood, a rowdy youth organization led by Gerard Lawless, which eventually merged into the Fianna Eireann, the republican youth movement.

In America the Clan na Gael had been shaking off its attitude of non-assistance to the IRA. As it revived politically, it divided into factions, being confused by the IRA splits. One Clan faction led by Joseph Stynes backed the IRA, as led by Tony Magan; but another faction, led by Tadgh Brosnon, supported Liam Kelly and his Saor Uladh and a tiny splinter group led by Brenden O'Boyle.* Another part of the Clan, under Patrick Smith, tried desperately to remain neutral and evenhanded.

The first planned IRA arms raid in England occurred on 25 July 1953 on the Combined Cadet Force armory at Felstead School, in Essex. Cathal Goulding from Dublin, Seamus Canning from Derry, and John Stephenson (later to call himself Sean MacStiofean) of London drove to the unguarded armory, broke the lock, and simply loaded arms into their van. They drove off from the armory with a machine gun, eight bren guns, twelve sten guns, a PIAT (Projectile, Infantry, Antitank), a small mortar, and 109 rifles—but no ammunition. According to Stephenson† they were getting away safely in their van when they fell into a speed trap; by chance the British policemen saw their load of weapons and arrested all three of them.

The more accurate facts are that the IRA men were using an old, decrepit vehicle; when they were ready to leave, the van was not able to move under the exceptionally heavy load, so a number of weapons had to be unloaded and left behind. Overloaded and swaying from side to side, the ancient van was speeding along the main road to London when it was stopped by a mobile police patrol who thought the vehicle was not in a roadworthy condition. A combination of bad planning, using an old and unreliable vehicle, and bad luck aborted this exploit. Goulding, Canning and Stephenson were convicted and sent to prison.

It was a year before the IRA was ready to make the next arms raid, this time in Northern Ireland, on Gough Barracks, the depot of the Royal Irish Fusiliers at Armaugh. It was a daylight raid on 21 June 1954. A twenty-man group led by Adj. Gen. Charles Murphy approached the

---

*O'Boyle was killed by a premature explosion and his group, never more than a dozen members, disappeared.
†*Memoirs of a Revolutionary*

barrack gates in a large cattle-truck. The sentry on the gate was tricked and hustled into the guard room where, with the remainder of the guard, he was bound and gagged.

The keys to the armory were taken from the keyboard in the guard room, its door opened, and the cattle-truck backed up. The IRA men loaded arms into it as fast as they could. An IRA man had donned the sentry's uniform and stood guard on the barrack gates. The few people who came through the gates while the raid was in progress were pushed into the guard room and tied up. The raid completed, Murphy and his men drove off in their cattle-truck with 290 rifles, thirty-seven sten guns, and nine bren guns. They were all well clear by the time the trussed-up prisoners were able to get free and raise the alarm.

The next IRA arms raid took place in England on 13 August 1954 by a small seven-man group led by Rory O'Brady, a member of the IRA Council. The target was the armory of a British regular army barracks at Arborfield, in Berkshire. Once again the sentry was neatly taken by surprise, and together with other soldiers of the guard, was quickly gagged and bound. This time the key to the armory was not on the keyboard in the guard room, as was customary in the British army in off-duty hours; the Garda had warned Scotland Yard Special Branch that British military armories might be IRA targets. The armory door had to be broken open, and then arms and ammunition were quickly loaded on to two vehicles. Within the hour the raid was over and the two IRA vans were well clear by the time the alarm was raised. They had taken ten bren guns, fifty-five sten guns, a rifle, a revolver, and over 60,000 rounds of different types of ammunition.

The van carrying Rory O'Brady, four of his men, and a small proportion of the arms and ammunition escaped successfully. The other, carrying the bulk of the arms and ammunition, was stopped by a mobile police patrol for speeding; the two men in it, Donal Murphy and Joseph Boyle, were arrested. The British police subsequently arrested another IRA man who had been involved in the raid, James Murphy. All three were eventually charged and sentenced to imprisonment. In accordance with IRA orders, they refused to recognize the British court or plead before it. One other man involved in the raid was Frank Skuse, a corporal serving in the British army; he had previously been stationed at Arborfield barracks, and his local knowledge had contributed greatly to the success of the actual exploit. He was not caught.

The next IRA arms raid was to be a carbon copy of the Armagh raid and was to be on the military barracks at Omagh, the depot of the Royal Inniskilling Fusiliers, in Co Tyrone. Led by Eamonn Boyce, a smaller raiding party of twelve men arrived at the barracks on 16 October 1954. Little went according to plan. There was initial difficulty in surprising and silencing the sentry and the soldiers of the guard, while yet other unexpected, stubborn individuals were encountered. A gun-battle flared up between the IRA raiding party and the guard; five British soldiers and two IRA men were wounded. By this time the alarm was fully raised, and the operation had to be aborted. The withdrawal was hasty, uncoordinated, unplanned, and chaotic. In all, eight IRA men were arrested; only four escaped back across the border into the Republic to report abject failure.

Among those IRA men captured was Phillip Clark, who, while in prison in 1955, was elected to the Westminster Parliament as the Sinn Fein candidate for Fermanagh; he was unseated because of his conviction for the Omagh Raid. Another was Thomas Mitchell, who was also elected as a Sinn Fein candidate to Westminster, while still in prison, and debarred for the same reason.

The failure of the Omagh arms raid caused some drastic rethinking at the IRA general headquarters. One of the main outcomes was the formation of an Active Service Unit in Dublin of specially selected trained men for such GHQ-nominated operations. The team that had raided Omagh Barracks had been an impromptu one because the prestige of the Armagh Raid had become so great that certain IRA men, anxious to win their spurs, used all their influence to be included at the last moment.

The IRA was expectantly working towards the promised Northern Campaign; but as little ever seemed to happen, there again rose murmers of complaint of GHQ inactivity, or even complacency. Many asked when the action was going to begin. Meanwhile, after his release from prison, Liam Kelly maintained his easygoing live-and-let-live relationship with the IRA. The IRA needed the Saor Uladh (which by this time had about fifty activists) more than Kelly needed the IRA in Co Tyrone. Suddenly, on 26 November 1954, with a group of Saor Uladh men, Kelly attacked the RUC post at Roslea, on the border. A gun-battle broke out, and the Saor Uladh attackers were repulsed.

One of Kelly's men, Con Green of Derry, was fatally wounded in the assault, but was taken over the border into Monaghan, where he died. This raid on the Roslea RUC post angered Prime Minister Costello, who declared that if such an incident occurred again he would take severe measures against the IRA and the Saor Uladh. The Saor Uladh was already proscribed in Northern Ireland, but not in the republic. The Irish Republican Publicity Bureau run by the Sinn Fein in Dublin denied IRA responsibility for this incident.

The IRA was now beginning to accumulate arms in some quantity and was able to train volunteers in their use. Two-week summer training camps in the mountains of Co Dublin became a regular feature of the IRA year.

Surprisingly, more raids were planned on both Armagh and Omagh barracks, but both were aborted. This did not show any brilliance on the part of Tony Magan and his GHQ, as security had been tightened up at all British military establishments, and especially in Northern Ireland had countermeasures been introduced. The second attempt to raid Gough Barracks, Armagh, was made on 5 March 1955, but information about it had been passed on to the RUC. Mobilized B-Specials were waiting for the attack, but the IRA never crossed the border. On that occasion, near Armagh, during the period of tension, RUC policemen shot at a car that did not stop when signaled to do so. An eighteen-year-old youth, Arthur Leonard, was killed, and his sixteen-year-old passenger, a girl, was wounded: they were the first civilian casualties caused by the RUC during the Northern Campaign.

Onto the scene of slow, ponderous IRA planning, preparation, and hesitation in the autumn of 1955, came Sean Cronin, who returned to his native Ireland from the U.S. to join the IRA. Cronin had been a regular officer in the Free State army before resigning his commission to work in America as a journalist. The majority of the IRA leadership had no formal military training at all, its vision was narrow, and its thinking often naive and amateurish. Cronin's expertise as a trained military officer with a flair for tactics was just what the IRA required. Moreover, Cronin was eager for action. He was appointed to the GHQ staff.

Tony Magan and his military committee envisaged a slow buildup of up to five years for the Northern Campaign, which would have meant launching it in 1960 at the earliest. Magan was thorough, but plodding. Charles Murphy, the adjutant general, wanted more immediate action — within twelve months if possible — and in this he was supported by Cronin. After some discussion the plans were passed over to Murphy and Cronin to work upon.

Squabbles seemed to be endemic within the IRA GHQ, and Murphy fell out with Magan, who had arbitrarily dismissed Michael Donovan, the editor of the *United Irishman*, for printing some material without his permission. Murphy resigned, but was persuaded to return to continue work with Cronin on the plans for the Northern Campaign. At the annual training camp in Co Dublin in July 1956, the IRA Council decided to launch the Northern Campaign in November 1956.

With the Magan-Murphy rift healed, all seemed once again to be going well in the IRA GHQ. It was beginning to regain some of its old confidence and prestige, although it still had problems with volunteers who were impatient for action. Then another deep rift rent it in twain: Joe Christle, a graduate student at the University of Ireland and a member of the GHQ staff, had a personality clash with Tony Magan. Christle had a flair and a liking for publicity and had engineered a number of dramatic publicity stunts that caused the introspective and staid Magan to wince.

As the months sped by and the IRA took no aggressive action in Northern Ireland, many began to think that Magan had no intention of fighting, but was simply dragging matters out in his overcautious manner. Criticism again began to mount of Magan's leadership; critics began to gravitate towards the popular, lively Joe Christle, who openly favored immediate action. Magan became increasingly jealous of Christle's popularity and influence.

Matters came to a head on 30 October 1955 when Magan banned members of his GHQ staff from membership in the National Student's Council, which Christle had organized the previous December. Christle left the GHQ staff but continued his other republican activities and interests. In April 1956 he organized the theft of one of the famous pictures in the Lane Collection from the National Gallery in London to publicize Ireland's claim to the collection.*

Joe Christle's reaction to his arbitrary dismissal from the IRA was to call a meeting at Dalkey, Co Dublin, at which he formed a rival IRA. He called his breakaway organization by its Irish title, "Oglaigh na nEireann"—the Army of Ireland. He immediately attracted considerable support; the larger part of the Dublin Brigade, then estimated to consist of about fifty men, defected to join him, as did the whole of the ASU, several members of the GHQ staff, and others who were tired of Magan's "wait and prepare" attitude. Gerard Lawless went over to Christle. The Magan-Christle split had its repercussions not only in IRA county units but also in the faithful Cumann na mBan and the Fianna Eireann. Many

---

* The famous Lane Collection of impressionist pictures had been lent by Sir Hugh Lane to the British National Gallery, which anticipated that in due course it would be bequeathed to it. Lane had been a director of the National Gallery of Ireland, and when he was lost in the *Luisitania* disaster in 1915, it was discovered he had made a codicil, leaving the Lane Collection to the National Gallery of Ireland; but the codicil was unsigned, and so unenforceable legally. Possession being nine points of the law, the London Gallery held onto it, and it was not until 1959, when an arrangement was made for part of the collection to be shown in London, and the other part in Dublin alternately, that the dispute died down. It was an issue that caught the public imagination.

loyal IRA members were appalled. The IRA was now virtually in two parts, which for convenience and clarity for the moment can be called the Magan IRA and the Christle IRA.

In July 1956, the Christle IRA convened to regularize the movement and determine future policy. It was agreed unaminously to begin its own Northern Campaign within three months. Although Magan had also set that date to commence the Northern Campaign, it was suspected that he would find some excuse to postpone it. The idea was to provoke the Magan IRA into action: if the Christle IRA began the fight, then both the Magan IRA and Liam Kelly's Saor Uladh would have to join in, and some sort of a wartime coalition could be glued together. There was bitter friction between the Christle IRA and the Magan IRA, especially in Dublin, where Christle had his main power base, which led to some factional brawling.

In September 1956 Gerard Lawless and a group of IRA men who had defected from the Dublin Brigade moved ostensibly towards the border, as though to start terrorist activity. It was a feint to try to provoke the Magan IRA into action, but Magan did not rise to the bait. After waiting for a few days, Lawless moved into Northern Ireland and joined forces with Liam Kelly in Co Tyrone to start a Christle-Kelly partnership. These two men tended to complement each other, as Kelly had little support in the south, and Christle little in the north. Both were unorthodox men with the same aim in mind: to start the Northern Campaign quickly. On 11 November 1956, the Christle-Kelly group made half a dozen pinpricking raids against RUC border posts; but the Magan IRA still did not respond. On the contrary, Magan postposed the Northern Campaign for another month, until December 1956.

7 The Northern Campaign: 1956–62

"The Irish Republic is a sanctum sanctorum for murderers."
—Brian Faulkner, Stormont minister for home affairs,
16 November 1961

CHARLES MURPHY AND Sean Cronin continued working on their plan for the Northern Campaign, which was code-named Operation Harvest,* but it was not nearly as specific or comprehensive as the old S Plan. Selected IRA team leaders were trained and briefed at the summer training camp in Co Dublin. The Dublin GHQ was to select the major targets, and small Flying Columns (another emotive designation resurrected from the Tan War days) would operate from the south into Northern Ireland against them and then quickly return across the border.

Four Flying Columns,† each of about twenty-five men, were organized and trained to strike at priority targets in the north. To observe the Geneva Conventions, members were to be in uniform, which in fact consisted of old combat-dress tunics and trousers obtained from shops that sold British, American, and Irish army surplus stocks. Later, some of the IRA men wore black berets, again cast-off military supplies, and some insignia.

The task of the local IRA units in Northern Ireland was to prepare the way for the Flying Columns: obtaining all details about the target, selecting the best approach and withdrawal routes, taking delaying, or diverting, action against the security forces, providing safe-houses, and generally giving backup support. Local IRA units were also expected to strike at opportunity targets. The basic assumption, once again without any solid foundation, was that the Republic of Ireland government

---

*A copy of Operation Harvest was found in Sean Cronin's apartment when he was arrested in Dublin.
†According to J. Bowyer Bell

would tolerate the IRA operating from its territory into the north provided there was no IRA activity in the Republic.

The Northern Campaign began on the night of 11 December 1956 with IRA attacks on six widely scattered targets. Not all were successful, and five IRA men were arrested while carrying them out. At Gough Barracks, Armagh, the attacking IRA team withdrew hastily after firing a few shots when faced unexpectedly with a new sandbagged watchtower. At the RAF radar installation at Torr Head, Co Antrim, the IRA attackers ran into an RUC patrol and were captured.

However, other IRA teams succeeded in destroying the BBC relay station at Derry, burning down a B-Specials' hut at Newry, damaging by explosion a Territorial Army center at Enniskillen, and setting fire to a courthouse at Magherafelt. There were also three ineffectual explosions at road bridges. These IRA attacking teams had each been given a main priority target and a secondary one, in case the first was too hard a nut to crack. The prompt turnout in force of the B-Specials in the early hours of 12 December surprised and disconcerted the IRA teams and did much to divert them to secondary objectives.

On the 12th the Irish Republican Publicity Bureau issued a campaign proclamation that stated more attacks must be expected. These frequent bureau statements were printed in full in the *United Irishman*; they were also issued to the media in Dublin, and to newspapers sympathetic to the republican cause elsewhere, some of which printed them in part.

After a pause of twenty-four hours there was a second wave of similar terrorist attacks on the night of the 13th. It did not cause much damage but did have the effect of arousing cold Protestant fury against the IRA. A rotation system was implemented for the B-Specials, so there was continually a proportion of them on duty at night and an additional number ready to turn out instantly, day or night, to take part in antiterrorist operations.

The strength of the security forces in Northern Ireland in December 1956 was about 2,800 men in the regular RUC, assisted by about 1,000 B-Specials on full-time duty and another 11,600 part-time B-Specials. This meant that there were about 15,400 active security personnel available to combat the attacks by the IRA, whose maximum active service strength was never more than 200 men, and usually very much less. There were also in Northern Ireland about 5,000 regular British soldiers in garrison and at regimental training depots, and also about 5,000 part-time Territorial Army soldiers, who assembled in various cities and towns across the province. These British soldiers were not involved in the campaign against the IRA, which was under civil government direction, except for some specialized assistance in defusing bombs and dealing with explosives. However, this British military presence in the background did give some substance to the IRA boast that it was "fighting a 30,000-strong British security force."

The reaction of the Protestant Stormont government was quick, hard, and uncompromising. Known IRA and Saor Uladh members were arrested where possible, and others were relentlessly tracked down. On 22 December, for example, over thirty were arrested. The Stormont minister for home affairs announced certain antiterrorist measures that confirmed the call-out and use of B-Specials for guarding key installations and posts and for patrolling the countryside, strengthened RUC border patrols, authorized the erection of semipermanent barriers on the many unapproved roads (that is, those that traversed the border but did not have any checkpoint at the actual frontier), and imposed a speed limit of ten miles per hour on all vehicles in the vicinity of the border. He also accused the Irish government of allowing illegal organizations to drill in the Scotstown area, in Co Monaghan. The Northern Ireland government proscribed the Sinn Fein movement, whose headquarters in Belfast was raided by the police; the IRA had remained proscribed from World War II days.

In the Republic, Prime Minister Sean Costello, who governed by a majority of only three in an uneasy coalition, feared that the IRA attacks in Northern Ireland would arouse a wave of republican enthusiasm. He did not want to seem to be clamping down too hard on the IRA, as his political enemies would accuse him of collaborating with the British; but quietly he did what he could to deter the IRA. On the night of the 16th, his Garda arrested thirteen IRA men who were about to raid north over the border; but they were later released because they carried no arms (they were to have picked them up inside Northern Ireland). Costello hoped this would be a timely warning, but the hint was not taken.

British Prime Minister Sir Anthony Eden was deeply enmeshed in the Anglo-French Expedition against Egypt, the controversy over the Egyptian nationalization of the Suez Canal, his enmity with President Nasser, American condemnation, and in fighting off his critics; his hands were more than full. However, on 19 December he found time at Westminster to make a statement on the Northern Ireland situation. He declared that the Ireland Act of 1949 made Northern Ireland an integral part of the United Kingdom, and he assured Lord Brookeborough, the Stormont prime minister, of his support.

A number of similar, scattered terrorist incidents took place in the remaining days of December but by this time the IRA had lost the advantage of surprise. On the night of the 30th an IRA team was ambushed by the RUC near Dunamore, Co Tyrone, and four men were captured. On the night of the 31st there were two unsuccessful IRA attacks: one against the Derrylin RUC post, the other against the RUC barracks at Brookeborough, both in Co Fermanagh. At Brookeborough two IRA men were killed, one being John South from Limerick, now immortalized in Irish ballad as "Sean Sabhat of Garryowen," and Feargal O'Hanlon. The other twelve involved escaped, although four were wounded, and crossed the border into the Republic, only to be arrested by a Garda patrol. Under the Republic's Offenses Against the State Act, they were all sentenced to six months in prison for refusing to answer questions.

Under the Northern Ireland Special Powers Act, the RUC rounded up and interned all the known IRA and Saor Uladh men in Crumlin Road Prison, Belfast. RUC barracks, posts, and offices were protected by barbed wire and sandbags and guarded by armed policemen; all posts were connected to an alarm system that enabled them to be quickly reinforced and to set up roadblocks and ambushes whenever necessary. Only seventeen of the major cross-border roads were left open, the actual crossing points being manned by armed RUC and B-Special personnel. All the other cross-border roads were spiked to prevent the passage of wheeled traffic.

The presence of over 15,000 watching and searching security men gradually caused the IRA to lose the initiative. By the spring of 1957 the local units, having been flushed out from the cities and towns, were reduced to hiding in dugouts in the hills and bogland, reminiscent of those in the trench warfare of World War I, while Flying Columns hesitated to cross into Northern Ireland because of the ubiquitous patrols. The Northern Campaign was kept going only at a very slow pace by the initiative and energy of a few local leaders, who managed to mount a few exploits. On 2 March, for instance, a train was wrecked on the buffers at Derry station.

In the Republic, Prime Minister Costello invoked the Offenses Against the State Act of 1939, which gave power to intern without trial, and ordered a series of arrests. Also, he said he would prevent the media from giving publicity to the IRA. The first batch of IRA leaders was arrested on 8 January 1957 and included Sean Cronin. On the 13th another batch of IRA leaders was arrested, including Tony Magan. Other arrests followed, and within a few weeks the IRA had been virtually beheaded. Most of those arrested were sentenced to imprisonment for refusing to answer questions.

Magan, Cronin, and others had been released by April and resumed their appointments. Charles Murphy, the adjutant general, and Sean Cronin, who was appointed director of operations, settled down to get the Northern Campaign moving again. In May 1957 there was a huge Sinn Fein rally in Dublin, at which open support for the IRA and its Northern Campaign was enthusiastically expressed, which indicated to the leaders that mass support for it was being generated. Then, later that month, came the blow — Eamonn de Valera returned to power in the Irish Republic.

At the election of 30 May 1957 his Fianna Fail Party gained 72 seats, which in a 144-seat Dail enabled him to form a government. The Sinn Fein party won only four seats, which they refused to take, causing de Valera to declare, "These men are living in the past."

The next event of note occurred on 4 July 1957 and became known as the Forkill Ambush. The reassembled IRA Council and GHQ staff had restarted the momentum of the Northern Campaign. One IRA team on that date ambushed an RUC Landrover at Forkill, near Carivegrove, Co Armagh. One policeman was killed and another wounded. The IRA team disappeared back across the border into the Republic.

Three days later Prime Minister de Valera struck at the IRA, and within three days had arrested over sixty top IRA leaders, including Tony Magan. Only Charles Murphy and Sean Cronin escaped the net for the time being. In one blow de Valera had imprisoned practically the whole of the IRA Executive Committee, Council and GHQ staff. The IRA was once again beheaded.

Somehow Murphy and Cronin managed to keep the Northern Campaign going. On 17 August an RUC sergeant was killed at Coalisland, Co Tyrone, when his Landrover went over a mine detonated by remote control. William Talbot and Kevin Mallon were arrested and charged with his murder; they later alleged they were tortured by the RUC. Other incidents in the month of August included an unsuccessful attempt to kill Albert Kennedy, the deputy inspector general of the RUC, with a car bomb; a bomb was exploded at the Strabane customs post; and a post office garage in Derry was set on fire.

In September the RUC barracks in Armagh were damaged by a bomb. In October an RUC patrol was shot at in Derry; the Roslea customs post was again attacked; and explosions damaged road bridges, a telephone box, and an electricity transformer. They were all small incidents near the border, so the IRA attackers could quickly slip back into the Republic or a sizable Catholic community, such as Belfast and Derry.

On 11 November 1957 in a farm cottage just south of the border at

Edentuber, near Dundalk, a small ASU of four men was preparing a land-mine when it prematurely exploded, killing them all and the farmer. In December an RUC vehicle was damaged by a land-mine; two policemen were wounded. In the Dail in Dublin on 30 October, Jack McQuillan, one of the founder-members of the Clan na Pobachta, put forward a motion that the United Nations organization be asked to send observers to Northern Ireland, but it was defeated by a large majority.

In the south the Christle IRA remained independent, although its strength declined as the Northern Campaign swung into action. Christle's men continued to raid for arms and explosives, especially gelignite; this angered the Magan IRA, and disclaimers by them were regularly published in the *United Irishman*. The Christle IRA still maintained a loose relationship with Liam Kelly's Saor Uladh; Kelly passed on arms and explosives he had seized. This also infuriated the IRA, as Kelly always seemed to have ample money and arms when the IRA was so short of them. Kelly did pass some arms over to IRA men on the run in Northern Ireland when RUC pressure was heavy on them, but not much or often.

Terrorist ambushes, bombing, explosions, shootings, and arson continued in Northern Ireland throughout 1958, the incidence being heaviest in the early part of the year. Early on the morning of 18 February an IRA unit of six men led by Sean Cronin made an arms raid on the British military camp at Blandford, in Dorset, England. One member of the ASU was Frank Skuse, the corporal in the British army who was stationed there. The sentry and the guard were taken by surprise, bound, and gagged; but shots were fired, which raised the alarm, so the raid had to be aborted. Skuse fled to the Irish Republic and went on the run but was eventually arrested under the name of Paul Murphy and detained in Mountjoy Prison.

In April 1958 Freedom Radio, the IRA pirate radio station in Belfast that had been broadcasting IRA propaganda, was detected and closed down. On 6 May there was an attempted mass breakout of IRA political prisoners from Mountjoy Prison, which failed. The real identity of Frank Skuse was discovered by the Dublin authorities during this incident.

The tempo dropped after July 1958. On 24 August James Crossman was shot dead by an RUC border patrol as he ran back into the Republic on being challenged. The IRA man with him was wounded and captured. On 9 September a bomb was discovered in Gough Barracks, Armagh.

Two soldiers born in the Republic and serving in the Royal Irish Fusiliers were interned, while two others involved had deserted and disappeared.

Toward the end of the year, the IRA was again losing its momentum. Only the Saor Uladh, which was down to about thirty active members, carried out any attacks. The IRA in the north, also drastically reduced in number, generally lay low in hideouts in the countryside or returned to the Republic.

Meanwhile, inside the Curragh Internment Camp which had been reopened in July 1957, leadership quarrels were again festering. Tony Magan smuggled out instructions to Sean Cronin, when he was chief of staff, on how the Northern Campaign should be conducted; but by expecting them to be followed, Magan was overlooking and overriding the strict IRA rule: once an IRA man was arrested, imprisoned, or detained, he immediately forfeited all rank and authority, no matter what position he had held. Someone else must be appointed or elected to take his place. Cronin ran the IRA his own way, which displeased Magan. When Thomas MacCurtain was transferred to the Curragh Internment Camp, he was elected prison CO, and so was the leader of all IRA internees. This was a disappointment to Magan, who thought he should have been automatically chosen because of his former position. However, Magan deferred to and supported MacCurtain.

Onto this festering, unhappy scene came another arrested former chief of staff, Charles Murphy. He disagreed with the MacCurtain policy and soon found himself to be the leader of the discontented. On 2 December, without permission from either IRA GHQ or Thomas MacCurtain, Murphy led a mass breakout of fourteen IRA internees, of whom only three were recaptured. The IRA GHQ and Sean Cronin, chief of staff, had to consider what disciplinary action to take against the escapers and Charles Murphy in particular; after some deliberation it was decided to overlook the matter.

A state visit of the Irish president, Sean O'Kelly, to the U.S. for the purpose of persuading American businessmen to invest in the Republic showed just how unpopular internment without trial was among the Irish Americans. On 23 December 1958 Prime Minister de Valera began gradually to release them, the last leaving on 11 March 1959, when the Curragh Internment Camp again closed its gates. It was officially stated that 207 internees had been held there without trial since July 1957. Both the British and Northern Ireland governments protested against the mass release of these IRA and Saor Uladh men.

The Irish government had to tread warily as it already had one case against it awaiting trial by an international court. Gerard Lawless, the youth leader who had joined forces with Joe Christle, had been detained in Dublin without trial from July to December 1957, when he was released upon pledging not to engage in illegal activities. Through the efforts of Sean MacBride, the ex-IRA lawyer-politician, Lawless filed a complaint against the Irish government with the Commission of Human Rights at the Council of Europe, claiming compensation for his detention. This was accepted as admissible in September 1958. The Lawless case was the very first one to come before the European Court of Human Rights, in April 1960; in October the court decided in favor of the Irish government, giving as judgment that Lawless's human rights had not been violated. Had this international court's decision been otherwise, there would have had to be drastic rethinking in regard to this particular antiterrorist measure in the Irish Republic, Britain, Northern Ireland, and perhaps elsewhere.

Internment without trial continued in Northern Ireland, the internees being held in Crumlin Road Prison under the Special Powers Act. The prison CO was the popular Thomas Mitchell, who had taken part in the Armagh Raid. Unlike the Curragh Internment Camp, there were no bitter quarrels or divisions. Escape was much more of a problem because this was a solidly constructed purpose-built prison, with watchtowers and huge, thick, high outer walls.

An IRA meeting in April 1959 was attended by released IRA leaders Tony Magan, Thomas MacCurtain, Charles Murphy, and others. The Magan group produced a statement indicating that the MacCurtain-Magan leadership in the Curragh Internment Camp had been correct, and inferring that the IRA GHQ had been wrong in not disciplining the Charles Murphy escapees of December 1958. This was opposed by Murphy and his supporters, and so the matter was left pending for the moment.

In the IRA convention of June 1959 the leadership squabble came out into the open, and the issue was put to the vote. The convention was attended by Cathal Goulding and Seamus Canning, who had carried out the abortive Felstead arms raid and had just been released from a British prison. The MacCurtain-Magan group lost out to those led by Goulding, who had immense influence and prestige, and Rory O'Brady, and Sean Cronin, all of whom simply wanted to get on with the Northern Campaign. This decision caused resignations, and others were asked to leave, but a few stayed on muttering discontentedly. Sean Cronin was appointed chief of staff, and Cathal Goulding adjutant general; they set to work to regain the momentum that had been lost in 1958, but they found themselves facing great difficulties. The Northern Campaign was fast running out. In 1959 there were only 27 recorded incidents in Northern Ireland, while in 1957 it was claimed there had been 341.

Cronin and Goulding found that the IRA was desperately short of arms and ammunition as so many arms dumps had been discovered by the police in both the Republic and Northern Ireland. The search for rocket-launchers to blast concrete buildings had been unsuccessful. More critical still was the fact that the IRA was short of money, particularly as it had the obligation to support the families of men in detention.

In the Tan War and the Civil War in the south, the mining of roads had been an extremely successful tactic, and somehow it had been assumed that this could be used again in Northern Ireland with similar effect. By this time the majority of the roads in Northern Ireland, even the minor ones, were paved with either asphalt or tarmac. To plant a mine in a roadway meant disturbing the surface, which was obvious and easily detectable. The IRA explosives experts had found another method, that of sawing the top from a five-gallon heavy metal milk churn, of which there were ample in use in the farming communities, packing it with gel-ignite, hiding it in the undergrowth by the roadside, and detonating it from a distance. This method had several successes, but the drawback was a shortage of gelignite.

On 25 September 1959 Sean Cronin and other IRA leaders were arrested in Dublin, which caused the momentum of the Northern Campaign again to slow down almost to a stop. Sean Cronin always tended to be secretive and was the exception to the general rule of his less well educated predecessors, who from the days and example of Michael Collins had the habit of writing everything down. Since being appointed chief of staff, Cronin had committed most details to memory, as he knew how dangerously incriminating documents could be if seized by the police. After all, he had been caught once, and a copy of Operation Harvest had been found in his apartment. The result was that when Cronin was arrested, John McGirl, who was appointed chief of staff in his place, did not know exactly what was happening and had to call a meeting of field commanders and others to discover what the plans were, what had been authorized, and what each unit was supposed to be doing.

Meanwhile, in June 1959, the aging Prime Minister Eamonn de Valera was appointed president of the Republic of Ireland, to be the nonexecutive head of state. His place as prime minister and as leader of the Fianna Fail was taken by Sean Lemass, a founder-member. Soon after assuming office Sean Lemass called for economic cooperation between the Republic and Northern Ireland, but this was sharply rejected by the hard-line Protestant government at Stormont, which accused the Irish government of harboring illegal organizations and allowing them training facilities. In reply, Lemass openly condemned IRA activity and stated he was drafting extra police into the border areas.

Sean Lemass was alarmed by the presence of the IRA and the activities of the Christle IRA and the Saor Uladh in the Republic. For example, on 24 October 1959, a Saor Uladh–Christle IRA armed raid for gelignite on the industrial explosives magazine at Blanchardstown, Co Dublin, was only narrowly foiled; on 10 November an arms dump was discovered in Dublin; and on 4 December, two Saor Uladh men were captured when raiding an Irish army armory, at Dundalk—the first such raid in the south since that on the Magazine Fort in Dublin in December 1939.

The British government also expressed concern that the Irish government was harboring the IRA; its ambassador formally complained to the Irish minister for external affairs, who explained there was little more that could be done. He pointed out that his government had invoked the Offenses Against the State Act, imposed censorship, and made extra police available to deal with the IRA problem; and that although internment without trial had ended, over one hundred IRA men were still in Irish prisons.

During the course of 1960 only thirty-six terrorist incidents in Northern Ireland were committed by the IRA or the Saor Uladh, some quite trivial. In February two arms dumps were discovered in Co Armagh; in March an RUC patrol was fired upon from south of the border near Roslea; in April a post office van was blown up near Augher, Co Antrim; in May a grenade was thrown at an RUC policeman at Keady, Co Armagh, and a large arms dump was found when an IRA man accidentally shot a comrade at Derry. From June until November nothing of any particular interest occurred; then David O'Connell, the IRA adjutant general, was ambushed, wounded, and captured by the RUC. In December there was an abortive attack on the RUC post at Belleek.

Under Liam Kelly the Saor Uladh had retained its good contacts with the Clan na Gael and received enough money and arms to continue operating in Northern Ireland. The Saor Uladh was responsible for the majority of terrorist incidents in the first part of 1960, but Kelly suddenly lost interest and in June emigrated to America. He gave over his arms, explosives, and ammunition to the Christle IRA. Less than twenty armed men remained in his Saor Uladh. A few of them went over to the Christle-IRA, but most simply disappeared—they also had had enough. Emigration to America attracted many despondent IRA members.

The Christle IRA carried out an occasional exploit in the south to obtain explosives and arms but became inactive during 1960 and began to crumble. Its one notable action had been to engineer the escape from a British prison in Wakefield, Yorkshire, on 19 February 1959 of James Murphy, sentenced for his backup part in the Arborfield raid in August 1955.

On 27 January 1961 an RUC policeman, Norman Anderson, was killed in an ambush near Roslea, when returning from a visit to the Republic. The Irish Republican Publicity Bureau issued a statement claiming that Anderson had been "executed because he had been engaged on espionage missions in the 26 counties under cover of social activities." The IRA was very much concerned about the activities of informers in that area, as information passed on to the RUC might result in units being ambushed; but there was considerable doubt whether this RUC policeman was deliberately spying, as he was well known in the locality and when on duty was a uniformed RUC man. The shooting of an unarmed policeman generated widespread repercussions and expressions of horror and disgust on both sides of the border. There were a few other incidents in the first five months of 1961, but none of any magnitude.

The Stormont government had been under pressure for some time from its nationalist members, that is the Catholics, and others outside the province, to suspend internment without trial; but it had hesitated, saying that it was reluctant to do so until the Irish government took more positive measures to restrict the IRA in the south. The Stormont minister for home affairs had said that he could not respond until "all those released from the Curragh in March 1959, were rounded up and detained once more." Pressure from the British government caused this hard line to alter.

Toward the end of 1959 the Stormont minister for home affairs stated that selected internees could be released if they promised to have nothing more to do with any illegal organizations, and there was no objection from the RUC. The Saor Uladh was an illegal organization in Northern Ireland, but not in the Republic. About forty IRA men were freed under these conditions during the first quarter of 1961, and they all kept their promises as far as the RUC could ascertain. Then after a pause of three months to ensure that none had become active again, further releases were made, the last seven IRA men being freed on 7 April 1961, when internment without trial in Northern Ireland was suspended. The Stormont government refused to grant amnesty to IRA and Saor Uladh men serving prison sentences.

The IRA had almost completely run out of steam, and its acts in Northern Ireland during the summer and autumn of 1961 were more in the nature of vandalism than terrorism. One exception occurred on 3 September when IRA men hijacked the Belfast to Dublin train near Kilnasggart and used it to block the main line.

On 12 November 1961 near Jonesborough, Co Armagh, close to the border, an RUC patrol was ambushed and fired upon; one RUC man was killed and three others wounded. The five IRA men involved in the shooting quickly escaped across the border into the Republic. The RUC policemen were monitoring people crossing from Northern Ireland to attend a commemoration for the Edentuber Martyrs, the five men who had been killed by a premature explosion in 1958. The Jonesborough Ambush caused Prime Minister Lemass to reintroduce the military tribunal, which began sitting on 23 November. Lemass claimed in the Dail that his government had reduced the number of illegal acts, and stated that there were over 600 police employed on special antiterrorist duties, of whom 250 were in the border area.

The elections in the Irish Republic on 4 October 1961 were disastrous for the Sinn Fein candidates, who gained only three percent of the votes cast. This was a big blow to republican hopes, and in particular to the IRA, as it meant that the people in the Republic had lost confidence in it and its cause. Probably the last deliberate IRA terrorist act in the Northern Campaign occurred on 26 November 1961, when an RUC vehicle moving out from barracks in south Armagh hit a land-mine. Three policemen were injured. Two days later Brian Faulkner, who had become minister for home affairs at Stormont, threatened to impose the death penalty for such terrorist crimes. He had already said, on the 16th, that "the Irish Republic is a *sanctum sanctorum* for murderers."

The Irish government, the Catholic Church, and the media in both the north and the south were now in unison in condemning the IRA and its campaign of terrorism in Northern Ireland. It was also openly condemned by politicians of most parties on both sides of the border. In Northern Ireland even the Catholics were sick and tired of the IRA, which had made such heavy demands upon them, treated them with scant respect, and neglected to give them any thanks; they would now respond only to IRA threats or force. In the south, ex-IRA men were harassed by the Garda and were at a great disadvantage when trying to obtain employment. Perhaps the final blow came in December 1961 when the Clan na Gael—for so long the main, and often only, supporter of the IRA, which had just been won over to the Irish government's way of thinking—stated that it would send no more money to the IRA from America.

Early in 1962 a saddened and disheartened IRA Council agreed to end the Northern Campaign. On 26 February the Irish Republican Publicity Bureau issued a statement announcing that the IRA was "to end the campaign of resistance to British occupation" in Northern Ireland, giving the main reason for this decision as being lack of support from the people, and blaming the "attitude of the general public, whose minds have been deliberately distracted from the supreme issue facing the Irish people—the unity and freedom of Ireland." It added, "All arms and other materials have been dumped, and all full-time active volunteers been withdrawn."

It emphasized that the IRA policy of not undertaking "aggressive action in the Republic remains," and claimed it still had the support of many Irish exiles in several countries. It said, "In the future an even greater volume of support would be needed so that the cause will ultimately triumph," and ending by pledging "eternal resistance to the British Forces in occupation of Ireland."

The bureau communique stated that during the "Resistance Campaign" from 1956 to 1962 the IRA had originated 600 operations, during which it had killed six and wounded twenty-eight of the "enemy," while it had lost two of its own "resistance fighters" killed in action, and seven more accidentally killed. It added that forty-three of its members were still in Northern Ireland prisons, three in prisons in England, and forty-two in Mountjoy Prison, Dublin.

The RUC estimated that during this IRA Northern Campaign there were at the maximum only about 150 IRA activists and about twenty of the Saor Uladh in the field, but that they were originally supported by "thousands of helpers." By February 1962 only thirty remained at large. The RUC stated that six members of the security forces had been killed, and thirty-two wounded or injured. The annual cost of the security forces to the Stormont government was assessed at over one million dollars, being taken up with such items as extra equipment and vehicles, overtime for the regular RUC and full-time B-Specials, and expenses for the other B-Specials called out for duty.

And so the five-and-a-half-year-long Northern Campaign by the IRA, dedicated to uniting Ireland by force had fizzled out in ignominious defeat. The excuse of lack of public support was but one of the reasons for its failure. The fact that the Catholic population had turned against the IRA was a most significant feature, but there were other contributory causes. These included the overwhelming defeat of the Sinn Fein Party at the October elections in the Republic; the acute shortage of money, and the abrupt refusal of the Clan na Gael to send any more; the acute shortage of weapons, especially rocket-launchers, and the scant hope of obtaining any; the frequent beheading of the movement by the Dublin government in successfully arresting top leaders; the leadership quarrels, and the thousands of B-Specials, who knew every inch of the countryside, continually patrolling and searching, reducing the IRA men in Northern Ireland to hiding in miserable dugouts in the hills and boglands. On 26 April 1962 the Irish government amnestied all its political prisoners, but the Stormont government showed no such magnanimity: all in Northern Ireland prisons had to serve out their sentences.

8 The Civil Rights Explosion in Northern Ireland

*"A quasi-Fascist organization masquerading
behind a clerical cloak"*
> —Harold Wilson, British prime minister, 28 June 1966,
> on the Ulster Volunteer Force

LITTLE IRA ACTIVITY took place between 1962 and 1967. On 7 March 1963 an explosion designed to destroy a republican monument to be dedicated by President de Valera killed one IRA man and injured another. In September 1965 the HMS *Brave Borderer*, a British torpedo boat, was fired on by IRA men when entering Waterford Harbor, where it was to be given a civic reception. Three men responsible were arrested, convicted, and imprisoned. On 7 March 1966 an early morning explosion blew off the top part of Nelson's Pillar in O'Connell Street, Dublin, adjacent to the general post office of Easter Rising fame, which had been one of the few remaining symbols of British Ascendancy.

Within the leadership of the IRA there was a searching reappraisal of why the Northern Campaign had failed; their conclusion confirmed that the main cause was lack of support from the Catholic people. This gave encouragement to the faction that had always wanted the IRA to adopt left-wing socialist causes and intertwine them with the ultimate IRA aim. Cathal Goulding, a political moderate, saw the value of such a policy and in April 1964 produced what became known as the Nine Proposals. Two of the proposals were of deep significance.

The first was the abolition of the policy of abstentionism, so that elected Sinn Fein members could take their seats in the Dail at Stormont or at Westminster, and so become involved in the constitutional processes. Cathal Goulding argued that without political activity in all available legislatures and among the people, any further terrorist activity would again fail. This alone caused controversy, as it seemed to be a complete sell-out of one of the longtime IRA principles that had been so rigidly adhered to throughout triumph and disaster. It also upset the militants who wanted terrorist action to continue in Northern Ireland.

The other controversial proposal was for the IRA to form a political National Liberation Front with the tiny Irish Communist Party. The underlying idea was that the IRA would first dominate and then take over this party, and perhaps others too of similar political persuasion. One authority, Sean MacStiofain, tells us that from 1964 until 1968 the seven-member IRA Council was almost equally divided on this issue. Cathal Goulding led those who wanted to take political action, and Sean MacStiofain those who wanted to take terrorist action. For some time one or two members of the IRA Council wavered between these two alternatives, so that neither faction obtained the majority it sought.

MacStiofain had learned to speak Gaelic in prison. He had a distinct Cockney accent, and seems to have had an inferiority complex about it* as it was definitely out of place in IRA circles. Maria Maguire wrote that he "had a London accent that was even more acute when he talked in Irish." There is a peculiar snobbishness about accents in Ireland, a land of several varying ones that identify a person as being from a particular locality. To most Irish Republican minds an English accent of any sort is one of the enemy and grates on their ears. Erskine Childers's English accent probably had much to do with his execution in 1922 and also with Michael Collins's intense dislike and suspicion of him.

A few of the older, left-wing, politically minded IRA leaders reappeared, all anxious to push forward extreme socialist views. In January 1966 Tomas MacGiolla, president of the Sinn Fein, admitted that it was not until 1965 that the republican movement had considered and actively begun to take an interest in, people's everyday problems and general welfare. Previously it had been assumed that all Catholic Irishmen, no matter where they lived, were automatically committed republicans and would do all in their power to help the IRA cause. It was something of a shock to the Sinn Fein and IRA leaders to realize that this was not necessarily so, and that the Irish people, the grass roots of their support, had to be considered, cultivated, and conserved. In June 1967 Cathal Goulding said that the IRA had been mistaken in concentrating solely upon ending partition, and declared that the basic IRA strategy would in future lay greater stress on social and economic aims.

In July 1966 MacStiofain, who was an abrupt personality and who

*Memoirs of a Revolutionary

had sharp differences of opinion with his senior colleagues, was suspended from all duties by the IRA Council. He was then a member of both the Executive Committee and the governing IRA Council. He had stopped the distribution of an issue of the *United Irishman*, the IRA newspaper, because it contained a criticism of the IRA practice of reciting the rosary, a Catholic ritual, at republican commemorations, such as the annual pilgrimage to Wolfe Tone's grave at Bodenstown. A convert to the Catholic faith himself, MacStiofain gave as his reason that "the real target of this Marxist criticism was not sectarianism, but religion . . . and was offensive." It was a blow in his struggle against the left-wing leadership.

At the IRA Convention in September, however, he was again elected to the Executive Committee and the IRA Council, being appointed director of intelligence. The twelve-man Executive Committee consisted largely of Marxist theorists who wanted political action and repeatedly expressed the view that the time was not yet ripe to reopen the war in Northern Ireland. The IRA Council remained teeteringly divided. MacStiofain was the spokesman for the activists, who thought that the Northern Ireland government should be given no respite. He was dismayed by the time wasted in discussing projects that never materialized, and thought "the IRA would end up as a paper army, both demilitarised and demoralised."* He decided to "soldier on, to turn up on time at every Council meeting, and take full part in discussions."

In Northern Ireland the Protestant majority rejoiced at the defeat of the IRA in 1962, deriving the comfortable feeling that their privileges and dominant position were secure. An attitude of arrogant confidence was obvious at both the Stormont level and in the lower political echelons. This was demonstrated in the annual Orange Marches in July, when their supremacy was flaunted.

In March 1963 Lord Brookeborough retired; his place as leader of the Unionist Party and prime minister at Stormont was taken by Capt. Terence O'Neill. Cast in the mold of Edward Carson, Lord Brookeborough had been a strong and determined Protestant leader who had preserved and consolidated Protestant rights and privileges. Although having much the same ideas and motivation, O'Neill was a lesser man. In December 1963 Prime Minister O'Neill released the last of the IRA prisoners serving sentences in Northern Ireland prisons. He and most of his compatriots considered that the IRA problem had been solved, but they remained wary and were determined to be vigilant to ensure that it did not arise again.

*Memoirs of a Revolutionary

The moderation of Prime Minister O'Neill did not please the more extreme of his supporters, who particularly criticized him for inviting Prime Minister Sean Lemass of the Irish Republic to Stormont on 14 January 1965 for a friendly visit. Even so, at the Stormont elections that year the Unionists were again returned to power with the comfortable majority of thirty-six of fifty-two seats. Terence O'Neill was unopposed in the election, as were certain other Unionist candidates.

There was considerable dissatisfaction among the Catholic population in Northern Ireland at the blatant way in which the constituencies, wards, and voting had been organized to enable the Unionist Party to gain and retain power. There had been gerrymandering and also a certain amount of plural voting, again in favor of the Protestants, by the universities and businessmen, some of whom had as many as six extra votes to cast. In the election of 1965, for example, the universities gave the Unionists an extra 16,500 votes, and the businessmen an extra 12,000.

The inequalities of the enfranchisement of the Catholics were again highlighted, and a surge of resentment began to rise against discrimination practiced in this respect by both the Unionist-dominated Stormont Assembly and the local councils. All top and a majority of medium grade positions in government and the professions were generally held by Protestants. Local councils mainly employed Protestants. Derry, for example, had a two-thirds Catholic majority, and only employed about thirty percent Catholics. There was also complete segregation in schools, and advantages in buildings, equipment, teachers, and facilities were given to Protestant ones.

However, when Harold Wilson, leader of the Labor Party, came to power in Britain the Unionists were disappointed. Wilson and the British Labor Party were unknown and perhaps unwelcome factors. They had what they considered to be a good understanding with the British Tory Party, which let them govern Northern Ireland in their own way without interference. The Labor Party had always seemed more sympathetic toward the Irish government than the Conservative Party, which had political links with the Ulster Unionist Party dating back to Carson's day.

Another factor disturbing to the Unionists was that Harold Wilson's own constituency of Huyton, Liverpool, was largely populated by Irishmen and those of Irish descent, upon whom he relied for political support. The Unionists noted that one of Prime Minister Wilson's early decisions was to allow the body of Sir Roger Casement to be returned to Ireland for reburial in Glasnevin Cemetry, Dublin, a request previously refused by British governments.

Staunch Protestants began to bristle and become vocal. One of the most staunch and vocal was the Rev. Ian Paisley, moderator of the Free Presbyterian Church of Ulster, which he had founded in 1951 and which he claimed had congregations totaling 200,000 people. Paisley's church had no connection whatever with the older established Presbyterian Church of Ireland. Born in Ballymena, Co Antrim, Paisley feared and distrusted the Church of Rome, which became his favorite whipping boy and the epitome of all that was wrong with Christianity and Northern Ireland. A powerful orator in the old style, his favorite sermons were based on the theme of "No Popery here."

Paisley appeared on the political scene in September 1964 when an Irish tricolor was being flown from a building in Divis Street, Belfast, a Catholic area, contrary to an Act of Parliament.* He threatened to lead his followers to Divis Street to remove it forcibly if the RUC did not do so immediately. On the 28th a Catholic crowd of about 2,000 people unsuccessfully tried to prevent the RUC from removing the republican flag. Two days later another tricolor was flown from the same building, and once again the RUC had to battle with a Catholic mob to remove it; eighteen RUC members and twelve others were injured. Paisley had been prominent in these two incidents, and so put himself on the political map of Northern Ireland.

In 1965 Paisley organized and led the Ulster Constitutional Defense Committee. He began addressing political meetings and organizing demonstrations, which roused anti-Catholic feeling in the province. He also campaigned against Prime Minister O'Neill, whom he feared might come to some agreement with the Irish Republic detrimental to the Northern Ireland Protestants. The Ulster Constitutional Defense Committee's associate movement, almost its militant arm, was the Ulster Protestant Volunteers, led by Maj. Ronald Bunting; together they organized rallies and meetings to propagate their political views throughout 1965 and 1966.

Sensing danger to the Protestant supremacy in Northern Ireland, the old Ulster Volunteer Force reappeared, bristling with energy and determination reminiscent of the days of Randolph Churchill's "Orange Card." One element took to terrorism against the Catholic population in Northern Ireland and also decided to take action against the IRA. In February 1966 the UVF began a series of terrorist exploits that mainly consisted of throwing petrol bombs against Catholic churches, schools, and houses; occasionally they attacked individuals. One of the first of the UVF exploits occurred on 16 April when members fired shots at the house of

*Flags and Emblems (Display) Act, 1954

John McQuade, a Stormont Unionist MP. The object was to give the impression that this had been done by the IRA, so that Unionist feeling against it would be roused. On the 28th the UVF announced that it was declaring war on the IRA, and that it would execute all known IRA members. On 7 May a petrol bomb was thrown at a Catholic pub but missed and crashed through the window of the house next door, in which lived an elderly Protestant widow, who received burns from which she later died.

Next, on 27 May 1966, UVF terrorists tried to kill a prominent Belfast republican; when they could not find him, they instead attacked a complete stranger in the street. John Patrick Scullion was stabbed and died a fortnight later. Late at night on 26 June UVF terrorists ambushed four Catholic barmen leaving the Malvern Arms, Malvern Street, Belfast. One, Peter Ward, was shot dead; two of the others were wounded. This incident became known as the Malvern Murder and is regarded as the commencement of confrontation between Protestant and Catholic extremists in Northern Ireland, which soon rose to crisis point. Four men, all Protestants, were arrested on the 28th for these crimes. The leader was Augustus (Gusty) Spence, a dockyard worker, alleged to be in charge of the UVF unit in the Shankill area; he was charged with the murder of both Scullion and Ward. The others were Arnold McLean, also charged with Ward's murder; and William Miller and George McCullough, both charged with the murder of Scullion.

On 28 June the Ulster Volunteer Force was declared to be an illegal organization by the Stormont government; in the Westminster Parliament, Prime Minister Wilson declared the UVF to be a "quasi-Fascist organisation masquerading behind a clerical cloak." Paisley openly disassociated himself from the UVF, declaring that he was a man of peace and that his Ulster Constitutional Defense Committee was not a subversive body.

Paisley's tub-thumping and his success in attracting and rousing crowds into enthusiastic loyalty to the Protestant cause drew reprobation from those who thought they were better fitted to guide the destiny of Northern Ireland Protestants. On 12 July 1966, the day of the annual Orange Marches, for example, Paisley was publicly denounced by Sir George Clark, grand master of the powerful Orange Order, in a speech to over 100,000 Orangemen assembled at Omagh. The grand master complained that Terence O'Neill, who was a member of the Orange Order—as practically all the ruling establishment had to be to survive—was under continuous and bitter attack from the Reverend Paisley, who, he said, had resigned from that Order three years before. Sir George Clark noted that

Paisley was still invited to speak from Orange Order platforms and asked the Order not to allow him to do so any more.

After the July Orange Marches in 1966, a section of Paisley's followers became rowdy; some vandalism occurred, resulting in the arrest of over forty of them. On 18 July Paisley and two pastors of his church were charged with unlawful assembly (on a previous occasion on 6 June), and as three of them refused to be "bound over to keep the peace," they went briefly to prison in Belfast. After these July Orange Marches and the troubles arising from them, the Stormont government banned all public meetings and processions in the month of August.

Another problem for the Unionists was the founding in February 1967 of the Northern Ireland Civil Rights Association. The CRA was modeled on and affiliated with the National Council for Civil Liberties in Britain. Initially nonsectarian, it was organized and run by a number of lecturers and students at Queens University, Belfast, including a very mixed bag of young activitists from New Left groups and the Communist Party. It came to be supported by such small political groups as the Republican Labor party and the Liberal Party. Feeling they should take some action against discrimination, some Catholics were attracted to the CRA movement. The Republican Labor Party, which had splintered in 1965 from the Irish Labor party, had an all-Catholic membership of about 500, and it followed a "united Ireland" policy. The Liberal Party, led by Sheilagh Murnaghan, was founded in 1957 and had about 1,000 members; it was in association with the British Liberal Party. Local CRA committees sprang up in some cities and towns, such as the Derry Citizens Action Committee and the Armagh Civil Rights Committee. At first the CRA, like its British counterpart, dealt with individual cases of discrimination and injustice.

In April 1967 the Stormont government banned all demonstrations in connection with the Hundredth Anniversary of the Fenian Rising; also banned were the newly organized and expanding Republican Clubs, which it considered to be fronts for the Sinn Fein and recruiting booths for the IRA. The republicans replied by organizing a series of public meetings, many of which were attended by CRA members. A few prominent Sinn Fein and republican characters were arrested. These meetings and incidents were well covered by television and other media, British and foreign, which was now beginning to show an interest in these disturbances in Northern Ireland.

CRA activities on behalf of individuals gained momentum, and on 28 June 1968, Austin Currie, a Catholic Stormont MP of the Nationalist party, staged a sit-in in a Dungannon apartment that was assigned to a young, single Protestant girl when there was a long waiting list of Catholic families badly in need of accommodation. One of the main complaints of the Catholics was that houses and apartments built and allocated out to tenants by local councils using government grants and subsidies were unfairly and unequally rented to Protestants. This incident was an example, and Austin Currie's interest and action turned the spotlight of publicity onto it, causing the apartment to be reallocated to a family instead of a single person. After this success in Dungannon, the CRA began to court publicity by organizing its own marches and demonstrations. Many with an axe to grind were attracted to its banner, including some of the restless IRA members.

During the summer of 1968 the leadership of the IRA had to decide whether to allow IRA members to take part in the CRA demonstrations in Northern Ireland, and indeed whether to involve the IRA as a body. Eventually, somewhat reluctantly, it was decreed that IRA members could take part in CRA activities if they wished, but only on an individual basis. Any involvement must be discreet, and no official IRA groupings or units were to take part as such; IRA personalities well known to the RUC should not attend any CRA demonstrations, marches, or meetings. At the September 1968 IRA convention, the seven-man IRA Council was suddenly enlarged to twenty members; many of those coopted were Marxist theorists who favored political activity rather than active terrorism. The activists, still led by Sean MacStiofain, were now very much in the minority in the leadership. MacStiofain said that the strength of the IRA was "a few hundred, half in the north" and that the IRA Council decision was still that "the time is not yet ripe for IRA action in the north."*

Next, the CRA announced that it would organize a march on 5 October right into the heart of Protestant Derry to hold a meeting. William Craig, the Stormont home affairs minister, banned the march; but on the appointed day it took place, some 2,000 people assembling. Emerging from the Catholic Bogside area into Derry City, the marchers were stopped by the RUC, and clashes between the two began. The RUC charged the marchers and drove them back into the Bogside area; withdrawing, they ran into RUC ambushes. Television cameras recorded the events, showing the strong police action in which seventy-seven civilians were injured. Gerry Fitt, the Catholic MP at Westminster for West Belfast, was later

*Memoirs of a Revolutionary

criticized by the Cameron Report* for seeking "publicity for himself and his political view" and because his conduct "was reckless and wholly irresponsible in a person occupying his public position."

The Protestant reaction to the attempt of the CRA marchers to enter the "Protestant territory" of Derry was manifested by the Rev. Ian Paisley, whose Ulster Constitutional Defense Committee, in conjunction with Ralph Bunting's Ulster Protestant Volunteers, was to organize counter-demonstrations and marches, which whipped up Loyalist frenzy. Ralph Bunting styled himself commandant of the Loyal Citizens of Ulster, who were in fact the extreme militants of his movement.

The immediate result of the Derry March was the formation of the People's Democracy, a political party that purported to be a militant civil rights group. Based at Queens University, Belfast, it was organized and led by a number of personalities involved in left-wing groups; its true aim was the total destruction of all existing constitutions and their replacement, both in Northern Ireland and the Irish Republic, by a Workers Socialist Republic of Ireland. The People's Democracy became closely associated with the England-based Revolutionary Socialist Students Federation, part of the Trotskyist Fourth International.

Four prominent leaders were Michael Farrell, Bernadette Devlin, Cyril Toman, and Eamonn McCann. Farrell, a lecturer, had been chairman of the Young Socialists Alliance, of which Devlin and Toman were members, and which also wanted a Workers Socialist Republic for Ireland. McCann had been involved with the now defunct Irish Workers Group and the Dublin-based Irish Workers League. People's Democracy members became active in the CRA and within a very short time had turned it into a political left-wing organization with over 1,000 members.

Previously, on 11 July 1968, Prime Minister Harold Wilson had told Prime Minister O'Neill that he must introduce reforms that would lead to "one-man, one-vote"; on 22 November O'Neill outlined his proposals in the Stormont Assembly. In short, they were a timid, slow, and gradual progression to equal enfranchisement for the Catholic population. Mild though they were, they immediately aroused fury and opposition from the bulk of the Protestants, who saw their supremacy slipping away. O'Neill suddenly became a most unpopular Unionist prime minister.

The CRA organized another demonstration march into Armagh on 30 November 1968 with the intention of holding a meeting at the War

*Published on 12 September 1969, an inquiry into the disturbances in Northern Ireland of this period that was conducted by Lord Cameron, a Scottish High Court judge.

Memorial in the center of the city. About 6,000 people were mustered by the CRA. Earlier in the day, however, a large group of Protestant demonstrators led by the Rev. Ian Paisley and Ralph Bunting occupied the center of Armagh with the intention of preventing the CRA marchers from entering. The RUC erected double barricades to keep the two hostile factions apart.

In the afternoon, the CRA marchers were halted at the first police barrier by their own stewards, some of whom were IRA members. The CRA demonstrators held their meeting where they were and dispersed when it ended. At the other end of the street, across the other police barricade, Paisley and Bunting held their rival meeting; eventually they and their followers dispersed too. The RUC later stated that over 200 weapons, mainly clubs and sticks, had been confiscated at police roadblocks on the city approaches, and that five people had been arrested for carrying firearms. Twelve civilians and eight policemen were injured.

Two press incidents occurred that day in Armagh. In one, as the Paisley supporters were dispersing, a television news (ITN) cameraman was attacked and injured; in the other a BBC TV news team alleged the police had deliberately broken its television cameras after it had filmed a police baton charge that had followed an attack on the RUC, in which rocks were thrown by Paisley supporters. Home Affairs Minister William Craig advocated stronger measures against the Civil Rights Association.

On 5 December the Stormont government announced measures for strengthening the police. The regular RUC, which was below its authorized establishment, was to be increased substantially to allow two more Special Duties Platoons to be formed. More vehicles, including armored personnel carriers and water-cannons, and other equipment were to be provided. Volunteers from the Ulster Special Constabulary, the B-Specials, were to be mustered while the "present tension exists," a few for a "fairly long time" and others on a daily basis as required. The B-Specials would not be used in areas where disturbances were liable to erupt, but to relieve RUC policemen from routine duties for this purpose. William Craig agreed to appoint a press relations officer for the RUC. During the major part of December there seemed to be an unofficial truce between the Stormont government and the CRA, ostensibly to give it a chance to implement its announced reforms; but in fact, the CRA had organizational and leadership problems.

In December 1968 a new issue came to be voiced openly by a small number of Protestants—the possibility of a unilateral declaration of independence (UDI) for Northern Ireland. This was an expression and an issue that had become universally familiar since Rhodesia had declared

UDI from Britain in 1965 and was at the time being economically block-aded by Britain and certain other nations. One of the main proponents of UDI was William Craig, who had stated that Northern Ireland could sur-vive economically without British aid, his view being that a turn-over tax or a value-added tax would make up any deficit due to the secession of British subsidies.

On the 11th Prime Minister O'Neill, who was appealing for support for his proposed reform policies and an end to the mounting disorders, dismissed Craig from his government. O'Neill stated that "Ulster's in-come is £200 million a year, but we spend £300 million." On the 12th O'Neill asked for and obtained a vote of confidence in Stormont. Although many Unionists had doubts, they all backed him. O'Neill then said he was determined to "preserve the constitutional position with Britain," thus totally repudiating any thoughts of UDI, an issue that faded into the background for some years.

On 20 December 1968 the leaders of the People's Democracy an-nounced there would be a CRA demonstration march from Belfast to Derry, a distance of seventy-three miles, to take four days. It was to leave Belfast on 1 January 1969 and go by way of Antrim, Randalstown, Toomebridge, Maghers, Dungiven, and Claudy, to be welcomed in Derry by the Citizens Action Committee. The People's Democracy (PD) statement also expressed dissatisfaction with the proposed O'Neill reforms; demanded that the "one-man, one-vote" be implemented im-mediately; demanded a total repeal of the Special Powers Act; and demanded a radical rethinking of solutions to the housing and unemployment problems.

On 27 December 1968 William Long, who had become the Stormont minister for home affairs, asked the PD to cancel its march to Derry; but it refused, despite the fact that the RUC said the march would meet with Protestant opposition all along that particular route, and there would be difficulty in providing the marchers with adequate police protection. Both the Reverend Paisley and Ralph Bunting called upon Protestant ac-tivists to harass this CRA march. Despite all this, William Long decided not to ban it officially. Bunting aggressively announced that his Loyal Citizens of Ulster group, his strong-arm men, would be "trooping the colour" in Maghera on the 2nd and in Claudy on the 3rd.

The CRA march began as planned on 1 January 1969 with only a small number of marchers, who, when prevented from entering Antrim by militant Protestants, were diverted round that city by the RUC. By the 2nd the CRA numbers had increased to over 600, but Loyalist dem-onstrators solidly barred their route and prevented them from entering

Randalstown. They had to take a circuitous route to Toomebridge, where they were again prevented from marching into town by Bunting's followers. Again, the CRA procession had to be diverted.

The CRA marchers spent the night of the 2nd outside Maghera, while inside that town a Protestant mob ran riot, smashing windows and overturning vehicles. Extra RUC men were quickly moved in to restore order, and four policemen were injured. Abandoning an attempt on the 3rd to enter Maghera, still packed with Protestant militants, the CRA procession walked to Dungiven, to be welcomed by the largely Catholic population. Numbering now over 1,000, the CRA marchers moved on to reach Claudy, only ten miles from Derry, by nightfall. By this time considerable interest had been aroused and television cameras and press were in frequent evidence.

On the 4th the CRA march was ambushed by Protestants at Burntollet, about eight miles from Derry. Some were dispersed by the attack but the majority continued marching, despite rock-throwing and harassment by Protestant activists. They eventually reached Derry, where they marched into Guildhall Square and were welcomed by John Hume and Ivor Cooper of the Derry Citizens Action Committee. Hume was the Catholic Stormont MP for the Foyle constituency (Derry was on the River Foyle). The CRA arrival passed off without violence, but later in the day disturbances erupted when about a thousand CRA members and others—many teenagers looking for trouble—surrounded the Derry Guildhall, where both the Reverend Paisley and Ralph Bunting had arranged to speak to their followers. Rocks were thrown and cars overturned. The RUC made repeated baton charges, and clashes continued for several hours. In all, some 126 people, including twenty policemen, were injured.

The whole Civil Rights Association project had been a blatant provocation exercise, moving as it did, or attempted to do, through solid Protestant areas right to the Guildhall, the very symbol of Protestant supremacy, within the ancient walls of Derry. As anticipated, Protestant elements reacted violently.

On the night of 4 January a group of RUC policemen, some of whom had been drinking, followed by gangs of Protestant youths, made a raid into the Bogside area, in which over 5,000 Catholics lived in squalid conditions. The Bogside lay in a shallow valley that was once a swamp beneath the towering city walls of Derry. It was a psychological setting for trouble. The police and their hangers-on smashed windows, terrified inhabitants, caused other damage, and beat up all who opposed them. The Catholics saw this raid as an uncontrolled act of revenge for Catholic temerity in penetrating into the sacred Guildhall Square in force.

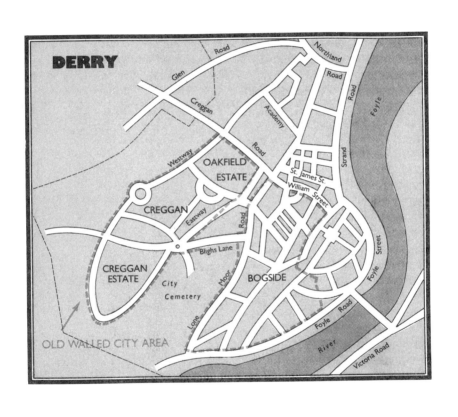

DERRY

Glen Road

Creggan

Northland Road

Academy Road

Westway

OAKFIELD ESTATE

St. James St.

William Street

Strand Road

Foyle

CREGGAN

Eastway

Road

Foyle Street

CREGGAN ESTATE

Blighs Lane

City Cemetery

Moor

BOGSIDE

Lone

Foyle Road

Foyle River

Victoria Road

OLD WALLED CITY AREA

A senior RUC officer inquired into allegations against the police in the Bogside, and eventually sixteen policemen were disciplined. The Cameron Report concluded that on the night of 4–5 January 1969 "a number of policemen were guilty of misconduct which involved assault and battery, and malicious damage to property in streets in the predominantly Catholic Bogside area . . . and the use of provocative sectarian and political slogans." The report also condemned the RUC for "the use of unnecessary and ill-controlled force in the dispersal of the demonstrators."

John Hume, Ivor Cooper, and Gerry Fitt went to the main RUC station in Derry, where they received an assurance that the police would not again enter the Bogside, provided all remained peaceful. The Bogsiders feared reprisals. Later on the 5th about 1,500 CRA members and others armed with clubs and similar weapons moved into the Bogside to protect the inhabitants from any recriminatory raids. The Protestant activists were getting their second breath and, as had become almost customary in such sectarian disturbances in Northern Ireland, they were preparing to take action against the Catholic population.

John Hume took charge of the CRA group in the Bogside and emphasized they were there only to protect the area, that no damage should be done, but that the area must be completely sealed off; no one was to be allowed to enter or leave. CRA barricades were erected at all entrances and exits. For six days, from 5–11 January 1969, the Bogside became the first "no-go area" in Northern Ireland, from which the RUC and others in authority were rigidly excluded. Television cameras and the world media reported these events, in which both the Stormont government and the RUC had to back down in the face of Catholic resistance.

On the 7th the Stormont government authorized greater use of the B-Specials, and more were mustered for full-time duty. This only further alarmed the Catholic Bogsiders, as they generally felt the B-Specials were a partisan paramilitary force recruited exclusively from the Protestant community. The strength of the regular RUC was quoted as being about 3,000.

The People's Democracy, which now had a firm grip on the CRA, decided to strike while the iron was hot. It planned a similar CRA march through Newry, a "mixed" town with both Catholic and Protestant communities. The RUC shortened the proposed march and attempted to reroute it, but the organizers were determined to enter the town. The CRA march to Newry began on 11 January 1969 with about 5,000 demonstrators in the procession; they tried to force their way through police barriers, erected to prevent their entering parts of Newry in which they would inevitably clash with Protestant activists. Paisley, Bunting, and other hard-line leaders decided they would not oppose this march, however, so it turned into a confrontation between the RUC and the CRA. Violence flared up and several RUC vehicles were set on fire or damaged. On the 12th William Long, Stormont minister for home affairs, openly accused the People's Democracy of brutal attacks on the RUC at Newry.

On 24 January 1969 Brian Faulkner, the Stormont minister of commerce (and virtually the deputy prime minister, although the constitution did not provide for that office), resigned in protest against the suggestion that an outsider should be appointed to inquire into the disturbances in Northern Ireland since October 1968, considering it to be an abdication of Stormont authority. William Morgan, Stormont minister for health, resigned a couple of days later for the same reason. On 30 January 1969 a letter signed by "Thirteen Backbenchers" (those MPs who held no government portfolio or office) called for a change in Unionist leadership.

On 4 February Prime Minister O'Neill dissolved his government. In his attempt, under British pressure, to implement a gradual program of electoral equality for the Catholics, O'Neill had run up against hard-liners in his own Unionist Party. By general consensus, O'Neill was described as being sincere, honest, but a slow plodder who was not able to carry his Unionist Party or the powerful Orange Lodges with him, while his reform proposals simply kindled the wrath of the Reverend Paisley and his extremist followers.

Elections for the new Stormont Assembly were held on 24 February, when candidates contested for fifty-two seats, of which seven (six Unionists and one Republican) were returned unopposed. Previously, Terence O'Neill had been one of those automatically returned without opposition; certain seats were regarded almost as rightful family ones. This time O'Neill was opposed in his Bannside constituency, Co Antrim, by Paisley, whom he defeated. Another Unionist member, James Chichester-Clark, a future Stormont prime minister, was also opposed for the first time—by the youthful Bernadette Devlin, whom he defeated. Ralph Bunting failed to win a seat and gradually sank into political oblivion.

The final result of this 1969 election was a victory for the Unionist Party, which gained thirty-six out of the fifty-two seats, a comfortable majority. Additionally, three seats had been won by "Independent O'Neill Unionists"—the first signs of an open split in the Unionist Party. The Nationalist Party, drawing support from the Catholic communities with a "united Ireland" policy, gained only six seats (a loss of three). Of the others, the Northern Ireland Labor Party won two seats. It had a registered membership of 2,550, had twenty-one trade unions affiliated with it, and was affiliated with the British Labor Party, having similar aims. Its members were both Catholic and Protestant. The People's Democracy contested the election but won no seats. O'Neill received votes of confidence from his Unionist Parliamentary Party, from the party's Standing Committee, and from the Unionist Council; he was once again firmly back in the saddle. This was the usual Unionist way of dealing with inconvenient elections.

On 20 March during a Stormont debate on amendments to the Public Order Act, nine opposition MPs were suspended for their unruly behavior. On the 25th Paisley and Bunting began short prison sentences for unlawful assembly in Armagh (on 30 November), their appeals having been dismissed. At a bye-election on 17 April 1969 for the mid-Ulster constituency for the Westminster Parliament, Bernadette Devlin beat the Unionist candidate. Her tiny figure belied her fiery oratory, and she was only twenty-one years old.

After the suspension of the nine Stormont MPs, a series of CRA demonstrations and marches was organized to protest proposed amendments to the Public Order Act. There were serious clashes and disturbances at only two of them—at Lurgan, Co Armagh, and Derry. On 4 April the People's Democracy organized an Easter Commemoration March from Belfast to Dublin through Lurgan, where it was to hold a meeting at the War Memorial in the center of town. The War Memorial site was occupied in advance by about 500 of Paisley's supporters, so about 150 CRA marchers staged a sit-down in front of them and had to be bodily removed by the RUC. About eighteen were arrested, and in the scuffling seven policemen were injured.

A CRA march from Burntollet into Derry was planned by the Derry Citizens Action Committee for 19 April, but it was officially banned by Robert Porter, who had been appointed the Stormont minister for home affairs. Instead, the demonstrators staged a number of sit-downs in various parts of Derry, one of which led to clashes with hard-line Protestant activists. Several hours of violence ensued, during which RUC stations were attacked. A group of about 400 policemen entered the Bogside and made several baton charges against the demonstrators, using their water-cannon. The RUC established themselves at several key points in and around the Bogside area.

In the early hours of the 20th the inhabitants of the Bogside, aided by CRA demonstrators, attacked the RUC and their vehicles with petrol bombs. Some of the police vehicles were burned or damaged. One policeman fired shots into the air when the mob tried to overturn his Landrover, but the reaction was so great that the RUC had to withdraw from the

Bogside. Tension again rose suddenly as the RUC moved back into the Bogside. For some years the pattern had been much the same: every now and again the Bogsiders rose against the RUC and drove them out of their area; then, after a pause for reinforcements, the police usually charged back in and took retribution with a heavy hand. It was part of the way of life in the more violent areas in Northern Ireland, and no one in Protestant authority took much notice of how the RUC handled such problems.

About 2,000 Bogsiders—in fact, all the able-bodied people, both men and women—together with about 2,000 CRA demonstrators armed with clubs and similar weapons stood ready to repel the anticipated RUC attack. For the first time television cameras and representatives of the international media were on hand to record the police invasion of the Bogside. Sizing up the situation quickly, John Hume, now the dominant on-the-spot leader of the CRA and the Bogsiders, persuaded them all to evacuate the Bogside area for two hours, and to move to an adjacent housing estate. He then warned the RUC that if policemen were still in the Bogside area when they returned, he would not be responsible for the consequences.

Both the Catholic and Protestant bishops of Derry appeared and appealed to the demonstrators and Bogsiders to keep off the streets, and avoid becoming involved in civil disturbances. The two bishops and other Church leaders saw John Hume's reasoning and personally made appeals to the Stormont government. Then John Hume spoke by telephone to Robert Porter, minister for home affairs, who ordered the withdrawal of the RUC from the Bogside. The policemen evacuated the area just a few minutes before John Hume's deadline. The residents of the Bogside and the CRA demonstrators accepted assurances from the RUC that only normal police patrols would be in their area. For the second time, the Bogside had become a temporary no-go area. During that weekend of violence at Derry, 209 policemen and 79 others were injured, while 33 people had been arrested. Apart from allowing individual members to take part, the IRA had not been involved in this explosion for the civil rights movement that was sweeping uncontrollably across Northern Ireland.

9 The No-Go Bogside

"You are now entering Free Derry"
— Sign daubed on a house wall in the Bogside.

RIOTING AND VIOLENCE in Derry subsided on 23 April 1969 when Vincent McDowell, chairman of the Derry Citizens Action Committee, called for a temporary suspension of street activities because "bands of Paisleyites were roaming the streets of northern towns." In other words, there was apprehension that gangs of Protestant youths might take reprisals on Catholic communities elsewhere. "Free Derry" had been established, and the now famous sign daubed on the end wall of a row of terrace houses read, "You are now entering Free Derry." Barricades on all roads leading into the Bogside were manned by determined volunteers.

Events in the Bogside alarmed the Stormont government and made it realize that the security situation in Northern Ireland was becoming extremely serious; it asked that British troops in garrison in the province — about 1,800 in all — stand by to help the RUC if necessary. On the 21st Home Secretary James Callaghan said that British troops could be made available but that they must be confined to a passive role and would use only the minimum force if attacked. That night British soldiers began guarding certain vulnerable installations.

The people in Britain were almost completely ignorant of the state of affairs in Northern Ireland and of the way in which the dominant Unionist party had been running the province for many years. Riots, disturbances, and demonstrations by Catholics seldom merited more than a few lines hidden away on some obscure page in British newspapers. Northern Ireland was an unimportant political backwater as far as Westminster was concerned, and few MPs knew or cared, just what was going on there. To the Tories, Northern Ireland had traditionally meant the support of the eleven Unionist seats when required; as long as this was given, they were content to let the Unionists govern the province in their own way, as long as there was no overt trouble or fuss. Although it had been in power since 1964, the British Labor government led by Harold Wilson had found no reason to pay any special attention to Northern Ireland and, despite the civil rights explosion, was reluctant to become involved.

113

The era of disinterest by British governments was suddenly brought to an end by two things. The first was the interest—carefully cultivated by the publicity-conscious CRA movement—of the British and foreign media, especially of television, which fully covered the disturbances and the behavior of the RUC. Violent scenes were seen on television screens in millions of British homes. Startled and horrified, people began to ask whether this was really happening on their own doorstep.

The second was the diminutive but extremely vocal firebrand, Bernadette Devlin, who had won a bye-election for the mid-Ulster seat at Westminster. Miss Devlin (whose grandfather had been a British soldier in the Boer War of 1899–1902) was one of the leaders of the CRA movement and had been extremely active during the weekend of rioting in Derry. Fully appreciating the value of publicity, she had been enticing and directing television crews to where the action was, or was about to be, so that it could be properly recorded.

Early on 22 April she left Derry for Westminster to make her maiden speech. Speaking before her in the British parliament was James Chichester-Clark, the Stormont minister of agriculture and Westminster MP. His speech was pedantic. He ascribed the cause of all the recent troubles in Northern Ireland to the IRA, alleging that it had resumed activity again in the north, and that groups of IRA men were openly drilling in the Irish Republic. He was wide of the mark. The disturbances were the result of the spontaneous welling up of discontent caused by discrimination, to which disruptive, rowdy, and trouble-seeking elements had been attracted.

Bernadette Devlin followed Chichester-Clark, and her speech, made on the eve of her twenty-first birthday, delivered emotionally and forcibly, was a memorable one, fully reported in the British media the following day. She told her listeners things they had never heard before. She described the situation in Northern Ireland as she saw it from her discriminated-against Catholic point of view. The tiny figure with the penetrating voice said, "I was engaged in building barricades to keep the police out of the Bogside," adding that, "I organized the civilians in that area to make sure they wasted not one solitary stone in anger."

Miss Devlin castigated the Unionists for their reluctance to embark upon reform and urged the British government to consider abolishing the Stormont Parliament and ruling Northern Ireland direct from Westminster. She warned the British government against the use of troops in Northern Ireland, saying that, "If you send in British troops, I would not like to be either the mother or sister of the unfortunate British soldier who stands there." It was an effective speech that presented the Northern

Ireland problem to the British people in a light they had never seen before. It aroused their interest, but it also caused them some unease. It also forced the Labor government to turn its cold, unsympathetic attention to the problem.

The British government began pressuring Stormont to hasten with its political reforms. This issue was discussed on the 23rd at a meeting of the Unionist Parliamentary Party when it was decided to accept the principle of universal adult enfranchisement and to put it into practice at the next election. This decision was not unanimous by any means: to many diehard Unionists it was an unpalatable one. Unionist power rested upon existing inequalities of the voting system in Northern Ireland, and despite the tense situation and British pressure, there was strong resistance to such reform. James Chichester-Clark, for example, resigned from the Unionist Parliamentary Party on this issue, his excuse being that the timing of this reform was not yet appropriate.

The flash point Derry (still Londonderry to the non-Catholics) was a city far too vital to their traditions to be allowed to pass completely under Catholic control, as would surely happen should the one-man, one-vote system be introduced; some two-thirds of the population was Catholic. Then a local Catholic council would be in a position to forbid the use of the walled city for Protestant demonstration and deprive them of the use of the esplanade overlooking the Bogside, on which they held their flaunting Orange Parades in July.

In what he hoped was an opportunity to internationalize the Northern Ireland problem, Irish Prime Minister Jack Lynch sent Minister for External Affairs Frank Aiken to New York on 23 April to ask U.N. Secretary General U Thant for his intervention. Aiken returned to Dublin emptyhanded.

On the 24th an explosion fractured water pipes in Silent Valley, and the following day there was another similar explosion. The water supply for Belfast was reduced by half. As these installations were so vulnerable to acts of sabotage, British soldiers carried out surveillance patrols in daylight hours using helicopters while at night the whole length of the exposed water pipeline was patrolled on foot by B-Specials.

The weekend of 26–27 April was comparatively quiet in Derry and the Bogside. The focus of discontent and demonstration moved to Armagh, where a rally of some 4,000 Paisleyite supporters was held to welcome home three of the men who had been imprisoned for involvement in disturbances in that city on 30 November the previous year. This led to clashes with the police, in which civil rights groups became involved.

On Sunday the 27th, Cardinal Conway, the Catholic Primate of All Ireland and Archbishop of Armagh, condemned from his pulpit in Armagh Cathedral the "conduct of irresponsible hooligans." That day the first contingent of British troop reinforcements arrived in Northern Ireland, consisting of about 500 soldiers.

On 28 April 1969 Terence O'Neill resigned as Stormont prime minister and as leader of both the Unionist Parliamentary Party and the Unionist Party. In the face of the solid wedge of Unionist resistence, he found the mounting pressure from the British government for immediate political reform more than he could cope with. O'Neill had been clearly out of his depth in the rough swirl of sectarian political strife that was engulfing the province.

On May 1969 James Chichester-Clark* was elected leader of the Unionist Party and so automatically became prime minister at Stormont. He had gained the leadership by only one vote. The other candidate was Brian Faulkner, considered by many to be tougher and more practical. That day, retired members of the RUC under sixty years of age were asked to return to full-time duty.

On 6 May Prime Minister Chichester-Clark announced an amnesty for everyone against whom proceedings had been or were being taken for involvement in civil disturbances as of 5 October 1968. This brought about the release from prison of the Rev. Ian Paisley and Ralph Bunting and the withdrawal of proceedings against Bernadette Devlin and Gerry Fitt, both Westminster MPs, and two Stormont MPs, Austin Currie and Ivor Cooper. On 21 May Chichester-Clark went to London to meet Prime Minister Harold Wilson, to whom he outlined in detail his proposals and the timetable for political reform in Northern Ireland. Later he claimed that both Prime Minister Wilson and Home Secretary Callaghan were satisfied with his proposals, but this was never confirmed by either man.

The annual Protestant July Orange Marches caused renewed violence in Derry that lasted for several days and also affected other towns, notably Lurgan and Dungiven. On the 12th regalia-bedecked Protestants marched and countermarched with drums beating along the esplanade of Derry, above the Bogside no-go area. This provoked a large crowd of Catholic youths to throw stones and petrol bombs at the police who were trying to keep them away from the Orange marchers. Property was damaged, shops were looted, and cars set on fire. By use of water-

---

*Not to be confused with his brother, Robert Chichester-Clark, who held the Westminster seat for Londonderry.

cannon, and by making a number of baton charges, the police managed to confine the rioting to a small area adjacent to the Bogside and Derry. The RUC, which made no attempt to enter the barricaded Bogside, stated that forty petrol bombs had been thrown that day and that sixteen policeman and twenty two civilians had been injured.

On the 13th there was more damage to property and vehicles, more petrol bombs thrown, and many incidents of looting. Twenty policemen were injured and over forty people were arrested. The Derry Citizens Action Committee issued a statement disassociating itself from the violence, condemning it and praising the actions of the RUC. In Derry the Catholic rowdies had shrugged off all semblance of any influence of the CRA movement and its leaders.

In the early hours of the 14th there was a shooting incident near the Bogside, one of the first; then during the daytime, violence again erupted and continued until the 15th. The fighting was now definitely between the rival gangs of Catholic and Protestant youths looking for trouble, and the area adjacent to Derry and the Bogside became a favorite sectarian battleground, a sort of rioters' no-man's-land.

Stormont Minister for Home Affairs Robert Porter alerted stand-by parties of B-Specials, which he said would be equipped only with batons. The Derry Citizens Action Committee immediately criticized this decision on the ground that they all had rifles at home. It announced it was forming a Citizens' Council, to include members of all religious denominations, with the aim of cooling the tension and preventing further outbreaks of violence. After the 15th the RUC succeeded in keeping apart the rival sectarian gangs for almost a month.

On 28 July the Derry Citizens Defense Association came into being. Its object was to organize the defense of the no-go Bogside against anticipated RUC and Protestant gang attacks when the annual Apprentice Boys March took place in Derry on 12 August.

However, before that, four days of violent rioting began in Belfast on 2 August 1969. Outside the Unity Walk block of apartments, occupied mainly by Catholics, stones had been thrown at a procession of Junior Orangemen. An angry crown of Protestants gathered and smashed windows in the apartments but were prevented from storming the buildings by a large detachment of the RUC that had been rushed to the scene. Behind the police and the angry crowd, Protestants began barricading the Shankill Road area to prevent any more RUC reinforcements being moved toward the Unity Walk apartments. Many petrol bombs were thrown and the violence continued until the early hours of the 3rd.

Elsewhere in Belfast on the 2nd, sectarian fighting broke out near the predominantly Catholic Crumlin Road area. Inhabitants constructed barricades with telegraph poles and lamp posts, blocking off the side roads leading to Crumlin Road. Cobblestones, known locally as "Belfast confetti," were torn up from the roadways to be used as offensive missiles. This fighting continued until the early hours of the 3rd, and at least fifteen houses were set on fire by petrol bombs.

On the afternoon of 3 August another large crowd of Protestant youths gathered threateningly outside the Unity Walk apartments but were eventually dispersed by the police using their water-cannon. That evening fresh rioting erupted as a large Protestant crowd of rowdies rampaged through the Shankill Road, causing damage and looting shops. On the 4th there were more sectarian clashes in the Crumlin Road area, in which three buildings were set on fire. Then the violence in Belfast subsided for the time being.

Real trouble began in Derry in the afternoon of 12 August during the closing stages of the Apprentice Boys March. As marchers passed through that part of the city bordering the no-man's-land near the Bogside, stones were thrown. This developed into a running battle between the police and the Catholic mobs, in which Protestant gangs of youths periodically joined. By early evening a force of about one thousand policemen with armored vehicles and water-cannon advanced to the barricades. Fighting and scuffling immediately broke out between the police and the defenders and went on for some time. At one stage the police were beaten back toward the city center, but they charged forward again. As a warning of the charge, the RUC beat a sharp tattoo on their riot shields with their batons. There were many such tattoos between that day and the next. By these tactics the police managed to advance some distance within the no-go area, using CS gas* in their efforts to disperse the mobs. By midnight several houses within the Bogside were on fire.

There was a similar pattern of violence in the Bogside the following day. An Irish tricolor was hoisted atop a ten-story apartment on the edge of the Bogside, as well as, for a while, the blue flag of the Easter Rising, usually known as the Plough and Stars banner. From the top of this

---

*The technical term was chloro-benzylidene alonontrile, but it was usually referred to as CS gas. It was already on official issue to thirty-six police forces in England and Wales for the exclusive purpose of "flushing out dangerous armed criminals." This was the first time that CS gas had been used by the RUC in Northern Ireland. At a press conference an RUC spokesman described it as a "CS anti-riot irritant" and stated that had it not been used the policemen in the Bogside would have been completely overwhelmed.

building the defenders showered the police below with stones, bottles and petrol bombs. It was a field day for the television crews and Bernadette Devlin, who with her colleagues was busily ensuring they were shown the most advantageous locations.

During the afternoon the rioting and fighting spread to the nearby Catholic Creggan estate, where the RUC police station was surrounded and attacked by gangs of youths throwing petrol bombs and other missiles. Fighting between the police and the Bogsiders continued until about 10 P.M., when John Hume, the Catholic Stormont MP, arranged a truce under which the RUC were to be withdrawn temporarily from the Bogside.

On the evening of 13 August Prime Minister Chichester-Clark spoke to the people of Northern Ireland over television and radio. He said the Ulster Special Constabulary (the B-Specials) would be mustered to relieve the RUC of duties other than riot control, as the RUC men were tired and needed rest. His speech was generally a negative one. He repeated his promise of working towards "one man, one job" and "one family, one house." He asked the people to have patience.

Meanwhile apprehensive Catholic communities in Northern Ireland, especially in Derry, were openly calling on the Irish government to send in soldiers to protect them against the RUC and the B-Specials. In a speech on the 12th, Prime Minister Lynch said that the Stormont government had lost control of the situation; he called upon the British government to ask the United Nations to bring in a peacekeeping force. Prime Minister Chichester-Clark called Lynch's speech an "intolerable intrusion into our internal affairs." On the 15th Prime Minister Lynch also announced that the Irish army was setting up field hospitals along the border, and that he was mobilizing 2,000 Irish army reservists to be ready for participation in peacekeeping operations. This raised false hopes among the Catholic communities and bred rumors that Irish troops were about to cross the border to protect them. On the 20th Irish Minister for External Affairs Patrick Hillery was allowed to address the U.N. Security Council to give the Irish government's view on the Northern Ireland situation. The Northern Ireland Civil Rights Association also called upon the Irish government for help and asked it to recall its troops serving with the U.N. peacekeeping force in Cyprus. All this had the effect of arousing cold hostility in the non-Catholics.

Fighting between the RUC and the defenders of the Bogside began early on the 14th. During the morning gangs of Protestant youths rampaged through Derry attacking Catholics, damaging shops and houses, and setting fire to vehicles with petrol bombs. Robert Porter instructed all B-Specials to report to their nearest police station, and he announced that the RUC could make full use of them if necessary. About sixty B-Specials joined the RUC on the streets of Derry in the afternoon.

In the late afternoon the RUC men were forced to withdraw from the Bogside because a sudden change of wind caused the CS gas they had been using in quantity to be blown back at them. As the RUC withdrew in ignominy, forced out by their own weapon, wild cheers broke out among the defenders behind the barricades. The Bogside remained a no-go area; additionally, the Creggan estate had become a partial no-go area too. A British Home Office statement later said, "During three days and two nights of continuous riot duty, the RUC had found it necessary to fall back on their police stations," thus "leaving the citizens of Londonderry exposed to the prospect of looting and danger."

The Stormont government sought permission to use British troops to help the RUC in Derry, and the first contingent, about 300 soldiers, arrived at the Bogside at 5:15 P.M., shortly after the RUC had been forced to withdraw. The soldiers cordoned off the Bogside but made no attempt to enter. The Catholic population within breathed a huge sigh of relief at the sight of the British soldiers and openly welcomed them: their enemies were the RUC and the dreaded B-Specials, both of which were armed.

The British commanding officer on the spot made an agreement with the Derry Citizens Defense Association, which had assumed the responsibility for the defense of the Bogside. All B-Specials were to be withdrawn from the Bogside and the Creggan estate; the RUC was to be confined to normal police duties; and the Derry Citizens Defense Association was to be responsible for keeping order within the Bogside. Thus the first Catholic no-go area in Northern Ireland was recognized by the British army in a *de facto* way. The barricades protecting the Bogside remained.

Bloody, but temporarily triumphant, defenders of the Bogside rejoiced because the police had been driven from Free Derry, but their exhilaration was mingled with apprehension as they expected inevitable harsh retribution. This was why the sight of British soldiers was so welcome, especially as it was becoming obvious that no active help would be sent by the Irish government. Catholic mobs had frequently risen to battle briefly with the police, but any advantage gained was only temporary. If the police were forced to withdraw they simply called for reinforcements and then charged back in again in strength, using rifle butts and batons to beat the rioters into the ground, after which all was quiet for a period.

This time it was to be different. Television cameras had recorded the Battles of the Bogside for the whole world to see. At Westminister, the Labor government looked towards this Tory preserve with suspicious anger. In the Stormont Assembly on 14 August an acrimonious debate took place in which Prime Minister Chichester-Clark defended the decision not to ban the Apprentice Boys March, the call-out of the B-Specials, the use of CS gas, and the conduct of the RUC. Gerry Fitt alleged that CS gas had been used indiscriminately and that hundreds, if not thousands of CS gas shells littered the streets of the Bogside. The Stormont minister of health replied that there had been very few casualties from tear smoke, and that none had reached hospitals. When a vote of confidence in the RUC was passed, seven opposition MPs walked out.

On the evening of the 14th serious disturbances erupted. In a clash between Protestant gangs and CRA supporters in Armagh, one man was shot dead and another wounded. In Belfast rival sectarian groups clashed in the Catholic Falls Road area, and in the Crumlin Road district shots were fired. In the Catholic Ardoyne area, sectarian fighting continued until the 15th. In Stormont, Prime Minister Chichester-Clark claimed that "well disciplined and ruthless men, working on an evident plan, attacked the police at a number of points in the city [Belfast]," and that the police were obliged to return their fire. He also referred to the rioting generally as "our darkest hour."

The RUC stated that throughout the whole province, casualties for the five days' rioting (12–16 August) had been eight killed (one in Armagh and seven in Belfast) and 414 civilians, 266 policemen, and one British soldier injured. Using his authority under the Special Powers Act, Robert Porter made detention orders for up to seven days against a number of political suspects who had already been held by the police for the statutory time limit of forty-eight hours.

On the morning of August 1969 a contingent of 500 British troops took up positions along a one-mile stretch of Belfast's Falls Road and Divis Street in an attempt to separate the warring factions. Throughout that day sectarian violence continued, with shots being fired at the police. On the 16th the areas patrolled by British troops were extended and a detachment entered the Ardoyne, where there had been intermittent fighting and gun-battles since the 14th. Rioters in the Ardoyne had seized over fifty buses, some of which were set on fire, while petrol bombs had caused several houses to be gutted. The following day violence diminished in Belfast, although tension remained. The plain fact was that the rioters and troublemakers were exhausted. On the 17th more British soldiers arrived in Northern Ireland, bringing their total strength in the province up to the 3,000 mark.

The widespread violence in Northern Ireland caused considerable anxiety in Britain, where people were suddenly taking an interest in what was happening and were beginning to ask why. On the 19th there was a top-level meeting in London, chaired by the prime minister, attended by the home secretary, the defense minister, and the chief of the defense staff on the British side, and Prime Minister Chichester-Clark and certain Stormont ministers on the other. Prime Minister Wilson was not amused, and he thought the Apprentice Boys March should at least have been banned, as it was so obviously provocative and had started the trouble. He also did not like the way the RUC handled the situation, nor did he like the Unionists' reaction to events. The Stormont prime minister wanted many more British troops, and while Harold Wilson promised to send some, he also laid down stringent conditions.

After the long meeting a communique was issued, which became known as the Downing Street Declaration. The British general officer commanding (GOC) in Northern Ireland was to be given the overall responsibility for all security operations, (later) with the title of GOC and Director of Operations, Northern Ireland. He remained directly responsible to the defense minister and only had to cooperate with Stormont ministers. He was also given full control over the deployment of the RUC, except with respect to normal police functions, for which the inspector general remained responsible. He was also given full control over the Ulster Special Constabulary, which could be armed or not at his discretion. In short, authority over the internal security forces had been wrenched from Stormont hands and given over to the resident British GOC. The Stormont ministers were casually pushed aside. This made a legal nonsense of the polite British fiction that the British soldiers in Northern Ireland were simply acting in aid of the civil power.

The remainder of the Downing Street Declaration included a reaffirmation of the local reform program, the establishment of a complaints procedure against the authorities, and the stationing in Northern Ireland of two senior British civil servants to report directly back to the British government in London on the situation. This was a hard pill for Prime Minister Chichester-Clark to swallow, but as he could not continue to govern without British soldiers, he had to take it and smile.

On the 20th the Northern Ireland CRA demanded the immediate disarming and disbanding of the B-Specials, alleging they were a sectarian armed wing of the Unionist Party; but in Stormont that day,

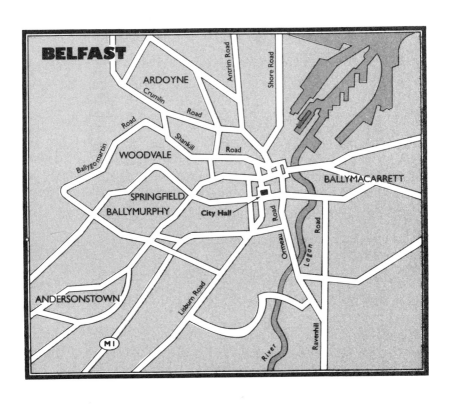

Chichester-Clark declared there was no intention of disbanding them, as they were to be included in the security plan to guard vulnerable points. Since 12 August about 4,000 had been mustered on full-time duty, and while this number was to decrease, they were still needed to protect such vital installations as the Belfast docks. The GOC ordered that arms issued to the B-Specials in Derry and Belfast be placed under central control, which meant the men would not longer be able to keep their rifles at home.

More British soldiers continued to arrive in Northern Ireland, until by 22 August they totaled about 6,500. The units were formed into two infantry brigades (equal to the U.S. combat regiment), one based in Derry and the other in Lisburn, near Belfast, which was also the location of the GOC's headquarters. A system of rotation for the British units was put into operation so that those sent to Northern Ireland would serve for a four-month period only. This did not include the resident units, of which there were three at this time; they stayed for an eighteen-month tour of duty and, being in permanent military accommodation, had wives and children with them.

On 23 August Cardinal Conway issued a statement in which he alleged that on 14 and 15 August "the Catholic districts of the Falls and the Ardoyne were invaded by mobs equipped with machineguns and other firearms. A community that was virtually defenseless was swept by gunfire, and streets of Catholic homes were systematically set on fire." The statement contained such sentences as "We reject the hypothesis that the origin of last week's tragedy was an armed insurrection," and "that among Catholics, belief in the impartiality of the USC is virtually nonexistent." Strong words indeed from the leading Catholic dignitary in the country, who was rather dramatically overemphasizing the facts. However, a few days later in a seemingly softer mood, he said that the proposed Stormont reforms were a "new deal," and "an enormous step forward, and something that would have been inconceivable a year ago." To embittered Unionists, the cardinal seemed to be telling them that Catholic violence had paid off.

On 12 September 1969 the Cameron Report on the January disturbances in Derry was published. It confirmed that the causes were the inadequacy of the housing provision; unfair allocation of such houses by local authorities; and the refusal to adopt a points system in assessing priorities of need (as was operating in Britain). It stated that there was early infiltration into the Civil Rights Association, both centrally and locally, by subversive left-wing and revolutionary elements prepared to use it to provoke and foment disorder and violence in the guise of supporting a nonviolent movement.

The Cameron Report also condemned the wide publicity given to particular episodes by the press, radio, and television which inflamed and exacerbated resentment against the police. It recommended a machinery for complaints against the police and could find no evidence of any Catholic members in the Ulster Special Constabulary. The Cameron Report was welcomed by Edward McAteer, leader of the Nationalist party, and by Frank Gogarty, chairman of the Northern Ireland CRA; but it was not liked at all by the Ulster Unionists.

The Hunt Report* on recruitment, organization, structure, and composition of the RUC and the USC, and their respective functions, appeared fairly quickly, being published on 10 October 1969. Its main recommendations were that the RUC should be disarmed; that the USC should be phased out; and that a locally recruited, part-time military force should be raised to replace the B-Specials. The organization and rank structure of the RUC should be patterned on that of the British police; its members should wear a dark blue uniform instead of a dark green one (the only point the dumbfounded Unionists agreed with); and an independent police authority should be established to control it, again on the British pattern. This meant responsibility for the police function in Northern Ireland would be completely removed from the Stormont government. The RUC element earmarked and trained for riot control would be named the Special Patrol Group. The Hunt Report urged the RUC to recruit more Catholics into its ranks.

The Wilson government accepted the Hunt Report recommendations and pressured the dazed Stormont government into accepting them. On 10 October 1969 Prime Minister Chichester-Clark announced that Sir Arthur Young, commissioner of the City of London Police, was appointed the first chief constable of the RUC; the incumbent inspector general was retired.

On careful examination, and especially in retrospect, it is difficult to see the reasoning behind the Hunt Report recommendations and to accept and agree that Northern Ireland, with its history of hatred and sectarian distrust, could be policed like a peaceful English county by solitary, unarmed bobbies on bicycles. The only explanation for this astoundingly perverse report, or the major part of it, is that Englishmen

---

*Lord Hunt was a former British regular officer who had led the expedition in 1953 that successfully climbed Mount Everest, the world's highest mountain. The report was prepared by an advisory body appointed on 21 August.

generally are convinced that everyone else thinks and feels as they do. The constitution, law, local government, police, and other institutions in England have been built on the principle of compromise—"if you give a little, I will give a little." It does not seem comprehensible to Englishmen that other nationalities should not think, feel, and act likewise whenever they have internal differences.

British Home Secretary James Callaghan again visited Northern Ireland in October to put more pressure on the Stormont prime minister to hurry his reform program; in return he vaguely promised the province economic aid in the form of industrial assistance, unemployment benefits, and short-term relief schemes. From September to December 1969 the Unionists in Stormont passed a number of reform bills, appointing a minister for community relations and a commissioner, independent of Stormont control to deal with complaints about local departments and other public bodies. A central housing authority was established and took over and assumed responsibility for allocating all the council-owned houses from the sixty-one local councils. The Wilson government in London was pulling the rug out from under the Chichester-Clark government in Belfast.

10 The Provisional IRA

"It was touch and go whether full-scale war would break out between the two organizations."
—Sean MacStiofean, March 1971

MEANWHILE WHAT OF the IRA, and what part had it been playing during the momentous events in Northern Ireland in 1968 and 1969? In brief, it had been completely taken by surprise and its part was minimal. During this period the IRA leadership had remained split between the importance of socialist activities and of militant terrorism in Northern Ireland. The GHQ order that the IRA units in Northern Ireland should take no military action remained in force and was generally adhered to, but IRA men as individuals began to take a prominent part in the many local street defense committees and action groups that were springing up in the Catholic communities against anticipated attacks by the RUC, B-Specials, and Protestant mobs. As the security situation worsened, many IRA leaders in Northern Ireland pressed for permission to take their units into action, but this was always refused with the old excuse that the time was not yet ripe for military action.

Despite its inactivity the IRA Council issued a surprising statement on 18 August 1969 under the signature of Cathal Goulding, the chief of staff, claiming that the IRA Council had placed all volunteers on the alert, that IRA units had taken part in operations in the Bogside and in Belfast, that a number of fully equipped units were in Northern Ireland assisting local defense committees, and that more IRA units were waiting to cross the border. This was pure fiction, and it simply evoked disdainful responses from both Catholics and Protestants. Nevertheless, it had the effect of causing Prime Minister Lynch to watch the border area more closely.

The following day John Hume, the Catholic Stormont MP who had been active in the Bogside, stated categorically that "there are no IRA" units present in the Bogside, nor have there been any." Edward McAteer, leader of the Nationalist Party, said pointedly that Catholic communities in Northern Ireland could expect little protection from the IRA. The reputation of the IRA in Northern Ireland sank even lower, and Catholic opinion of it was indicated by the many inscriptions of "IRA = I Ran

Away" that were suddenly daubed on many walls. Stung by the Catholic reaction, the IRA leaders in Northern Ireland complained bitterly to their GHQ in Dublin that they had neither the permission nor the means to protect the Catholic population, and that something should be done about both.

The reason for the unusual IRA statement was that, obsessed with the distant prospect of a socialist revolution in the whole of Ireland, the leadership thought the rather inept handling of the disturbances would cause the British government to abolish Stormont and impose direct rule on Northern Ireland from Westminister. The abolition of the Stormont government was to be a stage in the visualized socialist revolution, but the IRA was unprepared for it, and was following the Communist philosophy that if the masses were not ready for revolution, the revolution should be pended until they were. Under Cathal Goulding, the IRA leadership simply wanted the civil rights explosion to subside and Northern Ireland to return to normal. One concession the IRA Council made to its members was to form a larger Northern Command comprising the whole province of Ulster (that is, the six counties of Northern Ireland plus those of Donegal, Monaghan, and Cavan) but in practice this did not mean very much.

The Downing Street Declaration of 19 August came the day after the IRA statement and provoked the scattered, understrength IRA units in Northern Ireland to prepare to take unilateral military action in defense of certain Catholic communities without formal GHQ permission. Arms and equipment in small quantities were taken from IRA dumps in the south by those who favored a military line of action and were smuggled over the border into Northern Ireland, usually without the knowledge, and certainly without the permission, of the IRA GHQ in Dublin. In this way many IRA units in Northern Ireland tended to drift away from their GHQ.

An IRA convention in mid-December 1969 was poorly attended. Afterwards the militants alleged that many members who would have sided with them had been deliberately kept away by subterfuge. Two main resolutions were on the agenda, the first being that the IRA should enter into a National Liberation Front, and the second that it should end the traditional policy of abstentionism. The convention was dominated by Cathal Goulding, Seamus Costello, Tomas MacGiolla, and others who favored socialist action. They were opposed by those who wanted militant action in Northern Ireland, led by the Englishman Sean Mac-Stiofain, who was then holding the appointment of director of intelligence, Rory O'Brady, David O'Connell, and others.

The first proposal was that the IRA should merge with the Connolly Association, the Communist Party of Northern Ireland, and Irish Workers Party—all tiny, but extremely left-wing. The idea was that the IRA would at first work with them and then take them over. Bernadette Devlin's opinion of these left-wing travellers was not high, she being on record as saying, "The Communists, particularly in Northern Ireland, are as reactionary as the Unionists." The militants opposed the proposal, believing that the IRA would devolve into being simply a cog in the Marxist machine. The proposal nevertheless was passed, and so in theory the IRA merged into the National Liberation Front. The proposal to abolish the policy of abstentionism was also passed.

MacStiofain walked out, taking a group of militants with him—O'Brady, O'Connell, Seamus Twomey, Joseph O'Hagan, Billy McKee, Joe Cahill, and others, many of whom were from Northern Ireland. Anticipating how the convention voting might go and disliking the political direction the IRA was taking, MacStiofain and his group had been secretly planning for many months to form an active breakaway group. Although these two main issues were the official reasons for the split, divisions went deeper than that, hinging upon clashing personalities going back four years or more.

MacStiofain immediately went north to Belfast, where he intended to base his group. He wrote, "We had seven out of the 13 Belfast units already with us"; three weeks later he had nine. Billy McKee was appointed commanding officer and a new battalion staff was selected. In short, he ruthlessly pushed aside opposition and by mid-January 1970 had "nine units in Belfast, five in Armagh, four in Down, three in Tyrone, two in Fermanagh, one in Derry city, and one in southwest Antrim."* Many of these units were quite small, with less than half a dozen members, but were eager for action, tired of the old passive policy, and hurt by the Catholic sneers. The RUC estimate at that time was that the IRA had between 150 and 200 members in Northern Ireland, but not all were armed or active.

In late December 1969 the breakaway IRA group held a special convention at which it elected a "Provisional" Executive Committee of twelve members, which in turn elected a "Provisional" IRA Council of Seven. MacStiofain was appointed chief of staff, and he wrote, "The last decision taken by the Provisional Army Council that day was to appoint a Chief of Staff. Their choice was unanimous. I left the Convention with a greater responsibility than ever before." The Provisional IRA Council

*Memoirs of a Revolutionary

had also elected a Central Citizens Defense Committee to deal with immediate Catholic problems in Northern Ireland.

The term "provisional" appears to have been deliberately used at this convention, as the previous IRA convention held that month by Cathal Goulding was considered an irregular one, as were its decisions, and it was hoped soon to regularize the situation. Until it had converted the remainder of the movement to its way of thinking and had voted Cathal Goulding and others off the Executive Committee and Council, the breakaway IRA considered itself to be merely provisional. Also the word "provisional" had prestige revolutionary overtones from the Easter Rising Proclamation.

These proceedings were conducted in secret, of course, and the first news of the split within the IRA appeared in the Fianna Fail newspaper, the *Sunday Press*, on 28 December 1969, with the statement that some members of the IRA "had withdrawn from a Convention to form a Provisional Army Council." This was splashed in all Irish newspapers the following day. The original disclosure provoked the Provisional IRA Council, through its embryonic Republican Publicity Bureau, to issue a statement* giving its policy and aim and criticizing the IRA's obsession with politics, its failure to maintain a basic military role, and its inability to provide protection for the Catholic communities in Northern Ireland.

After this the media christened the breakaway faction as the "Provisional IRA" and the other group as the "Official IRA." The former became more familiarly known as the "Provos" and the latter as the "Officials" or the "Old Stickies." The Official IRA retained its link with its overt political arm, the "Official" Sinn Fein Party, which had an office in Gardiner Place, in north Dublin.

One of MacStiofain's initial problems was lack of money. He wrote that immediately after the split "the kitty contained exactly one hundred and five pounds." He also made the interesting revelation that "before the split occasional payments from funds provided by the Dublin Government went to the Finance Officer of the Belfast IRA." He claimed that the only money that came to him from the south in those early days was about 200 a week from the Dublin government. This was to pay men to organize Catholic defense committees, then operating ostensibly within the CRA movement. After the Provisional IRA Council had been formed, he insisted these payments continued for five weeks and then ceased altogether.

*Given in full at Appendix C

A convention of the Sinn Fein Party in Dublin in January 1970 was attended by MacStiofain and many of his Provos. He still wanted the seal of legality on his breakaway group, always a deep-seated yearning in IRA circles. He hoped to reverse the decisions recently taken, and also to get himself and his nominees elected to the Sinn Fein Executive Committee. Tom Maguire, the last surviving member of the Second Dail of 1919, declared at this convention that the decision to end abstentionism was illegal; so when it was put to the vote, it was reversed. But the proposal to approve of the merger of the IRA into a National Liberation Front was carried by a majority vote.

MacStiofain and his followers, about a hundred in all, immediately walked out of the convention. They realized they would have to go it alone, as the majority of the Sinn Fein members were against them. They met together and formed a breakaway political movement, the Sinn Fein Caretaker Executive, which was pledged to support the Provos. It became the political arm of the provisional IRA and published a newspaper, the *An Phoblacht* (The Republic), mainly in Irish. Later it published one in English, the resuscitated *Republican News*. This breakaway group became known as the Provisional Sinn Fein, and it quietly attracted the allegiance of diehard republican activists and workers, such as the Cumann na mBan and the Fianna Eireann youth movement. The *United Irishman* remained the newspaper of the Official IRA.

The main architect of the Provisional Sinn Fein was Rory O'Brady, who became its president. The Provisional Sinn Fein became the overt propaganda organization of the Provos, and its Republican Publicity Bureau issued statements from its tiny Kevin Street office in south Dublin. Both the Official and the Provisional Sinn Fein movements remained legal in the Irish Republic and Northern Ireland, while both the Official IRA and the Provisional IRA were proscribed in both parts of Ireland, but not yet in Britain. A GHQ staff was formed, the three key appointments being chief of staff, adjutant general, and quartermaster general, who were respectively Sean MacStiofain, Seamus Twomey, and Joseph O'Hagan. Directors were appointed to be in charge of intelligence, operations, training, and finance. Several people held more than one office or appointment, being field commanders or members of the GHQ staff while also having seats on the Provisional Executive Committee or Council. Arms and ammunition were procured initially from the old IRA dumps in the Irish Republic, some of which were simply taken without permission; others were forcibly seized by Provo raiding parties and smuggled across the border into Northern Ireland.

The IRA split caused bitterness and friction, especially in the struggle for arms and for membership. In January 1970 there were several fights and clashes between the Officials and the Provos. The Provos were openly poaching men from the Officials and seizing their arms and equipment by force. In Belfast and certain other towns, the Provos were more successful that the Officials; but the Provos made only slow progress in Derry, while the Catholic Falls Road area in Belfast remained an Officials' stronghold. Niether the Officials nor the Provos at this stage were seeking a clash with British troops, the former because of their policy decision and the latter because they were not yet sufficiently organized and armed.

During the spring of 1970 the Provos began a campaign of sabotage, mainly against electric power supplies, roads, and bridges. The first Provo casualty was Michael Kane, who was killed by the premature explosion of a device he was planting against an electricity installation in Forge Lane, Belfast.

In the first five months of 1970 there was intermittent rioting and violence in Northern Ireland, but generally the annual Catholic Easter marches and commemorations passed off peacefully. There was trouble, however, when a Catholic mob attacked a police station in Derry, and there was rioting for two days and nights in the Ballymurphy district of Belfast. On 9 May twenty-seven British solidiers were injured in a night of violence in the New Lodge Road area. Another day and night of rioting in the Catholic Ardoyne area followed, but the pattern of violence was spasmodic rather than continuous.

The Provos were having difficulty establishing their credibility with the Catholic communities, but one incident that helped them considerably in this respect was their defense of the Catholic Ballymacarret district on the night of 27 June. Ballymacarret was a Catholic enclave that jutted into Protestant territory near the Belfast shipyards. That night, led by the militant Ulster Volunteer Force, Protestant mobs invaded Ballymacarret and rampaged through it, starting over one hundred fires. Their ultimate aim was to panic the Catholics into evacuating their homes, thereby eliminating this Catholic salient.

The Provos mustered and took to the streets to oppose the invaders. In the fighting one of them was killed and several were injured. Five Protestants were also killed and others injured. The attackers were gradually driven out. This was a Provo victory, its first; it established itself firmly in Ballymacarret and prevented the inhabitants from leaving, as many wished to do. For the first time a Catholic community had been vigorously defended. Next the Provos gained a firm grip on the Ardoyne area and were soon taking pinpricking action against security forces making sweeps and searches.

Just after the Provos broke away from the Officials, an anonymous document entitled "Fianna Fail and the IRA" circulated in both the Irish Republic and Northern Ireland. It alleged that the new organization was the "armed wing of the Fianna Fail, operating exclusively in the Six County area, as a prelude to Fianna Fail political control there." MacStiofean, the Provo chief of staff, vigorously denied this allegation, insisting that "the whole chain of events and sensation . . . was started by the NLF itself."* There was certainly bitterness in the Officials' camp, and the successful expansion of the Provos was perhaps sufficient reason for a smear campaign to be launched against them. The Provos bore no love for the Officials and always slightingly referred to them as the NLF, and never as the IRA or the Officials.

In March and April 1970 attempts were made—allegedly by the Fianna Fail using its official influence in the government—to obtain arms secretly from a dealer in Vienna. The arms were assumed to be for the Provisional IRA; MacStiofean said he expected a consignment but did not know where or when they might arrive, or any precise details. A serving Irish army captain, James Kelly, was sent to the Continent to arrange the deal, alleged to be for 500 Czechoslovakian 9mm pistols and 180,000 rounds of ammunition. The £30,000 alleged to be paid for the weapons and ammunition came from an account in the fictitious name of George Dixon. The arms and ammunition never arrived in Ireland, but were resold by the dealer to a Latin American country. There had been at that time a degree of panic in Dublin government circles that the Catholics in Northern Ireland were about to be subjected to a pogrom of some sort, and that something must be done to help them. Certainly, the Irish government had set aside £100,000 as a general relief fund for Northern Ireland.†

On 6 May two Irish MPs, Charles Haughey and Neil Blaney, were suddenly dismissed from the government by Prime Minister Lynch, and

---

*Memoirs of a Revolutionary
†In the May 1980 issue of the Dublin Magill Magazine, editor Vincent Browne stated that of the £100,000 voted by the Dail as aid for victims of violence in Northern Ireland, £31,500 went directly to the IRA—£22,000 to the Provos and £9,000 to Officials, approximately —and was distributed by giving £5 to single men and £10 to married men who were either manning the barricades or prevented from working or collecting their unemployment dole. Browne wrote that only £29,000 reached its destination; £65,000 was paid into two private accounts in a Dublin bank. At the trial, Captain Kelly had stated that £32,500 was used for the purchase of arms in Germany and £1,600 for an abortive arms purchase in England.

a third, Kevin Boland, resigned. On his return to Dublin from the Continent on the 27th, Captain Kelly was arrested, as were Haughey and Blaney. They were all charged with offenses relating to an attempted arms conspiracy. The trial was held in Dublin in October. Kelly admitted his part in negotiating to buy arms but insisted that he had been acting under government authority, and that he had been officially instructed to do so. On the 23rd all charges against the defendants were dismissed. The evidence had been inconclusive and prevaricating, and the judge had dryly remarked at the end of the trial, "Someone has been lying."

On the Protestant side of the fence in Northern Ireland, there was continuing dissension and discontent within the Unionist Party. Five of its Stormont MPs were expelled on 19 March 1970 for either voting against the Unionist Party line or abstaining from voting. On April the Rev. Ian Paisley took his seat at Stormont, having won a bye-election.

On 31 March 1970 the Ulster Special Constabulary, the B-Specials, was officially "stood down." The RUC establishment was increased from 3,500 to 4,940, and a new RUC Police Reserve was formed with an initial establishment of 1,500. The following day, the new Ulster Defense Regiment (UDR) came into being to replace the B-Specials. Its task was to protect the border and the state against sabotage; it was to be manned by part-time volunteers assisted by a regular army staff, on the lines of the British Territorial Army. Commanded by a regular brigadier, its initial establishment was set at 3,000, and as a military formation it came directly under the command of the GOC. Many disbanded B-Specials joined either the UDR or the RUC Police Reserve. On 3 April the GOC issued a warning that people found making, carrying, or throwing petrol bombs were liable to be shot by the security forces.

On 20 April 1970 the Alliance Party was formed, which aimed to attract both Catholic and Protestant members and so form a bridge between the two communities. It was led by a Catholic, Oliver Napier, the former leader of the Liberal Party of Northern Ireland. Other founder members included two former Unionists, Robert Cooper and John Hunter, and Brian Walker, leader of the New Ulster Movement (which had been formed just before the February 1969 elections to support Terence O'Neill, and which merged into the Alliance Party).

The other new political party was the Social Democratic and Labor Party (SDLP). Formed on 21 August, it claimed to be nonsectarian but in practice came to represent the Catholics. It was led by John Hume. Other founder-members were Gerry Fitt, Patrick Wilson, and Patrick Devlin, all of whom had deserted the Republican Labor Party, and Ivor Cooper, Austin Currie, and Patrick O'Hanlon.

The general election in Britain on 18 June 1970 ousted the government of Harold Wilson and ushered in a Tory one, under Edward Heath. As prime minister, Heath appointed William Whitelaw as his home secretary. The Unionists in Northern Ireland had had an uneasy relationship with the Labor Government and obviously hoped for a better understanding with their traditional ally, the Conservative Party, now that it was back in power. They were to be disappointed. No sooner had the new Tory government settled in office than it was faced with a riotous and explosive situation in Northern Ireland.

Contrary to RUC advice, the British army regarded the Catholic Falls Road area in Belfast as a "psycho-social" target, ideal for selective saturation in its cordon-and-search operations, designed as much to intimidate the population as to unearth arms and explosives. On 3 July the discovery of weapons by troops searching a house in the Catholic Lower Falls Road sparked off three days of violent rioting, the worst that had occurred so far in Belfast. Barricades were rapidly erected in many side streets, and even the main thoroughfares were blocked by burning vehicles. The Provos were just beginning to penetrate into the Falls Road area, which had been regarded as Officials' territory. The Officials remained generally passive during the three days of rioting, as did at first the Provos; but after a few hours the Provos took action against the security forces with firearms and grenades. Although not ready yet for terrorist activity, the Provos could not pass up an opportunity that would give them added prestige among the people.

A curfew was imposed on the area and CS gas was used liberally. On the morning of the 5th the disturbances died down: all were exhausted. Three civilians were shot dead by the security forces, another died later of gunshot wounds, and a fifth died after being crushed by an armored vehicle. Eighteen soldiers were wounded, thirteen by gunshot and five by grenade fragments. After this outbreak an "extended peace line" was created by the army in the Crumlin Road area to keep the sectarian militant groups apart.

Large military reinforcements amounting to about 3,000 soldiers arrived in Northern Ireland to cover the 1970 annual July Orange Marches, at which trouble was expected. However, in general they passed off peacefully. Prime Minister Chichester-Clark saved his "Orange prestige" with discretion: instead of marching in the procession in his Orange Order regalia, as the Unionists wanted him to do to show he was a solid Loyalist and was not weakening, he rode overhead in an army helicopter.

Incidents now occurred daily, but a long list would only bore and serve little purpose. One of note was an explosion on 25 July at the home of the Northern Ireland lord chief justice who had previously sentenced Bernadette Devlin to imprisonment.

Rioting again broke out in Derry in the late afternoon of 10 October when a group of youths from the Bogside moved into the center of the city with the intention of breaking up a Unionist meeting there. The RUC and soldiers moved in, separated the two sides, and dispersed the Bogside group; but they regrouped and attacked again, using petrol bombs and other missiles. The police used CS gas, and the British soldiers fired rubber bullets for the first time. Rioting continued until the early hours of the next morning.

Trouble flared up again in Derry in the afternoon of the 11th, but troops surrounded the Bogside, still a no-go area, and contained the rioters. Later that night a Catholic mob attacked an RUC station and set police vehicles on fire with petrol bombs. The RUC stated that over sixty petrol bombs were thrown, and a grain warehouse was set on fire. The injured included forty soldiers, six policemen, and four civilians.

The next outburst of sectarian fighting erupted in the Ardoyne area of Belfast on 29 October. It quickly spread to the Divis Street area and Springfield Road, and lasted for three days.

On the 30th the Provos came into action for the first time in an offensive role against the security forces. They threw seven homemade gelignite bombs at soldiers and also fired many shots. British officers at the scene stated that men wearing black berets were seen giving orders and directing the mobs, whose activities were described as vicious. Credence was given to this when, on the morning of the 31st, the disturbances stopped suddenly and the rioters dispersed quietly and quickly. The Provos were successfully imposing their hard discipline on the Catholic communities. Forty-one British soldiers were injured in these three troubled days.

The remainder of the year was one of progress for the new Provisional IRA and its chief of staff, Sean MacStiofain, who was reelected at a Provisional IRA convention in September 1970. Aspects of his character, his leadership, and his flaws were becoming evident. He had a vision of a Gaelic-speaking united Ireland, a vision not necessarily shared by his northern colleagues. Although he was still only "first among equals" in the Provisional Executive Committee and Council, his confidence was growing and with it a lust for absolute power. He began denigrating or removing any who opposed him or did not agree with his hard military line; but he had to tread carefully when dealing with established IRA characters, such as Rory O'Brady and David O'Connell, in case they ganged up against him. MacStiofain was impatient with political argument and dialogue, which it is suspected he understood only imperfectly. He professed to be more at home with military matters and liked to give the impression he understood them perfectly.

MacStiofain came to be feared and suspected for his ruthlessness, dour attitude, and secretiveness. A teetotaler himself, he disapproved of drinking and decreed that all Provos on duty must not drink, an unpopular rule that was not always obeyed. He was a cheerless character who seldom joked and, like most converts to the Roman Catholic faith, he took his religion extremely seriously. One critic, Maria McGuire, wrote that he "had a typically narrow Irish Catholic mentality that seemed at odds with the 'new Ireland' movement it aimed to create."

In October 1970 the Provisional Sinn Fein held its convention in Dublin, and Rory O'Brady was reelected president. O'Brady now took the lead in formulating and dominating the political thinking of the Provos. The prestige of the Provisional IRA continued to increase in the Catholic communities. For example, at the annual Edentuber Commemoration in November, there was a huge turnout of Provos and their supporters. There was yet another massive turnout in December in Monaghan at the unveiling of a memorial to Feargal O'Hanlon, who had been killed in an unsuccessful attack on an RUC barracks in December 1956.

The year 1970, the first in the history of the Provisional IRA, had been one of slow but solid progress in Northern Ireland. It was attracting support, volunteers were rushing to join it, cash and arms were beginning to trickle in, and the Provos were gradually being accepted by the Catholic communities. They were succeeding in turning the Catholic communities against the once-popular British soldiers. During the year two members of the RUC and twenty-three civilians were killed, while 191 members of the RUC, 99 soldiers and members of the UDR, and over 1,000 civilians were injured due to terrorist activity or involvement in rioting or disturbances. The toll of Provo terror was mounting rapidly.

The first quarter of 1971 was taken up with rioting, some instigated by the Provos, but some spontaneous; fighting between the Provos and the Officials; and Provos taking over territory and running it like the traditional Mafia. In January, starting on the 10th, there were seven days of violent rioting centered on the Ballymurphy estate. This was instigated and organized by the Provos. Their hand to some extent was forced, as RUC men were gradually returning to their beats on the streets in the district. The Provos wanted to establish Ballymurphy as another no-go area, but were not yet sufficiently strong and ready for such a big step. However, they did not want the RUC to regain control, so riots were organized. On the night of the 12th, the Provos rounded up Catholic youths and young men and forcibly made them join in the rioting.

On the 14th the security forces carried out a large cordon-and-search operation in the Ballymurphy area, in which the only weapons found were a submachine gun and some signal flares. The women in Ballymurphy took action against the security forces both by throwing missiles and garbage at them and by banging their metal trash-can lids on the ground as a general warning that the RUC or soldiers were approaching. This deafening clatter came to be one of the ugly sounds of the insurrection. That night thirty-two petrol bombs and three acid bombs were thrown at soldiers and policemen, mainly by Provos.

On the 15th Prime Minister Chichester-Clark stated that the British troops would remain in Ballymurphy until the situation calmed down, as the object of the Provos was to force them out to create a no-go area. That night there was excessive violence in Ballymurphy: shops, houses, and a library were set on fire by petrol bombs, and vehicles were destroyed. There were also other riots that night in both the Falls Road and the Ardoyne areas. The British GOC wanted the situation to be calmed down in Ballymurphy, and so did the Provos, but for different reasons, and it was tacitly agreed that if the troops and police stayed away from Ballymurphy it would be policed internally by the Provos. The Provo strategy at this stage was limited to defense only in such circumstances.

The Provos were beginning to operate protection rackets, collecting money and organizing the people under domination. They seemed to be less concerned with popularity than with compliance, which they enforced by fear, threats, and punishment. No Catholic now dared be seen talking to a British soldier, let alone giving him a cup of tea. In January at least five cases of disciplinary tar and feathering were reported, as were another twenty-two before the end of the year.

Volunteers were now flocking to join the Provos, but they had to undergo a thorough character selection process before being accepted to ensure that informers were not planted within the organization. Invariably local lads were preferred because it was easy to check on their backgrounds and their families were in some way hostage to their behavior when enrolled. Adventurers and idealists from outside local Provo areas, especially if non-Irish, were severely discouraged. In those early Provo days and for some time afterwards, ideology was not the paramount motive for joining the IRA, the real ones being those of excitement, belonging to a popular cause that was doing something active, and the prestige, which the Provos were rapidly gaining.

As recruits were trained and disciplined and as arms and explosives arrived in Northern Ireland, the Provos were able to extend their activities, which so far had been limited to the defense of Catholic communities and the sabotage of communications and electric installations. In February 1971 it was decided that British soldiers should become Provo targets; the Provos referred to this tactic as "antipersonnel operations." On 6 February, during rioting in Belfast, a British army vehicle was ambushed in the New Lodge Road area and the first British soldier was killed. Four other soldiers in the same vehicle were wounded, one of whom later died. As a matter of interest, the first six British soliders to be killed in Northern Ireland were Roman Catholics. On 28 February another British army vehicle was attacked and set on fire by a petrol bomb, one soldier being killed in the incident.

The other Provo tactic adopted about this time was to use children to harass British troops. Mothers encouraged their young sons to throw missiles at them in the streets and to vilify them in a taunting manner. Many of these children were under twelve years of age. In February 1971 a fourteen-year-old boy had his hand blown off by the premature explosion of a gelignite bomb he was about to throw at soldiers.

In January 1971 the focus of trouble turned to the Shankill Road area. Eight policemen and eleven soldiers were injured. The month of February was much the same, with spasmodic rioting in the now familiar trouble spots. Rioters threw assorted bombs, including those made of gelignite, petrol, and acid, and also nail bombs. The security forces used CS gas, rubber bullets, and water-cannon in reply. On occasions the Provos opened fire and the soldiers fired back. On the 9th five people, including two BBC technicians, were killed when their vehicle hit a land-mine.

One of the Provos' main objectives was to curtail and disrupt the special preparations for the Protestant commemoration, "Ulster '71," the fiftieth anniversary of Stormont-ruled Northern Ireland. The next objective was to provoke the British troops into overreaction, especially in their treatment of child offenders throwing missiles at them, in order to win over the Catholic moderates, who were becoming increasingly alienated by terrorist tactics. The longer-term objective was to prod the Catholic population into a popular uprising for a united Ireland.

At this stage there seemed to be an unusual degree of tolerance on the part of the security forces in dealing with the terrorists. For example, it was known to the authorities that certain IRA leaders, both Provos and Officials, regularly crossed the border into Northern Ireland to attend meetings in Belfast, but they did not bother to arrest them. The reason given was that if they did, they would not be able to charge them with anything more serious than membership an illegal organization — if that — owing to the difficulty in obtaining sufficient evidence to convict in a court of law. Witnesses were intimidated, biased, or perverse. There was also a degree of tolerance of IRA demonstrations; for example, on 9 February, at the funeral of two IRA men who had been killed in Belfast, an IRA escort and guard of honor, wearing black berets, green combat jackets, and arm-bands, fired a volley of shots over the coffins.

The feud between the Officials and the Provisionals continued, with hostilities frequently breaking out between them as each struggled for territory and dominance. The Officials were beginning to commit terrorist acts in Northern Ireland, but on a much smaller scale than that of the Provos. This was permitted by Cathal Goulding, as much as a safety valve to prevent his remaining militants from defecting to the Provos as a tacit agreement to what he was unable to prevent. On 12 February 1971 Cathal Goulding indulged in a little sabre rattling and pledged his organization would "kill two British soldiers for every Irishman killed." The RUC estimate was that in 1971 about twenty percent of the terrorist incidents were committed by the Officials, the remainder by the Provos. The RUC also estimated in March 1971 that the strength of the IRA in Belfast was about sixty hard-core Official activists, and that there were about 150 Provos, each faction having "several hundred" additional active supporters.

Basic differences divided them still: the Officials wanted a political revolution on the traditional communist pattern and the Provos wanted a Vietnam-type guerrilla war. There was an outbreak of internecine violence between them in Belfast in March 1971, when a number of bodies were found at dawn on the streets or in ditches, usually shot in the back of the head. In the underground struggle between the two factions, kangaroo justice was often dealt out in a ruthless manner. A number of informers and defectors were killed, and shootings and beatings were administered for other alleged IRA crimes. Punishments often included shooting the victim in the kneecap; apart from being extremely painful, this shattered the bones of the knee joint, which seldom healed properly. Concrete blocks or heavy weights were dropped on hands or feet as a punishment for theft, disobedience of orders, and other IRA misdemeanors.

In late March open friction suddenly flared up between the two IRA factions in Belfast when a boy of the Fianna Eireann youth movement was seized by the Officials and beaten up for working with the Provos. The commanding officer of the Provo Belfast Brigade assigned two men to investigate this case; they were also seized by the Officials, beaten, and tortured in two separate pubs, where they "had their fingers broken by a gun-butt."* When they learned of this, a group of Provos attacked one of the pubs concerned, set it on fire, and was on its way to do the same with the other pub when it was ambushed and fired on by the Officials. A shoot-out ensued, and that night a Provo named as Charlie Hughes was shot and killed by the Officials. Leaders of the Provos and the Officials came together urgently, and a truce was called within a few hours. MacStiofain wrote, "It was touch and go whether fullscale war would break out between the two organizations. But common sense prevailed in the Belfast leadership. The national interest must come first."

However, early the following morning Tom Cahill, brother of Joe Cahill, the Belfast Provo leader, was shot and wounded while on his milk round. Joe Cahill had consistently led the fight that drove the Officials out of many Catholic parts of Belfast; he had taken command of the Provisional Belfast Brigade when Billy McKee was arrested. Tom Cahill was arrested by the RUC and imprisoned for possessing a firearm. The Officials who had shot him hastily apologized for this incident and blamed it on their "poor communications." The truce wobbled but, after three months in which the Officials and the Provos spent more time fighting each other than fighting the security forces, it held. This armed truce was occasionally broken, and a number of dead bodies, shot through the head and sometimes bearing marks of torture, were found in ditches and alleyways during the remainder of the year, especially in and around Belfast.

The Provos were becoming well established in Northern Ireland, and MacStiofain wrote that "by April [1971] new units were springing up all over the place, creating tremendous problems for the Republican supply organization, but the Supply Department had one overall brief, to work miracles, and gradually they began to. There was enough equipment to step up the campaign." In March the Provos had already stepped up their antipersonnel operations; on the 10th of that month the bodies of three young Scottish soldiers in civilian clothes were found at Linoneil, three miles from Belfast. Two had been shot through the head, the other through the body. They had been granted a five-hour leave pass from their unit and were more than two miles off limits. Two were brothers, aged seventeen and eighteen years respectively. After this incident all British soldiers under eighteen years of age were withdrawn from Northern Ireland. At that time the British army enlisted men at the age of seventeen and a half years. In April four more British soldiers were killed.

Chief of Staff Sean MacStiofain claimed his Provos carried out forty operations in Northern Ireland in April 1971, fifty in May, and another

*Memoirs of a Revolutionary

fifty in June. A number were abortive but others were not. The Provos also suffered casualties, news of which they suppressed if they could for prestige and morale reasons. Otherwise, Provo fatal casualties were admitted in military fashion. For example on 15 May a British army patrol stopped a car, and the occupants of it fired at the soldiers; the soldiers fired back and killed one man. His obituary in the *Republican News* described William John Reed as a lieutenant in the Provisional Belfast Brigade and announced that "he had been killed in action, when one of our Active Service Units ambushed a patrol of British occupation forces in Academy Street."

Another British soldier was shot dead on the 22nd and others wounded; on the 24th a suitcase containing gelignite exploded in a Protestant pub, demolishing the building and injuring eighteen people. The following day a similar suitcase, also containing gelignite, was thrown into the Springfield Road RUC station, jointly occupied by police and troops. It exploded, killing one soldier and injuring two more, eight policemen, and seventeen civilians, including a two-year-old girl. In June a Provo arms factory was discovered in a cordon-and-search operation in Ballymacarret, as was another in the Falls Road area a few days later. The Provos were hitting their stride; 1971 was the year of optimum terrorism for them.

11 Internment without Trial

"The Queen's writ does not run everywhere in the Province."
—Lawrence Orr, Ulster Unionist MP, 19 March 1971

THE BRITISH GOVERNMENT'S reaction to the IRA terrorism that developed in 1971 was uncomprehending, hesitant, and piecemeal. British Defense Minister Lord Carrington visited Northern Ireland in January and agreed to increase the new Ulster Defense Regiment to 6,000; promised that the army would have an early delivery of new anti-riot weapons and equipment specially developed for the Northern Ireland situation; and approved the army's implementation of techniques of dispersing crowds, riot control, control of mass movements of people during disturbances, and the identification of active instigators and their arrest by army "snatch squads."

The GOC, General Sir Ian Freeland, was conditioned by colonial methods of dealing with insurrections, which were hardly suitable for a Northern Ireland setting. He was an advocate of showing the flag, of dominating the battlefield, of massive searches, of cordons, and of numerous roadblocks and checkpoints. Even in those days the RUC wanted a more subtle approach to the problem. Freeland had established the army's dominance and the RUC's subservience, as he had persuaded the British government to let the army—himself as GOC—to be responsible for overall security within the province.

However, he disappointed many. At first hailed by the apprehensive Catholic communities as a deliverer from Unionist oppression, his handling of the July 1970 disturbances turned their plaudits to condemnation. He was criticized heavily by the Protestants for his support of disarming the RUC and disbanding the B-Specials; he upset his military superiors by forecasting trouble and by his miscalculation in demanding unnecessary massive army reinforcements in July 1970. Although he still had over a year to serve as GOC, he suddenly applied to retire from the army and left Ireland on 4 February 1971. He was succeeded by Lt. Gen.

Sir Harry Tuzo,* who brought with him the superior army-is-in-charge attitude.

In a Stormont debate on 2 March the tactics used by the army were discussed and criticized. The Unionists recommended that a military presence should be maintained in the "riotous and subversive enclaves," and that whenever possible there should be hot pursuit of anyone using offensive weapons against the army. Otherwise a cordon should be thrown around the area and then rigorous house-to-house searches made for gunmen. The Stormont MPs had in mind the no-go Bogside and the partially no-go Creggan estate. Prime Minister Chichester-Clark said, "I believe the only way to drive out the terrorists is to make the country too hot to hold them . . . to make the risks of showing themselves so great that their movements of men and weapons will be wholly disrupted." The MPs said that many more British soldiers would be needed.

British Home Secretary Reginald Maudling began a three-day visit to Northern Ireland on 4 March. He was not a Northern Ireland specialist by any means; he knew little about the problem, and was very much influenced by the views of the "men on the ground," tending to accept them without too much question. He agreed that the campaign against the IRA should be intensified at every level, that there should be greater physical presence on the ground, more army patrols, and more control over the movement of civilians, both in Belfast and throughout the province—in short, more vigorous and more visible action, as recommended by the army. Many Unionists gained the impression that Maudling's attitude was one of bored disinterest, but as long as he agreed with the strong measures they recommended against the IRA, they were content.

Having sold his policy to the British government, Prime Minister Chichester-Clark demanded more British troops to carry it out. On 18 March, he was able to announce that it had been agreed to send another 1,300 soldiers to the province, which would bring their total number up to about 9,700. He also said that he had obtained a British promise that the troops would stay "until the job was done."

The murder of the three Scottish soldiers on 10 March released another flood of Unionist criticism. They complained that the army policy of simply sealing off subversive areas enabled the terrorists to control the people in them forcibly. The Unionists demanded the no-go areas be opened up and properly policed by the RUC. They complained bitterly at the disbandment of the B-Specials and the disarming of the RUC, say-

---

*Technically, Lt. Gen. Vernon Crum succeeded Freeland, but he suffered a heart attack a few days after assuming office and died on 17 March.

ing that if this had not happened, the IRA terrorist situation would never have developed.

Chichester-Clark had tried to persuade Prime Minister Heath to order the army to reduce the no-go area in Derry and Belfast, but Heath repeatedly refused, mainly on the ground that strong resistance would be encountered and might result in casualties, perhaps of women and children. The army advisers had emphasized that this course would mean casualties and damage to buildings, as they were sure the IRA was determined to defend them. The thought of women and children being killed by British soldiers made the British government hesitate.

In Stormont both the Rev. Ian Paisley and William Craig were loud in their criticism of Chichester-Clark, saying that the British army had been charged with the sole responsibility for law and order and now it was not able to cope with the situation. Regulations were made under the Special Powers Act to help combat the IRA. One forbade the wearing in public of any quasimilitary uniform, including the black berets, combat jackets, and arm-bands worn by the Provos. Another made it mandatory for anyone having knowledge of people being killed or injured in disturbances to report details to the authorities. The Provos were carrying away their dead and wounded to conceal their losses and to avoid the injured being arrested and interrogated.

On 12 March 1971 over 5,000 Protestant workers from the Belfast shipyards marched in a demonstration demanding that internment of IRA suspects be introduced.

On the 19th Prime Minister Chichester-Clark faced a hostile Unionist Council, which accused him of agreeing to disband the B-Specials and disarm the RUC in return for the dispatch of British troops to Northern Ireland. This he firmly denied, but the council passed a motion of "No Confidence." The ground was falling away from Chichester-Clark. Hardline Unionists began to express dissatisfaction with the way the army was dealing with the situation and to voice the suspicion that it was rather enjoying this taste of semiactive service, and was in no hurry to terminate it. And there was truth in that. The British army had just withdrawn from "East of Suez." Glamorous and exciting overseas stations, once so plentiful when the British Empire was at the height of its glory, were fast disappearing. There was little doubt that this stint of duty in Northern Ireland was a welcome change for many soldiers from boring garrison duty in Germany.

The British chief of the defense staff was rushed over to Belfast to assure the Stormont government that it was not like that at all. He tried unsuccessfully to persuade the Stormont MPs that a very long haul was the only sure way to defeat the IRA terrorists. Later on the 20th, Chichester-Clark resigned from all his political offices and appointments. The job of prime minister of Northern Ireland had proved too much for him: he had gone above his ceiling.

On 23 March 1971 Brian Faulkner, the son of a factory owner, was elected leader of the Ulster Unionist Party, which meant that he automatically became the prime minister at Stormont, even though he had been expelled from the Unionist Parliamentary Party in March 1970. In his policy statement, Prime Minister Faulkner, who spoke with a Northern Irish accent instead of that of the British upper class and was a harder and more practical man than his predecessor, declared that direct rule from Westminster would be a disaster, that he would continue with the reform program, and that he would give special attention to the RUC.

When the insurgency began in 1969 the RUC had no counterinsurgency expertise at all; when the British troops arrived and were given the overall responsibility for security, having some considerable experience in this art, they assumed this task. As the Provos gained a grip on the Catholic communities, people were afraid to pass on information to the authorities, even secretly, and so for a time there was a distinct lack of what was known to the British army as tactical intelligence.

Beginning in April 1971 members of the RUC attended tactical intelligence training courses at the British Army Intelligence Center at Maresfield, Surrey. Special interrogation aids and techniques were demonstrated and explained. They included "sensory deprivation," wherein the brain is deprived of the constant supply of oxygen and sugar it must have to function; "bread-and-water diet" to weaken physically; being "hooded" to confuse the senses; being deprived of sleep to tire the brain and body, and to lessen physical resistance to interrogation; and such apparatus known as the "Wind Machine" and the "Music Room." They were taught how to keep a suspect spread-eagled against a wall for long periods. Back in Northern Ireland, certain RUC detectives later put these techniques into practice in what became known as deep interrogation.

Republicans in Northern Ireland complained, with much truth in some cases, that the army was acting illegally by carrying out searches without search warrants, and commandeering houses for its own use and evicting families. British army photographers in plain clothes attended IRA funerals and Sinn Fein demonstrations and meetings to photograph suspects. There seemed to be some evidence that the army was in certain respects becoming a law unto itself. The RUC was also bending the rules with respect to carrying firearms; Prime Minister Faulkner later wrote with seeming approval that Graham Shillington, who had succeeded Sir

Arthur Young as chief constable of the RUC, had "commenced withdrawing unarmed RUC patrols in Belfast, and issuing them with arms again."*

The British public was becoming disgusted and alarmed by the news
pictures they saw on their television screens of the disturbances in Northern Ireland, and of the teenagers and even children throwing missiles at
British soldiers and reviling them. Many pictures printed in the media
were also unsettling to the people in Britain. James Callaghan, now in
opposition at Westminster, complained of the British media sending their
correspondents secretly to interview IRA leaders, and went so far as to
mention *The London Times* in this respect.

Provo Chief of Staff MacStiofain alleged that this exposure of hostile
activity against British soldiers was sheer "black propaganda" and was
being deliberately organized by the British government to turn the Catholic population against the Provos and to show the British people they
were a violent, sadistic terrorist group. He claimed he was unable to re-
but this "black propaganda" as his financial resources were limited. At
this time the Provos had only two newspapers: *An Phoblacht*, mainly in
Gaelic, for issue in the Irish Republic; and the *Republican News*, in English, for issue in Northern Ireland, Britain, and America.

Occasionally the Provos took violent action against the media. For
example, on 17 July 1971, a large explosion wrecked the Belfast printing
plant of the *Daily Mirror* and the *Sunday Mirror*, British newspapers
that had a Northern Ireland edition. The Republican Publicity Bureau
issued a statement from Dublin claiming responsibility for the Provos
and giving as the reason hostile British propaganda.

MacStiofain alleged that the British Special Air Service Regiment
(SAS) began operating in Northern Ireland in May 1971. This was firmly
denied by the British government and the military authorities, but they
based their denial on a tenuous technicality. It was true that the whole
regiment was not in Northern Ireland, but it was also true that SAS personnel were operating there in small sections. In those early days the SAS
teams came directly under the command of GHQ, Northern Ireland, but
later some were attached to individual units.

The SAS was the British counterinsurgency unit that had gained a
considerable reputation for efficiency and was popularly regarded as a
cloak and dagger outfit. Officially it was assigned to NATO, and its role
was one of "deep penetration behind the enemy lines for sabotage and
reconnaissance missions." Its brief in Northern Ireland was later officially
described as one of surveillance and gathering intelligence. The Provos

Memoirs of a Statesman

alleged this brief was exceeded and that the SAS was selectively assassinating members of the Officials and the Provisionals, hoping that each would blame the other and so start internecine fighting.

The SAS operated in small four-man teams, of which one member was an expert in all types of weapons from a Thompson submachine gun to a Soviet Kalishnikov automatic rifle; another in explosives and sabotage; another in all types of communication; and the fourth in either medical skills or languages. SAS personnel were equipped with special weapons, equipment, and surveillance apparatus, and were trained to lie out in hidden stakeout positions for days on end. Because of their furtive role and the general introverted nature of the SAS men, rumors of their deeds and capabilities had been magnified over the years by the British media. The British government was embarrassed that information on the SAS operating in Northern Ireland had leaked out to the press, as it dreaded being branded with the stigma of using a private assassination force.

During the second quarter of 1971 the hard areas, such as the no-go Bogside and Ballymurphy, generally were left alone by the security forces, and so there was little trouble from them. Occasional riots erupted in them whenever a British army "snatch squad" made a lightning raid to seize a particular individual for interrogation. Starting in early July the Provos began to fire shots from the Bogside and the Creggan estate in Derry at British army patrols and manned road checkpoints. The soldiers returned the fire selectively. Often the Provo gunmen crawled on their hands and knees amid children in school playgrounds. British snipers watched and waited for the Provos to open fire and then instantly fired back at them. This neutralized the Provo gunmen to the extent they became known as "One Shot Snipers": they would fire one shot only and then hastily evacuate the area before they could be located. On 8 July 1971 in a sniping shoot-out between the Provos and British army snipers, the British killed at least two Provos and fatally wounded another.

By July the Provos were ready to intensify their sabotage and antipersonnel campaigns. On the 12th of that month two British soldiers were shot dead in Belfast by Provos in retaliation for the murder of two Irish citizens in Derry on the 8th.

It was decided that the function of the security forces—that is, mainly the army—was not only to contain disorder and violence, but to find the terrorists and root out the organization behind them. This was the policy of the new GOC. On 23 July the largest search so far, involving over 1,800 soldiers, was made at dawn in Belfast and several other parts of the province. Arms, ammunition, equipment, and Provo documents were found. That day a British Home Office statement explained that this search "marks the beginning of a new phase in the battle against the IRA." On the 27th Reginald Maudling said it was now open warfare between the IRA and the security forces, and that the British government could not allow the IRA to win. He rejected a suggestion for a people's militia under Stormont control, as his government had no intention whatever of handing back any security responsibility to the Stormont government.

The Catholic communities now accused British soldiers of being trigger-happy and heavy-handed; while this may not have been generally justified, the troops were under great provocation by the attacks on them and the insults hurled at them, and they were occasionally abrupt and careless. One incident occurred on 7 August when a soldier on duty outside the Springfield Road RUC station fired at a small van on the roadway and killed a man. The official account was that shots were fired from this van as it drove past the RUC station, so the soldier fired back. This was later amended to say, "The car halted, and was moving off when troops fired at two people in the van, one of whom was killed." Witnesses were produced who said the van had slowed down as it passed the RUC station and then backfired but continued on a short distance until it halted at traffic lights, when it was fired on by the soldier. Conflicting versions were common in regard to most incidents.

Hard-line Protestants were becoming angry because Provos were not being arrested and brought before the courts since no one dared appear to give evidence against them. They demanded such men be detained without trial, and internment became a live issue in Northern Ireland. On 5 August Prime Minister Faulkner went to London to demand even more British troops and to obtain approval to introduce internment. The request for more troops was approved to bring the number in the province up to 11,900. However, the British government was not keen on internment and instead wanted Falkner to ban all processions, especially the forthcoming Apprentice Boys March in Derry and other provocative Orange Marches. Because of strong Unionist feeling and his own views, Faulkner was loath to do this. Finally it was agreed that he could introduce internment if he would ban marches.

On the 9th Prime Minister Faulkner introduced internment without trial in Northern Ireland and banned all public processions for six months.* Suspects could be detained for thirteen days for interrogation and then

---

*He later wrote, "We decided to move internment forward twenty-four hours" after the Springfield Road death on the 7th.

brought before a court and either charged, released, or interned indefinitely. Technically a person could be held by the police for forty-eight hours anyway, after which he became a "detainee"; when the fortnight lapsed, unless he was released or brought before a court, he became an "internee." Usually the expression "internee" was used for all suspects detained.

Usually arrests of suspects by the RUC and the army had been discrete, swift, and silent; a knock on the door in the early morning, and the person taken away with as little fuss or publicity as possible. In contrast, internment was heralded with a loud, ostentatious operation. It was a psychological exercise in mass intimidation with women giving the alarm by banging trash can lids on the ground. It was a Faulkner operation, and he wanted to demonstrate to his Unionists that he was taking strong action. Army trucks full of suspects were deliberately routed through Protestant areas to let the people see what was happening. The initial swoop netted 337 people, the object being to pick up not only suspects, but also others to provide a large pool for interrogation and for general effect.

The Republican Publicity Bureau stated that only fifty-three Provos were interned on the 9th; indeed, the majority had been Officials. The reason was that most of the Officials were already known to the RUC, while Provo personnel, belonging to a newer organization, were less well known to the police. MacStiofean had crossed back into the Irish Republic the previous night and so by sheer chance escaped internment. He claimed that internment caused several units of Officials to come over to his Provisional IRA, including a whole company from Strabane.

On the 11th the Stormont government announced that detention orders had been made against 230 people. Arrests continued to be made under this legislation, and on the 16th an army spokesman claimed that over eighty officers of both the Officials and the Provisionals had been arrested since internment was introduced. From the point of view of controlling the insurrection, internment came six months too late. To have been really effective it should have been brought in when the first British soldier was killed in February 1971. Intransigence on the part of the British government had given the Provos six months' grace in which to organize, train, and develop their strategy.

Prime Minister Lynch's reaction to internment was quick and inflammatory. On the same day, the 9th, his government stated that five refugee camps were being established for refugees from Northern Ireland, and that over 500 had arrived that day. Jack Lynch met Catholic Stormont MPs and sent Minister for External Affairs Patrick Hillery to London to protest. On the 11th an Irish army spokesman said there were

4,339 refugees from Northern Ireland in the camps; they had been accepted without regard to their religion. A Stormont spokesman said they were all Catholics. This mass exodus of refugees had been organized by the Provos, who marshalled whole families and transported them over the border. Most trickled back home again within a few days.

Three days of rioting followed the internment order. The GOC called out the Ulster Defense Regiment for full-time duty to relieve British soldiers manning road checkpoints and guarding vulnerable installations. The UDR was then quoted as having 4,150 members. Catholic areas in Belfast were barricaded off, and the inhabitants within them were organized and directed by the Provos, who shot at British troops, their posts, and vehicles. In all nine people were killed on the 9th. That day Protestants living in about forty houses in the Catholic Ardoyne area were ejected by the Provos, and their homes set on fire to prevent their being occupied by militant Protestant groups. The UVF had reappeared for the first time in the year since it had been defeated by the Provos in the Ballymacarret district. Tartan Gangs—crowds of Protestant youths wearing tartan scarves—roamed the streets looking for trouble. Three more civilians were killed on the 10th and another six on the 11th as gun-battles raged between British troops and Provos.

In Derry buses were set on fire, a church hall was burned to the ground, a garage was damaged by an explosion, and an RUC station came under automatic fire. Soldiers and police using CS gas and armored vehicles drove the rioters back into the Bogside and the Creggan estate; but they continually emerged again, throwing petrol bombs and other missiles. Five British soldiers were wounded by gunfire, and thirteen others were injured. On the 11th there was an all-day battle around an RUC station in Derry, more buses and vehicles were seized by the rioters and used as barricades, and a British soldier was shot dead near the Creggan estate.

In Newry shops and business premises were destroyed by fire when petrol bombs were thrown; the local offices of the *Belfast Telegraph*, a Protestant newspaper, were also set on fire. One man was killed in the cross fire during rioting in Armagh; at Claudy a member of the UDR was shot dead. There was also rioting at Coalisland, Dungiven, Omagh, and Strabane. In all, in three days, twenty-two civilians were killed.

The disturbances subsided considerably on the 12th due to exhaustion on the part of the rioters and a shortage of ammunition on the part of the Provos. That day in Belfast, British troops using bulldozers removed barricades; and although they met some opposition, there were no gun-battles in the city that day. Troops also removed barricades in and around Derry, but when they tried to remove those enclosing the

Bogside and the Creggan estate, they ran into considerable opposition. CS gas was used and a large number of rubber bullets were fired, but the army gave up and the no-go areas remained. Children collected the rubber bullets and sold them as souvenirs.

In Belfast the 12th was a day of mass population movement, set in motion by fear and intimidation. Hundreds of Catholics and Protestants left their homes in the mixed areas for the safety of their respective communities. Under threats from the Provos, Catholic families moved into Catholic ghettos, and many Protestant families were ejected to make way for them. Some of the abandoned houses not required for incoming Catholic families were deliberately set on fire so they could not be used by the security forces or hostile sectarian militants; but some were also destroyed so the owners could claim insurance benefits or compensation from the government. A Stormont spokesman later said that over 350 houses in Belfast had been gutted. The 12th also marked the beginning of the "political robberies": £2,000 was stolen from a post office in Belfast and £600 from business premises in Derry, both by gunmen who were suspected to be Provos.

On the 14th the population movement continued and there were more robberies and spasmodic disturbances. The next day the GOC repeated the warning that persons throwing or about to throw grenades or bombs would be shot.

The British army adopted the practice of holding fairly frequent press briefings, rather than formal press conferences, in the hope of improving its image. At one held on the 13th, the spokesman claimed that "most" of the barricades had been removed in Belfast and alleged that the IRA was intimidating people into leaving their homes and moving into sectarian ghettos. He claimed that in the three days' fighting the army killed at least fifteen gunmen, and said the IRA always did its best to conceal its casualties. The spokesman also claimed that internment had brought in seventy percent of the men wanted by the RUC. Before internment the RUC estimated there were about 200 active terrorists in the province, mainly in Belfast.

On the same day, at almost the same time, the Provos also held a well attended press conference of their own in a school in Ballymurphy, Belfast. It resulted in wide publicity for the Provos, especially overseas, and generated a great deal of support. The press conference was brought to an abrupt end when a British army patrol appeared in the vicinity.

The star of the press conference was Joe Cahill, commanding officer of the Provo Belfast Brigade, a veteran IRA leader by this time, who had been interned in Crumlin Road Prison from 1957 until 1962. Introducing him was Patrick Kennedy, a Stormont MP. Also on the platform with them was John Flannagan, a member of the Northern Ireland Police Authority; Eugene McKenna, a member of the Belfast City Council; and John Kelly, former chairman of the Belfast Citizens Defense Committee. Kelly was an officer in the Belfast Brigade and a former defendant in the Dublin arms trial of 1970. Cahill said, "The battle of the British army has not been won." He added that supplies were short, especially of ammunition, as the expenditure had been heavy. His losses in three days' fighting had been slight, and he would only admit to thirty men interned. Kennedy said the situation was desperate and appealed for military assistance from the Irish Republic. Cahill had just handed over command of the Belfast Brigade to Seamus Twomey, and that night made his way safely across the border to Dublin.

Deciding to cash in on the publicity gained by the press conference, the Provo Council sent Cahill on a fund-raising tour in the United States. British diplomatic pressure intervened. Cahill was detained at Kennedy Airport, New York, on the technicality that he had not declared a 1942 conviction for murder (he had been involved in the Williams incident). He was kept in custody for a few days and then sent back to the Irish Republic; but in the meantime the sympathetic U.S. media had given tremendous publicity to this incident.

Until this moment MacStiofain and some other Provo leaders had not fully realized the value of overseas publicity, but the Cahill press conference and abortive visit to America changed their minds. So they embarked upon a new policy of deliberately seeking American media support and linked it to a fund-raising campaign. One authority wrote, "We did ensure that when Provisionals flew to the United States they would not encounter the same difficulties . . . and we enlisted the help of the prominent Civil Rights lawyer, Paul O'Dwyer. A phone call from [Senator Edward] Kennedy's office to the American Embassy in Dublin would result; and all difficulties would magically disappear."*

After internment had been introduced in Northern Ireland, the new Provo policy was to intensify its bombing campaign of selected targets and also to step up the antipersonnel campaign, especially against British soldiers and UDR members. The object was to cause confusion and terror and to take the pressure from Catholic areas, as extra troops and police were required to deal with each incident. There were also many deliberate

*McGuire

false alarms, again to cause wasteful dispersal of security forces' personnel and means. The Provos' strategic objective was to bring the economy of Northern Ireland to a halt in the hope the British government might be forced to meet them at the conference table.

On 15 August the opposition MPs at Stormont called for a civil disobedience campaign as a protest against internment, calling on all elected representatives to withdraw from their offices. About one hundred Catholic councillors responded to this call. They also called upon the people to cease paying rent and rates to the authorities. The following day there were strikes in Derry and Coalisland. On the 19th Prime Minister Lynch sent a message to Prime Minister Heath in London, saying he would support the Northern Ireland civil disobedience campaign.

On the 18th, the day the British army made another unsuccessful attempt to remove barricades from the Bogside and the Creggan estate, there was rioting in Strabane, on the border, resulting from a mass meeting addressed by Bernadette Devlin, during which Eamonn McDevitt, a deaf-mute, was shot dead by soldiers. An army spokesman said McDevitt had a gun, but this was found not to be so. On the 22nd a gelignite bomb was thrown from a passing car in front of Crumlin Road Prison, where some 120 internees were still held. It injured four prisoners and two prison officers.

One of the worst explosions so far occurred on 25 August 1971 at the Northern Ireland Electricity offices, Belfast; it killed one person and injured thirty-five others, mostly women and girls. The Provos claimed responsibility and said everyone had been given reasonable warning time to leave the building, but the RUC said it was only ninety seconds. By September the indiscriminate detonation of bombs and explosives in public places without warning, or warnings that gave false locations, became an almost daily occurrence. For example, on 2 September three such explosions in the center of the city injured forty people. Intimidation tactics to deter Irishmen from joining the British army, or persuading them to desert from it, were not forgotten; on 19 August two such soldiers on leave at home in Ballymurphy were shot and wounded by the Provos.

In the early hours of 29 August two British ferret scout armored cars accidentally crossed the border near Crossmaglen, traveling about one hundred yards into the Irish Republic before realizing where they were. As the vehicles attempted to return, they were blocked and surrounded by a hostile crowd. One of the vehicles was set on fire but the crew managed to get into the other, which made its way back to the border. Shots were fired, deflating a tire. While the wheel was being changed, more shots killed one British soldier and wounded another. A British army spokesman said the soldiers were actually inside Northern Ireland, and that the shots came from the Irish Republic. The Provos insisted that the British vehicle was still ten yards inside the Irish Republic. Prime Minister Lynch declared there had already been thirty such illegal crossings of the border.

On 15 September Prime Minister Faulkner announced that orders had been made detaining 219 of the 337 people arrested on 9 August, and that an internment camp was being constructed at Long Kesh, near Lisburn. On 7 October he said that since the 9 August swoop, another 70 internees had been arrested, and that "63 officers and 93 volunteers of the Provisional IRA, and 35 officers and 28 volunteers of the Official IRA, were held in Internment." That day three more British units arrived in Northern Ireland, bringing the total army strength in the province up to 15,500, the highest figure yet. Previously, on 15 September, the British Ministry of Defense had announced that the UDR was to be expanded to seven battalions, one for each county and one for the city of Belfast. It was to be mainly deployed in the country areas.

Provo Chief of Staff MacStiofain had a military mind rather than a political one, and he tended to overlook or play down the importance of the political aspects of the insurrection. So far the Provisional IRA had not put forward a political program and so had no answer to that of the Official IRA (whose objective was a Marxist-type regime of a united Ireland). Internment caused him to rethink; on 21 August 1971 he called a press conference in Monaghan, at which the Provos said they wanted a Democratic Socialist Republic of Ireland, somewhat on the Western European pattern, although they were vague about the precise doctrine. The idea was that regional governments would evolve, each with its own parliament or Dail, based on the four provinces of Ireland. That of Ulster, which would comprise its original nine counties, would be the first to have its own "Dail Uladh."

Next the Provos produced a five-point program to put to the British government and said that if it was accepted by 9 September, they would suspend all operations. On the 4th this program, which was really a list of demands, was delivered to the British embassy in Dublin. Its timing had a propaganda aspect: it was meant to anticipate a projected Heath-Lynch meeting and to gain publicity for the Provisional IRA. Briefly, the five points were the ending of violence, the abolition of Stormont, free elections for Dail Uladh, the release of all political prisoners, and compensation. It was rejected outright by Prime Minister Faulkner.

Prime Minister Lynch and Prime Minister Heath met on 6 September for two days at Chequers (the British prime minister's official country residence). Lynch did admit that "we must recognize there are two communities in the north," and also claimed "there are no IRA activities south of the Border." The latter statement was far from the truth, and he could hardly have expected Edward Heath to believe it. The next talks, also held at Chequers, were tripartite ones between Prime Minister Heath, Prime Minister Lynch, and Prime Minister Faulkner, but they were negative. Harold Wilson, now in opposition at Westminster, had tried to preempt the talks, when on 8 September he issued his twelve-point program for Northern Ireland. It basically included proposals for an "All Ireland" council of representatives from both Stormont and the Dail, and it was also rejected outright by Prime Minister Faulkner.

The state-owned Radio Telfis Eireann (RTE) had been in the habit of interviewing leaders of both the Officials and the Provisionals—both illegal organizations in the Irish Republic—from time to time without hindrance. However, in September the RTE gave considerable time on the air to both Cathal Goulding and Sean MacStiofain, the respective chiefs of staff, and only a comparatively short interview to Prime Minister Lynch, which seemed to hurt his feelings. Lynch banned IRA leaders from appearing on RTE; so Rory O'Brady, president of the Provisional Sinn Fein, which was legal in the Irish Republic, became the indirect Provo spokesman. The RTE was under direct governmental control and was subjected to a certain amount of censorship, unlike the British Broadcasting Corporation, which had absolute editorial freedom.

John Taylor, the Unionist Stormont MP, called for all cross-border roads, except the twenty or so that had manned checkpoints, to be "spiked" to deny mobility to the terrorists, but the British army planned to go one better. It had become concerned in case it inadvertently clashed with the Garda or the Irish army, especially as the border crossing points were not always clearly marked. With the Crossmaglen incident of 29 August very much in mind, it began instead to "crater" the unapproved roads to impede terrorists flitting across the border in vehicles at night, and also to prevent British army vehicles from accidentally going too far. About fifty roads were cratered before the policy was abandoned. It caused ill feeling as it hindered local movement, especially of farmers who had land on both sides of the border. Encouraged by the Provos, crowds were mustered and it became a Sunday afternoon sport to fill in the craters. Several shots were fired at British troops from the Irish Republic during some of these confrontations.

Bank and post office robberies continued. On 3 October in Newry, troops shot and killed three men trying to rob a night safe at a bank; on the 15th two plainclothes policemen sitting in a car in the Ardoyne district, guarding a bank, were shot dead by the Provos. The Europa, a new, modern hotel in Belfast, was attacked by Provos on 20 October; the staff was held up by gunmen and a bomb was placed in the foyer'. The second attack came two days later, when a similar attempt was made. Both bombs were defused by army bomb disposal experts.

By this time many people in Britain were beginning to question British involvement in Northern Ireland. In September 1971 the *Daily Mirror*, a popular mass circulation British newspaper, published the results of an opinion poll it had commissioned, which showed that fifty-nine percent of the people interviewed were in favor of British troops being withdrawn from Northern Ireland. This was a surprise and a shock to both the British Government and the Unionists, who had automatically assumed that the British people, being naturally against lawlessness and terrorism, were with them in their policies. The following month in America, Senator Edward Kennedy spoke in support of a resolution calling for the withdrawal of British troops from Northern Ireland, and in favor of an immediate meeting of representatives of all parties for the "purpose of establishing a united Ireland." This upset the British government, which was committed to maintaining the border and the democracy of Unionist majority rule.

On 17 October in an interview on BBC television, Roy Bradford, the Stormont development minister, stated that the civil disobedience campaign had so far cost the Northern Ireland government £500,000 and that twenty percent of the tenants living in "council houses" (about 26,000 out of 140,000) were withholding rent and rates. Also, a large but unknown number were neglecting or refusing to pay vehicle taxes, television license fees, mortgage payments, hire purchase payments, or electricity bills.

A weekend wave of violence erupted in Belfast on 23–24 October, during which two Catholic women, Dorothy Maguire and Marie Meehan, both members of a Belfast Women's Action Committee, were shot dead by soldiers who had been fired at from a speeding car with its horn sounding continuously. This was the usual Provo method of warning people that British troops were approaching. On the 27th a bomb was lobbed into an army post in Derry killing two soldiers. The Republican Publicity Bureau in Dublin claimed responsibility for the Provos and said that it was a reprisal for the killing of the two women in Belfast on the 23rd.

The Provos had reestablished old arms smuggling links with Irish-American republican groups, but many more weapons were required than could be obtained from these sources. Usually the illicit arms were smuggled from America on aircraft and ships in small quantities of half a dozen at a time, or even less. They were mainly Garrand .300 M-1 carbines and old British .303 Lee-Enfields, which had been sold to U.S. arms dealers for sale as hunting rifles in the 1950s, when the British army reequipped itself with the self-loading rifle. Others included the old IRA favorite, the Thompson submachine gun, which fired a low-velocity bullet that did not penetrate the British flak jackets; and some French .222 Magnum high-velocity rifles, which posed an acute ammunition supply problem. By this time thousands of dollars were being collected in America from Irish Americans, ostensibly for the families of IRA men fighting in Ireland; a large proportion was diverted into the Provos' coffers and was available to pay for arms.

Other sources also were sought. Despite many difficulties, David O'Connell, a member of the Provo Council, made arrangements to purchase a consignment of arms from the Czech Omnipol armaments organization near Prague, which would sell to practically anyone who could pay in hard currency. Some of the Provo leaders did not like having to trade with a communist country, even through mysterious middlemen, but their urgent need for arms and especially ammunition overcame their scruples. However, on 17 October seventy-one crates of these Czech arms, weighing nearly four tons, were detected and seized by the authorities at Schipol Airport, Holland. Destined for the Provisional IRA via fictitious addresses, they included submachine guns, automatic rifles, rockets, grenades, and ammunition. Two days later a small quantity of arms destined for the Provos was discovered on board the British transatlantic ship, the *Queen Elizabeth II.*

A further extension of the Provo antipersonnel campaign against the RUC began on 27 October 1971, when the homes of ten RUC men had bombs thrown at them from passing cars. This was designed to intimidate RUC families. On the 29th one RUC man was killed and another two injured when a bomb wrecked an RUC station. On 12 November what had become a fact was announced officially: automatic weapons would again be made available to the RUC for the defense of their police stations. Individual policemen were already allowed to carry revolvers and shotguns for their own protection, but their other weapons had been taken from them by the recommendation of the Hunt Report. Concrete ridges almost a foot high appeared at right angles to the roadway outside the gate and entrances to RUC stations, barracks, offices, and premises, and at checkpoints outside towns and close to vulnerable installations. Known as "sleeping policemen," they forced all vehicles to slow almost to a stop to surmount them. This discouraged the hit-and-run terrorists who were using vehicles to throw bombs and shoot at people.

Yet a further extension of the Provo antipersonnel campaign was added in November, this time against firemen. A large fire was caused in Belfast on the 26th by an explosion, and a second explosion occurred as firemen were fighting the fire, injuring five of them as well as four civilians. This was the first deliberate Provo attack on firemen, who so far had been allowed to fight the many fires caused without being molested or endangered.

MacStiofain and his Provo Council members had carefully studied recent insurgent campaigns, especially those in Cyprus, Aden, and Algeria. His first antipersonnel target had been to kill 36 British soldiers, the same number as he mistakenly thought had been killed in the Aden insurrection (actually it was 181), the incident that was still fresh in most British minds. He achieved this target on 9 November 1971. He declared that the fight against the British army had changed from a "defensive one to an offensive campaign," and boasted that on the weekend of 27–28 November he launched "a co-ordinated wave of almost a hundred operations throughout the North." That was by no means the Provos' norm, even if it were true, which is doubtful. Despite the brave words, the Provo council was beginning to wonder whether it could really win the war against the British army, but this doubt had not yet been voiced openly. The Provos admitted that it was becoming risky to pick off a British soldier, even with their one-shot sniping techniques. In Belfast, for example, a whole area could be sealed off within three minutes and then searched for the gunman. Outside Belfast there was far less risk of Provos being captured in such circumstances.

The RUC reckoned that by November 1971 there were about 500 active IRA men in the province, of which about 200 were in the Bombing Section; about 20–30 were snipers who would probably only fire one round a week. The Provos now began wearing their black berets and green arm-bands more openly, especially when on duty at their barricades.

A few women were enlisted into the Provo organization; most of them became involved in intelligence, supply, and propaganda work, although a few were trained to handle firearms. A number of women were used to carry weapons to the Provo snipers: hidden in clothing, the gun was handed to the sniper just before he wanted to use it; when he had fired his shot, he quickly handed it back to the woman. At that time the RUC did not have regular policewomen and was short of female searchers. The British army began using members of the Women's Royal Army

Corps for searching suspects and in cordon-and-search operations. Unofficial contact between the Provos and the RUC was maintained through the Social Democratic and Labor Party. Whenever the Provos wanted to claim or deny responsibility for an incident, they were able to telephone the RUC or even the media; a special code-word indicated the message was a genuine one, and not a hoax.

Kangaroo justice was still meted out or encouraged by the IRA. On 9 November in Derry, three Catholic girls were tied to a lamp post, had their heads shorn, and then had red paint poured over their heads and upper bodies by a crowd of jeering women. A Provo spokesman said this was the punishment for being friendly with British soldiers. However, pictures of this particular incident caused such a wave of revulsion both in Northern Ireland and abroad that the Provos, who were now looking to their public image in America, called a press conference to deny any implication; the Officials also hastened to condemn it.

Intimidation against Irishmen serving in the British army continued. On 1 December 1971 the body of a soldier from Dundalk, in the Irish Republic, was found near Crossmaglen. On leave, he had crossed the border to visit his fiance. The Republican Publicity Bureau stated that a Provo squad had executed him. The Provos stepped up their antipersonnel campaign against the UDR, many of whose members lived in isolated farms and houses in the country districts. The seventh member of the UDR to be killed by the IRA was shot dead in bed at his home on 3 December; on the 8th another was shot dead in his home in Belfast while watching television; on the 10th another was ambushed and killed near Claudy; and on the 14th yet another member of the UDR was killed on his doorstep in Belfast. Magistrates were also singled out for intimidation: on the 13th seven separate attacks were made on their homes.

Perhaps the first purely political murder was carried out by the Officials, who on 11 December shot and killed John Barnhill at his home near Strabane, in front of his wife. His house was then destroyed by an explosion. Barnhill was a Unionist member of the Northern Ireland Senate. The Officials stated they had not intended to kill Barnhill, but that as he struggled he "received a wound from which he died." The Officials said they merely intended to destroy his house as a reprisal for Catholic homes that had been destroyed by British troops. During November the security forces carried out a number of successful searches; on one of these they found a large arms cache near Ballymena that included modern U.S. carbines and an antitank weapon. Many Provos were arrested, including fifty-two on the 4th and another thirty-eight on the 9th.

On 16 November nine Provo prisoners awaiting trial escaped from Crumlin Road Prison. Rope ladders were flung over the high outer wall and the Provos, who had been playing football, scaled them and escaped into waiting vehicles. Disguised as priests, two of the escapees were re-captured on their way to the border, but the other seven made it to Dublin. On the 25th they were presented at a press conference, at which they complained they had been ill-treated at the Holywood Barracks Interrogation Center near Belfast. On the 29th the report of the International Committee of the International Red Cross, which had been commissioned by the Stormont government, was published. It stated that Crumlin Road Prison was antiquated and overcrowded and that Long Kesh Internment Camp was also overcrowded, but otherwise made no remarks derogatory to the Northern Ireland authorities. On the 30th the Irish Republic government decided to refer to the European Court of Human Rights certain allegations of ill treatment of internees against the British government.

The next escape from Crumlin Road Prison was made on 2 December by three Provo leaders who scaled the outer wall in a similar manner. They were Martin Meehan, commanding officer of the Ardoyne Battalion of the Belfast Brigade, who had been arrested a few days previously; Anthony ("Dutch") Doherty; and Hugh McCann. They were also presented at a press conference in Dublin on the 14th by Sean MacStiofain himself, supported by John Kelly and Patrick Kennedy. At this conference MacStiofain produced the new Provo booklet entitled *Torture: The Record of the British Brutality in Northern Ireland.*

One of the worst explosions so far in Northern Ireland occurred on 4 December at a pub known as McGurk's Bar, in Queen Street, Belfast. The building was wrecked, fifteen people killed, and others injured. In the rioting that followed, seven people were shot dead. Witnesses said that a man was seen getting out of a car and putting something by the pub door. As it was a Catholic pub, both the Provos and the Officials naturally disclaimed all responsibility, which was claimed by the League of Empire Loyalists, an unknown organization assumed to be a Protestant cover-name. None of the known Protestant militant groups would admit responsibility. MacStiofain openly accused the British of this outrage. He said that as the explosion was caused by plastic explosives which neither the Provos, the Officials, nor the Protestant militant groups possessed at this time, but which the British army did, it must be guilty. MacStiofain also claimed that British Mobile Field Reconnaissance squads (MFRs) and SAS teams were operating in the province, and that the finger of suspicion should be pointed at them. He said the MFRs operated in threes, in unmarked cars, wearing civilian clothes, and using Thompson submachine guns, a weapon familiar to the IRA but which the British army did not have.

On 17 December 1971 Prime Minister Lynch put forward a five-point plan in the Dail basically aimed at Irish unity through negotiation, containment of the IRA, and full support for the Wilson initiative for a Council of Ireland. He also made a vague attack on the IRA, urging it "to get out of the way," and accusing it of "seeking a united Ireland of shambles." Patrick Kennedy, the Stormont MP, boasted that Jack Lynch could take no action in the Irish Republic against the Provos because they had too much local support. MacStiofain considered this statement to be dangerously provocative, and a rift appeared between these two men, who until this moment had been firm friends. This statement also touched Lynch on a raw nerve. MacStiofain's house at Navan was searched in his absence and a single round of ammunition was found. So far he and other top Provo leaders had been moving about openly in the Irish Republic, but now as it was obvious that the Garda's hand was being turned against them, he had to go underground.

It was no part of Lynch's policy to break up the IRA or to stop terrorism in Northern Ireland; but he wanted to be able to curb it when necessary and to cut it down to size, so he began to take a less lenient attitude towards the Provos. The first serious confrontation between the Garda and the Provos occurred on 22 December at Ballyshannon, Co Donegal, when the Garda arrested three Provos who were immediately transferred to Mountjoy Prison in Dublin. The Provos called this an act of treachery, and alleged that Lynch was acting under British pressure. There were demonstrations in Dublin against the Garda.

On 23 December British Prime Minister Edward Heath visited Northern Ireland and in a televised speech said, "You can count on us; we are with you. We will not weary of this struggle to free you from the nightmare of violence in which so many of you have to live." His words pleased the Unionists, but they wanted more drastic action against the terrorists. The Provos and the Officials declared a three-day Christmas truce which was generally adhered to. The Provos admitted, "Our volunteers in the Six Counties are very tired now."

The year of 1971 ended on a note of disaster for the Provos when on 30 December one of their best leaders, Jack McCabe, who was in charge of the Bombing Section at GHQ, was killed in an explosion in a garage in Dublin. Gelignite and other industrial explosives upon which the Provos had come to rely for their bomb-making and which they had been in the habit of stealing from industrial establishments in the Irish Republic, were now much better guarded and more strictly accounted for. McCabe was trying to develop alternative explosive bases, and was experimenting with various chemical compounds, like agricultural fertilizer. He had been mixing them with a shovel on the floor of the garage when his shovel caused a spark that ignited the explosion.

McCabe's death increased MacStiofain's influence in the Provo Council, as McCabe had been an ally of Joe Cahill and both of them opposed MacStiofain in his power struggle. MacStiofain's principal supporter was still Seamus Twomey, but both David O'Connell and Rory O'Brady were now ranged against him.

The year of 1971 was the worst so far for terrorism, as a few brief figures will indicate. In that year, 48 British soldiers were killed, as were 11 policemen and 114 civilians, while 2,398 people had been injured as the result of terrorist activity. There were 6,984 recorded terrorist incidents in Northern Ireland, over 1,000 explosions, 261 attacks on RUC stations, and 437 armed robberies in which over £500,000 was stolen. The British army had been fired on 1,741 times; had defused 520 "devices"; seized 3,700 pounds of explosives, 158,800 rounds of ammunition, 605 firearms (including 26 machine guns of various types and 243 rifles), 150 grenades, and 1,531 nail bombs. The volume of terrorism was staggering.

12 Bloody Sunday and Bloody Friday

"One day it may be our job, if the politicans fail,
to liquidate the enemy."
—William Craig, leader of the Vanguard Unionist
Progressive Party, 18 March 1972

THE PROVISIONAL IRA was now in its full flush of terrorist activity, and it could be said that 1972 was the "Year of the Car Bomb"—among other spectacular activities. Without any warning at all, on the first day of the year a bomb placed in a stolen truck exploded in the center of Belfast, injuring sixty-two civilians. On 7 January a "school for bombers" was discovered in Andersonstown; seven Provos were arrested and a quantity of gelignite recovered. On the 21st land-mines detonated by remote control from south of the border killed a British soldier. On the 25th one Provo was killed and another injured by the premature explosion of a bomb they were positioning near the RUC station at Castlewellan, in Co Down. On the 28th there were forty-five explosions in the province. And on the 31st the Europa Hotel was again rocked by an explosion.

The Provo antipersonnel campaign against the RUC was intensified. On 24 January several attempts were made to kill both regular policemen and police reservists in different parts of Northern Ireland, which resulted in eight of them being wounded. The next day three more were shot and wounded. On the 27th an RUC man was killed in an ambush outside Derry; and on the 28th another was shot and killed in Belfast. This was the pattern for the rest of the year.

On 27 January at Forkill, South Armagh, there was a cross-border gun-battle between Provos in the Irish Republic and British troops. Although many shots were fired, there were no casualties. This activity displeased Prime Minister Lynch, and at nearby Dungooley that day, the Garda arrested seven Provos suspected of being involved in the battle. They had in their possession seven rifles and an antitank weapon. Two of the men arrested were Martin Meehan and Dutch Doherty, who had escaped from Crumlin Road Prison the previous month. Charges against them were dismissed by the Dundalk magistrates on 16 February. This also displeased Lynch, and the two men eventually appeared before a Dublin court in May. On 17 January seven Provo internees escaped from HMS *Maidstone*, and a press conference was held for them in Dublin on the 23rd.

Despite protests from the 100,000-strong Orange Order, all public processions and demonstrations were banned for a further twelve months; but the Civil Rights Association chose to disregard the ban and organized a march to the Guildhall in Derry on Sunday, 30 January 1972, as a protest against internment. Over 7,000 people joined in the procession, which was watched warily by the IRA. The IRA would not cooperate with the CRA because it accepted the existing boundary, but it was prepared to take full advantage of any resulting disturbances. The procession was halted when it reached the police barriers. Stones and other missiles were thrown at the police and soldiers by the unruly elements. The police used their water-cannon with water dyed purple so as to be later able to identify offenders. The demonstrators withdrew and then formed up again and advanced from several directions.

The troops used CS gas and fired rubber bullets, while the rioters frequently threw the gas shells back at the security forces. The soldiers tried to make arrests by using their "snatch squad" techniques, but this merely exacerbated the fighting. At this stage the Provos came into the picture. Suddenly shooting began. When the rioters and marchers withdrew, thirteen people had been shot dead and another sixteen wounded by gunfire. An army spokesman said that the soldiers had come under fire from snipers in certain blocks of apartments occupied by Catholic families, and that both nail bombs and acid bombs had been thrown at them before they returned the fire. The Provos alleged the British troops fired at random into the crowds. This day became known as "Bloody Sunday" to all republicans, and the British unit involved, the Parachute Regiment, was at the receiving end of all the odium that went with it. All activity in Derry came to a halt until 2 February, the day of the funerals of eleven of the victims. Five prominent members of the Fianna Fail Party, all ministers in the Lynch government, attended.

The Widgery Report on the events of Bloody Sunday, published later, stated that four of the dead appeared to have been firing weapons or using bombs; but in the case of the remaining nine, evidence was either inconclusive or indicated they had no possession of arms.

The action by the British troops in Derry on Bloody Sunday was widely condemned by the Social Democratic and Labor Party and all

Catholics generally. The Monday after at Westminster, Bernadette Devlin compared it with Sharpville (in South Africa, when on 21 March 1960 police fired on a rioting mob, killing 67 people and injuring 186) and then physically attacked Home Secretary Reginald Maudling, scratching his face, knocking off his spectacles, and calling him a "murdering hypocrite." On the same day the British embassy in Merrion Square, Dublin, was attacked by a mob throwing petrol bombs and smashing windows.

February 1 was declared to be a day of national mourning in the Irish Republic, and both President de Valera and Prime Minister Lynch attended a memorial service. On the 2nd mobs again attacked the British embassy in Dublin, setting it on fire, but there were no casualties, as the staff had been previously evacuated. The Garda were particularly inactive. The Irish government quietly accepted responsibility for failing to protect the embassy and paid compensation to the British government.

In February 1972 three Englishmen were arrested in Dublin and charged with armed robbery and causing explosions at a police station. They were Kenneth and Keith Littlejohn and John Wyman. The Littlejohn brothers claimed they were reactivated British intelligence agents hired by the British government to kill Sean MacStiofean. The Provos claimed that there were over thirty British intelligence agents operating in the Irish Republic.

Irishmen serving in the British army remained priority targets. On 6 February the body of one such soldier, who was on leave from his unit in Germany, was found at Crossmaglen. On the 13th another body of a soldier on leave was found, this time hooded and bound. He had been to see his mother in Newtownhamilton, Co Fermanagh. On the 25th a Provo execution squad made an unsuccessful attempt to kill John Taylor, the Protestant Stormont MP. Shots were fired at him as he was getting into his car in Armagh, and he was seriously injured. On the 29th two members of the Ulster Defense Regiment were murdered in their homes.

Forgetting their planned communist-type revolution, the Official IRA was now competing in terrorism with the Provos. It also had its execution squads and selected victims. One was Marcus McCausland, a local landowner, whose hooded and bound body was found near Derry on 5 March. A former high sheriff and an officer in the UDR, he was accused by the Officials of working for British intelligence.

The terrorist tentacles of the Officials stretched into England, where on 22 February 1972 their most notorious exploit so far occurred at the garrison town of Aldershot. A car bomb exploded outside the officers' mess of the Parachute Regiment, killing seven people and injuring nineteen. The Officials claimed responsibility from Dublin before the full facts were known, and said that the explosion had killed several high ranking officers and that it was in retaliation for Bloody Sunday. The explosion had been planned for lunchtime when the mess would have been full of officers, but the bomb went off too soon and the mess was almost empty. The only officer killed was the Roman Catholic chaplain to the regiment; the others were a gardener and five women staff.

This action was widely condemned by prominent leaders in Ireland, including Prime Minister Lynch, who was angry because the announcement had been made by the Officials from Dublin. That day, eight leaders of the Official Sinn Fein and the Official IRA were arrested and charged with being members of an illegal organization. Among those arrested were Cathal Goulding, the chief of staff; Michael Ryan, editor of the *United Irishman*; Derek Kellaher, vice president of the Official Sinn Fein; and Anthony Hefferman, secretary of the Official Sinn Fein.

In Northern Ireland on 23 February, the High Court delivered a judgment that certain of the British army's activities were *ultra vires* (beyond their legal authority) under the Special Powers Act (Northern Ireland) of 1922. However, this was anticipated and the British government was prepared. The same day in Westminster, the Northern Ireland Act of 1972 was passed, making retroactive legislation authorizing certain activities in which the troops in the province had already been engaged, such as searches, dispersing crowds, and certain other "police duties." The bill was unopposed by all except Bernadette Devlin.

The Provos' bombing campaign continued with increasing tempo. To cause maximum civilian casualties in streets and shops, the explosions occurred without warning or with deliberately false information regarding the timing or location. On 4 March a bomb exploded without warning in the Abercorn Restaurant, Castle Lane, Belfast, killing two women and injuring 136. Both the Provos and the Officials denied responsibility, but the RUC was convinced the Provos had been the culprits. On the 6th there was yet another explosion at the Europa Hotel. On the 9th four Provos were killed by the explosion during a lecture on bomb manufacture in a house on Clonard Street, in the Catholic Falls Road area. The RUC stated that this brought the number of IRA men killed by their own explosives since August 1971 to at least sixteen. The Provos claimed that the British army was using an electronic device to sweep the area to activate bombs. The Provos claimed that later, when they realized what was happening, they were able to detect its waves and home its signals back to it on simple transistor equipment. This enabled the British eletronic devices to be located, usually on a vehicle, which could then be ambushed.

According to Peter McMullen, the technique of remote-controlled bombs was gained from a colonel in the Irish army who had thought up the idea of using photoelectric cells as booby traps. "He introduced us to remote-control bomb detonation by radio signals like those radio-controlled toy airplanes." McMullen claimed that some British bomb disposal experts were killed or wounded when they lifted the covers from the bombs. "What we would do is cover the cell [of the detonator] with black paper, arm the bomb inside the box, and then slip out the black paper. When the British bomb disposal experts lifted the covers off the boxes and light hit the cells, the bombs were detonated."*

On 20 March 1972 a car bomb exploded in Donegall Street, in the center of Belfast, which killed six people and injured 147. A misleading warning telephone call as to location had been received by the RUC. The next day, car bombs in Derry injured twenty-six people; on the 27th in Belfast, car bombs injured another seventy-eight people. In all cases false locations had been given in the warnings.

Before the advent of the car bomb, Provo sabotage operations were limited to what three or four men could carry and place in position. This method had the twin drawbacks of an explosion of a fairly low yield and the much greater risk of detection when placing the bomb near its target. The car was both a container and a means of delivery that could be casually left where it was required, without arousing suspicion. The bomb itself was usually a nitrobenzene mix in a container, detonated by a simple timing device. Security forces found it difficult to detect. Within weeks the centers of Belfast and most other towns in the province were off limits to vehicular traffic, and parking was not permitted anywhere unless one person remained in the car all the time. Empty parked cars were viewed with deep suspicion, and several were blown up by rockets or controlled explosions after the surrounding area had been cleared. After a while the British bomb disposal personnel brought into use an electronically controlled robot on tracks that could be moved toward the suspected vehicle and could use its mechanical arm to break a side window or otherwise detonate any explosives that might be wired up in the automobile.

Thinking it had the British government reeling under its bombing campaign, on 10 March the Provo Council ordered a truce for seventy-two hours, in the hope the British would now be more prepared to accept Provo demands. These were: withdrawal of British troops from the streets, a declaration of intent to evacuate Northern Ireland, the abolition of the Stormont government, and an amnesty for all political prisoners. Previously, on 1 March, the Provos had revised their former five-point program of September 1971 to three points: British withdrawal from Northern Ireland, the abolition of Stormont, and an amnesty for political prisoners.

*Boston Globe, September 1979

The British ignored the Provo demands and the Provo truce; the Provos complained that thirty-four of their men were arrested in this period. Both the Provisionals and the Officials observed the truce to the extent they refrained from bombing, although there were incidents of shooting, some of which were internecine. The no-go Bogside, for example, contained several feuding families who had their own private shoot-outs; the Provos and the Officials also still had a go at each other on occasions, as they were struggling for supremacy in Free Derry. The Provos maintained contact with the Social Democratic and Labor Party, through which they communicated with the British and Stormont governments and the RUC; but the Provos began to distrust the SDLP, alleging that it was being supported by Irish government funds.

In Dublin, when it was known that the Officials were also observing the seventy-two-hour truce, the prosecution withdrew charges against Cathal Goulding and the other Officials who had been arrested on 22 February, and all were released. Prime Minister Lynch hoped he had made his point. During the truce, Harold Wilson visited Dublin and secretly met David O'Connell, Joe Cahill, and John Kelly. The Provos considered this to be a kind of victory, enhancing their status. MacStiofain, the chief of staff, and Rory O'Brady, the president of the Provisional Sinn Fein, stayed in the background, considering themselves leaders who wanted to talk to the British prime minister of the day, and not the prime minister of yesterday. In the main, however, since there was no response from the British government, the Provos resumed their terrorist campaign, as did the Officials.

A Provisional IRA land-mine offensive began in the summer. Some were now fitted with remote-control detonators, and antihandling devices. Telephone exchanges were priority Provo targets: during the first six months of 1972 over thirty were damaged or destroyed by bombs.

The first months of 1972 saw the emergence of the Vanguard Unionist Progressive Party (VUPP), a militant Protestant force. It had been launched as a mass rally on 12 February 1972 by William Craig (who had been dismissed from the O'Neill government in 1968). Its declared aims were to defend and maintain the existing constitution in Northern Ireland and to oppose direct rule from Westminster which was becoming an increasingly ominous issue to Unionists. The Vanguard Unionist movement was really an umbrella organization that included the Orange Association, the Apprentice Boys of Derry, the Ulster Special Constabulary Association—including many former B-Specials in its membership—and the Loyal Association of Workers led by William Hull, one of the senior shop stewards at the Belfast docks.

On 18 March Craig addressed a rally of over 50,000 members and sympathizers in Belfast, at which he said, "One day it may be our job, if the politicians fail, to liquidate the enemy." Later, when asked to clarify that statement, he said that he had meant to say "ostracize the enemy," and that he had no intention of organizing liquidation squads.

Another militant Protestant organization that suddenly swelled in strength was the Ulster Defense Association (UDA) which had been formed in September 1971 in the Protestant Shankill Road area, having developed from street gangs. One of the principal leaders was Charles Smith, chairman of the Inner Council, the UDA's highest executive body. The UDA spread to other Protestant communities and eventually claimed company strength in eight of them. The members took on vigilante tasks, began to specialize in sniping, and started to outrival the Ulster Volunteer Force.

Direct rule from Westminster for Northern Ireland was foretold by Prime Minister Heath on 24 March 1972; two days later William Whitelaw was designated secretary of state for Northern Ireland. This British move was welcomed by the SDLP and Catholics generally, as it broke the rigid, overbearing Unionist government control that had dominated the province since it was formed as such. The Alliance Party also welcomed it. On 28 March the Stormont government under Prime Minister Faulkner met for the last time—to resign. On the 30th direct rule formally came into effect.

In protest there was a Protestant general strike, organized and instigated mainly by Craig's VUPP, which caused considerable disruption on the 27th and 28th. Prime Minister Faulkner complained that the British prime minister had treated Northern Ireland "like a Coconut Colony," and that he had completely lost faith in him. Faulkner added that he disapproved of the Vanguard activities. Later on the 27th, at a mass rally of over 100,000 Protestants outside the Stormont Assembly building, there was a public reconciliation between Faulkner and Craig, but it did not last long.

On Easter Sunday, 2 April 1972, there was a large rally of Catholics in support of direct rule, and MacStiofain crossed the border specially to attend the IRA Easter Rising commemorations. Both the Provos and the Officials paraded in some strength, many in uniform; and while the British army watched and photographed, it did not interfere. The soldiers did not know the Provisional IRA chief of staff was on parade. MacStiofain was concerned that too much enthusiasm for direct rule might water down support for his Provisional IRA, and he was also concerned about the attitude of the Catholic women of Derry, who were not by any means the wholehearted supporters of the Provos they had been previously, mainly because they were disgusted by the excessive terrorism.

A few days after direct rule had been imposed, MacStiofain called a meeting of the Provisional Executive Committee, the Council, and all the commanding officers in Northern Ireland to discuss the situation and the falling off of support by the Catholic population. The decision was made to fight on, to enforce Catholic support, and to try to provoke the Protestant backlash so that the British army would be compelled to take harsh, restrictive measures against the non-Catholic population.

MacStiofain admitted that during April and May 1972 he received requests to blow up certain houses and premises so the owners could claim the insurance money, but he insisted he always rejected such invitations.* He wrote that he did not want the Provisional IRA to become tainted by criminal and nonpolitical acts. He also asserted that he punished some of his men who had destroyed houses for this purpose. As Provo protection rackets of the most blatant type were in full swing in the Catholic communities, it was a case of his conveniently adjusting his moral measures.

On 15 April Joseph McCann, commanding officer of the Officials in Belfast, was shot and killed when he failed to stop when ordered to do so by British soldiers. The next day three soldiers were killed, two in Derry and one in Belfast, in retaliation. On the 18th Cathal Goulding, the Officials' chief of staff, came secretly to Belfast to give McCann's funeral oration; Bernadette Devlin also attended the funeral. On the 19th the body of a member of the Ulster Defense Regiment was found in a sack near Newtownhamilton. He had been kidnapped, taken across the border, and killed. His body had been brought back into Northern Ireland in a sack, dumped, and booby-trapped.

Tarring and feathering and similar punishments continued to be meted out to those who infringed the IRA code or committed criminal offenses or acts of immorality; there were twenty-eight separate instances recorded by the RUC during the year. On 9 April a Catholic Belfast woman was dragged from her home, beaten with hurley sticks, tied to a lamp post, and covered with paint and feathers. Her husband, who was in Armagh Prison on charges of possessing arms, was alleged to have been an informer. Another sad case occurred on 10 May when a fifteen-year-old girl was found tied to a lamp post in the Falls Road area, Belfast, covered in paint and feathers. The girl had been abducted from her home five days previously, held in a house, regularly beaten, and then had her

*Memoirs of a Revolutionary

hair shorn or pulled out. The Officials claimed she was part of a British spy ring.

Sectarian rioting and battles with the army continued. At a press conference on 11 May the new secretary of state for Northern Ireland, William Whitelaw, rejected the suggestion that British troops should forcibly move into the no-go Bogside and Creggan estate, as he said this would mean a large military operation and might put women and children at risk. This statement upset the Protestants. Whitelaw's policy was to give the British troops a low profile and not to attempt anything provocative. He was trying to be conciliatory, and had already begun on 7 April to release internees in batches.

On the 21st the Ulster Defense Association established a no-go area in the Shankill and Woodvale districts of Belfast, hijacked vehicles, and erected barricades. About 500 UDA men in uniforms of sorts manned the barricades and confronted the soldiers and police who came to remove them. For some time the UDA had been threatening to do this unless the Catholic no-go areas were opened up again. Troops used CS gas and fired rubber bullets and after some negotiation the UDA agreed to remove the barricades; but each weekend symbolic ones were reconstructed.

On 21 May the body of nineteen-year-old Pvt. William Best, a native of Derry who was on leave from the British army, was found on the edge of the Bogside, hooded and bound, with signs of having been severely beaten. The Officials stated that Best had been tried by an IRA court-martial and sentenced to death in retaliation for the ruthlessness of British troops. The Officials also stated through their Republican Publicity Bureau that "the IRA will continue to ignore appeals for peace from slobbering moderates" as long as British soldiers remained in Northern Ireland. Private Best was understood to have been an intending deserter who had been out on the streets stoning the British soldiers.

There was an immediate wave of revulsion against this killing amongst the women of Derry, especially the Catholic ones living in the Bogside and the Creggan estate; about 300 of them took to the streets to demonstrate against the violence. On the 23rd, the day of Best's funeral, which was attended by twenty-five Catholic priests and over 5,000 people, about 1,000 inhabitants of Derry, mainly women, met in the Creggan school and voted unanimously in favor of stopping hostilities against the British army. Officials' leaders at the meeting were shouted down and refused a hearing. Officials still predominated in the Creggan estate and the Bogside, although the Provisionals had gained territory in Derry city. A countermarch by supporters of the IRA ended in scuffles in which women, usually first supporters of the IRA, were involved.

On the 24th five Catholic women from the Bogside who claimed they represented ninety percent of the women in the district went to Belfast to see William Whitelaw. One was Margaret Doherty, whose brother had been killed on Bloody Sunday and whose sixteen-year-old son, who had joined the Officials, had been accidentally shot and killed some months previously. They said there were IRA men hiding in Free Derry, but as no one would hand them over to the authorities, they asked Whitelaw to consider an amnesty for them. Whitelaw hesitated and prevaricated as usual, but he charmed the women with his bland and pleasant manner.

The wave of resentment against terrorism which culminated with the murder of William Best caused the Officials to declare a truce with the British army on 29 May 1972. This was announced in Dublin by the executive of the Northern Republican Clubs. The Official Sinn Fein had been almost completely superceded in Northern Ireland by the Republican Clubs which, being legal, performed the same function. The reason given for the truce was to avoid the "danger of a sectarian civil war, which the Provisional IRA bombing campaign is threatening to provoke." The Officials, who had always favored political action of the communist sort, had somehow been forced into competitive terrorism simply to save face.

Divisions deepened within the Provo leadership, with MacStiofean struggling to keep his position and to increase his power base. The Provos' bombing campaign in Northern Ireland was causing controversy within the Provo Council because it inflicted so many innocent casualties, but MacStiofean was determined to continue with it. At first he had been rather timorous in launching the campaign because of the lives it would take, but he soon got over his squeamishness, became hardened, and took a callous attitude toward the death and suffering it brought.

One critic, McGuire, wrote that at one time, "Ruairi, Dave and I agreed in our opposition to Mac's actions and attitudes, now discussed quite seriously, whether it would be best for the movement if MacStiofean were assassinated." Rather dramatic words, but they indicated the unease felt at the leadership level. MacStiofean, however, was too strongly entrenched to be voted out of office or off the Provo Council. The same critic said that stomach ulcers were the most common ailment in the Provo leadership and that both MacStiofean and O'Brady suffered from them.

The day after the Officials declared their truce, the Provo Republican Publicity Bureau in Dublin issued a statement declaring that "the guerilla war in the north will continue until the British Government agrees to end internment, withdraw its troops, and grant political amnesty to all political detainees." It added that activity was aimed at the "destruction of the Capitalist system and big business, and not at the Protestant and Catholic worker." MacStiofean said that the "bombing campaign will continue for tactical and strategic reasons . . . because it ties down thousands of enemy troops, and enemy armour, which would otherwise be employed by the British military in continuous raids and searches in Ballymurphy, Andersonstown and Ardoyne, and other nationalist areas."

This statement was too strong for Prime Minister Lynch. The following day both Joe Cahill and Rory O'Brady were arrested in Dublin; but the removal of Cahill simply strengthened MacStiofean's position. The Provo leaders in the Irish Republic now went underground, as they feared Lynch might mean business.

On 10 May 1972 a referendum was held in the Irish Republic to decide whether the country should become a member of the European Economic Community, or Common Market. Both Fianna Fail and Fine Gael, the two largest parties, were in favor of what Lynch called "stepping away from the mists of our Celtic twilight." Voting was 1,042,000 in favor, with only 212,000 against; this overwhelming majority decision gave Prime Minister Lynch confidence to take firmer action against the IRA—but he realized he still had to tread carefully. MacStiofean had taken a belated interest in this issue and persuaded the Provisional Sinn Fein, the Provisional IRA, and other republicans to vote against it. He lacked political acumen.

On 18 May there were serious riots in Mountjoy Prison, mainly by Provos and other political prisoners, who wrecked a complete wing of the building. Prime Minister Lynch invoked emergency powers; Curragh Internment Camp was reopened and political prisoners transferred there from Dublin. On the 26th the Special Criminal Court reappeared and sat without a jury.

Meanwhile the Provos continued with their campaign of bombing and shooting. On the 26th car bombs in Belfast injured forty-one people; on the 28th a premature explosion demolished two houses in Belfast, where Provos had been assembling a bomb, killing six men and injuring eighteen; on 2 June two British soldiers in Co Fermanagh were killed by an explosion detonated from the other side of the border; on the 12th the Derry Guildhall was destroyed by an explosion; on the 18th two British soldiers were killed by a booby trap when searching a building; and on the 24th a land-mine explosion killed three soldiers and injured two others. The 26th was a bad day in Belfast of car bomb explosions and robberies.

Three gunmen disguised as nuns robbed a post office, and two soldiers were killed. Again it was much the same pattern of terrorism repeating itself.

On 11 June the UDA had again set up barricades in Belfast; there were over seventy that weekend. A new barricade was erected across the Old Park Road area, one of the few remaining mixed districts in the city. Troops were sent to remove it but met opposition that resulted in a gun-battle.

In June 1972 on the second anniversary of his revolution, the Libyan leader, Col. Maummar Gaddafi, who was anxious to be seen supporting revolutionary and terrorist causes, said, "There are arms, and there is support for the revolutionaries of Ireland." This surprised both the Provos and the Officials, because as yet no arms had been received by them from Libya. The previous month a representative of the Provos had been invited to attend what was virtually an international terrorists' conference at the Badawi refugee camp in Lebanon. Arms were still a problem, and a big one too.

Before the first British soldier was killed in Northern Ireland in February 1971, the Provos had been able to buy a few arms from various dubious sources; most of the arms were originally stolen from UDR members, even Protestant dockworkers, and from people who worked for establishments that held arms legally, such as rifle clubs.* Although small in total number, they were very welcome in the early days. In 1971 the Basque ETA terrorist group traded fifty revolvers in exchange for some training in the use of explosives. According to MacStiofean there were several visitors from the Palestinian and other terrorist organizations who all expressed cordiality but gave no concrete help.†

The one steady reliable trickle of arms from America was revealed in July when five Americans were indicted at Fort Worth, Texas, on charges of gunrunning to Ireland. A certain amount of interesting information on this point comes from Peter McMullen, a deserter from both the IRA and the British Parachute Regiment, who had been sent to America in 1972 to obtain arms for the Provos. He said that five suitcases packed with weapons were put on board the *Queen Elizabeth II* once a fortnight, and that "IRA men took care of them." He said, "There were a lot of people buying arms for us, and they were not necessarily IRA people, but often people sympathetic to the Republican movement." He explained that the

---

*In 1972 over 140,000 licenses were issued, mainly for shotguns, but the RUC was of the opinion that there were three times as many unlicensed guns in the province.
†*Memoirs of a Revolutionary*

guns were stored in his New York apartment, and that two methods were used to transport them to Ireland. One was the "QE II route," which he said had been perfected by a New York union official who had been involved in operations dating back to "when the *Queen Mary* was still making runs across the Atlantic." A suitcase full of arms would be put on board the liner and eventually collected by Irish customs agents based in Cork, who were supplied with claims tickets. "This was stopped when Joe Cahill failed to pick up a consignment, and the U.S. authorities arrested five men in the U.S. in July 1972."*

The other route, McMullen said, was to conceal the guns in household and office furniture sent direct to Dublin on container ships. Customs were "never a problem. Someone took care of that here and on the other side too." From Dublin the guns were taken to a warehouse in Monaghan and then moved to the border town of Dundalk, when women in the cars used to take the weapons into Ulster on busy Sunday afternoons. McMullen stated that the source of finance for at least one shipment was the Irish Northern Aid Committee (Noraid) based in New York. MacStiofean claimed that the intelligence services of Britain, the Soviet Union, and of European countries were all actively involved in preventing the IRA from obtaining arms from the Continent.

Eight Catholic women had formed a small peace movement in April in Andersonstown after a mother of ten children was killed by crossfire in a gun-battle between the IRA and British troops. On 1 June this movement announced that it had collected over 40,000 signatures on a petition condemning violence, which it thought was a ninety percent support for ending terrorism. A meeting organized by this movement was deliberately broken up by the local Provos. When Whitelaw visited Derry on 5 June, he was handed a petition condemning violence bearing some 13,700 signatures. Some IRA leaders had also signed this petition, including Martin McGuiness, who added after his name "Peace with Justice." On the 13th MacStiofean, wearing an eye-patch to conceal an injury from a parcel bomb, held a press conference in Derry, flanked by Martin McGuiness, now in charge of the Derry area, Seamus Twomey, commanding officer of the Belfast Brigade, Sean Keenan, commanding officer of the Derry Battalion, and David O'Connell. MacStiofean offered to suspend operations for seven days if Whitelaw would talk to the Provos and suspend arrests. There were no other conditions. Whitelaw rejected MacStiofean's offer and rejected an offer to meet MacStiofean in Derry; but O'Connell did establish secret telephone contact with Whitelaw. Two

*A series of interviews published in the *Boston Globe* in September 1979.

days later, the five-women Derry Peace Committee met MacStiofean and forcibly put their case to him; but he was not moved.

In late May 1972 Billy McKee, the former commanding officer of the Belfast Brigade being held in Crumlin Road Prison, went on a hunger strike, demanding to be treated as a political prisoner and not as a criminal. On 17 June it was rumored that McKee, who had been on his hunger strike by then for a month, had died, and this caused disturbances in Belfast. The next day Whitelaw gave in and granted political prisoners a special category status which meant they were separated from the other prisoners, did not wear prison uniform, did not have to work, and had less formal discipline. On the 20th, after nineteen days on hunger strike, Joe Cahill was released from a Dublin prison.

On 22 June the Republican Publicity Bureau of Dublin issued a statement on behalf of the Provos, saying that a truce would be observed if the British would make a reciprocal gesture. The same day William Whitelaw indicated that "HM Forces would obviously reciprocate." The truce went into effect at midnight on 26 June—a few minutes after the 102nd British soldier had been killed in Northern Ireland. Having arranged a truce after only three months in office, Whitelaw regarded this as his own personal triumph. The truce was welcomed by most Catholics, but the Protestants were not so happy. Brian Faulkner said that it had "come 378 lives, 1,682 explosions, and 7,258 injuries too late." William Craig, leader of the Vanguard Unionist Progressive Party, said that the truce declarations were meaningless. Generally, though, the truce held in the province. An incident did occur in the Ardoyne area on 2 July, when British soldiers were fired upon by Provos. The Provo commander of that district said he would discipline his men, and both Provos and British troops agreed that the incident did not amount to a breach.

The Protestants in Derry objected to the truce and set up barricades around their community areas, manned by UDA members in quasi-uniform. To go from one end of Derry to another, a vehicle had to pass through seven checkpoints, two manned by the IRA, three by the British army, and two by the UDA. On 29 June Whitelaw admitted that his officials had accepted an invitation to go into Free Derry to talk to IRA leaders about the possibility of removing barricades. That day the Provos, who by this time had gained dominance over the no-go areas, said they would immediately dismantle three of the about forty barricades, partly for convenience and partly because they were a health hazard.

On 1–2 July in Belfast, the UDA began erecting barricades. Whitelaw had met UDA leaders a fortnight previously and persuaded them to delay this plan, but their anger at the truce caused them to cease cooperating with him. On the 3rd the British army stepped in to prevent the UDA putting up twelve permanent concrete barriers near Springfield Road. A confrontation was avoided only when it was agreed that the soldiers would man these barriers and that the UDA would patrol the streets behind them.

Secret telephone contact between the Provos and Whitelaw resulted in the Provo leaders being secretly flown to London to meet Whitelaw and other British representatives on 7 July. The Provo party consisted of MacStiofean and O'Connell, and also Gerry Adams, Seamus Twomey, Ivor Bell, and Martin McGuiness, the latter all Northerners. The Provos demanded that the British withdraw from Northern Ireland by 1975; and in the meantime, British troops should withdraw from sensitive areas. MacStiofean suggested that another act be passed at Westminster to change the status of Northern Ireland. The talks were sterile, and the Provo party returned to the province that night. The same day, after attending a party in the early hours of the 7th, two British officers wandered by mistake into the Bogside, where they were held for eighteen hours before being released. MacStiofean was angry because the officers were released before he and his party had returned to Free Derry, as he regarded them as hostages for his safe return.

The truce broke down on 9 July, and both the British and the Provisional IRA blamed each other. The incident usually blamed occurred on Lenadoon Avenue, in the Suffold estate in Belfast. On 6 July Seamus Twomey, commanding officer of the Belfast Brigade put five Catholic families into houses evacuated by Protestants. The UDA organized a protest against Catholics moving into Protestant homes, and the British army was called out to separate the two sides. On the 9th a large crowd of Catholics organized by the Belfast Provos, with a symbolic furniture removal van leading the way, moved towards Lenadoon Avenue and came into confrontation with the British troops. A British armored vehicle pushed the van aside, and soldiers stayed in the area to prevent the empty houses from being occupied.

Then followed ten days of explosions and gun-battles in which a British army spokesman said there were seventy-four separate shooting incidents. This caused more sectarian displacement, as more families from mixed areas sought the shelter of their own communities. Shops and pubs now shut at 6 P.M., when people hurried to their ghetto homes, after which the streets were left to the security forces and sectarian groups manning barricades. On the 15th there was a mass evacuation of Catholic families, led by a priest, who temporarily left their homes in the Lenadoon area as a protest against the presence of British soldiers. The troops had remained to try to prevent Provo domination of the whole Suffold estate. On the 17th the Provos suspended their operations in this district, and the Catholic families were allowed to return to their homes.

Despite British denials, the Provos continued to insist that the Special Air Service Regiment (SAS) was operating covertly in Northern Ireland. One incident quoted to make their point took place on 22 May when five Provos in a stationary vehicle in Andersonstown, Belfast, were fired at from a passing car. At first this was blamed on the UDA; but at an inquest in November the British army admitted that one of its plainclothes squads had been responsible. The Provos alleged that SAS personnel were used in small Mobile Field Reconnaissance (MRF) squads and that they deliberately committed several sectarian murders to stir up internecine strife. In August the Provos in the Greencastle area of north Belfast stopped a car and arrested an Englishman in plain clothes, whom they named as Peter Holmes. They insisted he was an SAS man and handed him over to the RUC.

One SAS activity upon which there was definitely more information available was its running of the Four Square Laundry. With the help of the Women's Royal Army Corps, the SAS set up this laundry in Belfast, collecting washing from hard-line Catholic areas with the object of examining clothing for explosive stains to locate the bomb-makers and the bomb-carriers, and also for any blood or other incriminating stains. This operated successfully for several weeks in the summer of 1972, with at least three large laundry vans collecting and delivering laundry. This covert operation was eventually blown on 2 October when one of the laundry vans was attacked by Provos on the Twinbrook estate; the driver and two other SAS men hidden in an observation compartment near the roof of the van were killed.

British troops were becoming disillusioned over what they saw happening in Northern Ireland. At first they thought they could somehow help the people, but on returning for their second and even third four-month tour of duty, they saw the situation had not changed one iota. They were appalled by the rigid sectarian attitudes and the poverty of the slum areas, where there was a third generation of unemployed. In many cases the will to work had vanished, and the menfolk often stayed in bed until noon; sleeping late, especially after a previous night's drinking, had become a habit. This was an IRA weakness, but their excuse was that they operated at night. Dawn or early morning was the favorite time for the security forces to make arrests; they knew they would catch their suspects in bed.

On the one hand, the GOC Sir Harry Tuzo wanted a military victory and was always claiming the IRA was near defeat; on the other hand, Whitelaw was trying a course of conciliation, hoping to splinter the once monolithic Unionist Party. Whitelaw's charm with the "peace women" was worrying the Provos more than they cared to admit. July 21 became known as "Bloody Friday" because twenty explosions in Belfast, all within minutes of each other, killed eleven people and injured over 120 others. According to McMullen, "All the bombs had to be in position at 1400 hours to be exploded one hour later. Twomey, who was then CO of the Belfast Brigade, said 'There's another one. Ah, did you hear that then? This is a great day for us.' "* The explosions on Bloody Friday shocked William Whitelaw, who terminated his policy of reconciliation. On the 24th at Westminster he declared he would never talk to the IRA again.

At last Whitelaw gave General Tuzo permission to enter Free Derry by force. An extra 4,000 British troops had been drafted over to Northern Ireland for the task, bringing their total number up to 21,000. Named "Operation Motorman," 5,000 soldiers moved into Free Derry at dawn on 31 July 1972, spearheaded by a squadron of Chieftain tanks, some with bulldozer blades affixed and all with their guns reversed, and about a hundred other armored vehicles. The Chieftains had been specially brought over for the purpose and were taken away again as soon as Operation Motorman was concluded; contrary to Provisional IRA and other propaganda, they were the only battle tanks the British ever used in the insurrection in Northern Ireland.

Geared and conditioned to expect fierce resistance, the British contingent was a sledgehammer to crack a small nut: the entire Provisional Derry Battalion and the small scattered units of Officials had decamped westward during the night. A few shots were fired by some Provos who had stayed behind or been forgotten in the hasty IRA evacuation. Two of them were killed and two others injured; there were no British casualties at all. By 7 A.M. British troops were in complete occupation of both the Bogside and the Creggan estate, and the barricades were being bulldozed away. Searches uncovered quantities of arms and ammunition, and a bomb factory with a ton of explosives and about forty bombs. The Provo excuse for such prompt evacuation was that they wished to avoid a confrontation that would result in heavy civilian casualties.

*Boston Globe

The Protestants were delighted and removed all their barricades. There was only one incident that day: car bombs exploded at Claudy without warning, killing seven people and injuring thirty-two. The next day in Dublin, the Officials announced they would continue their truce but would ostracize British soldiers. Whitelaw responded by releasing in batches Officials who were interned. The next incident of note occurred on 17 August when a pub in the Protestant Shankill Road area was wrecked by an explosion in which fifty-five people were injured. The Provos claimed responsibility, alleging that "it was frequented by persons responsible for sectarian assassinations." The UDA said it would patrol all Protestant areas.

August was indeed a bad month for sectarian assassinations—they occurred at the rate of almost two a day on average. This showed a black side of the Irish character that had not been readily apparent in the past: deliberate torture was added to murder. The RUC stated that in August there were at least thirty instances in which the person had been horribly tortured before being finished off with a bullet in the head. Official rewards of up to £9,000 were offered for information leading to detection and convictions, but they were never claimed. Anyone discovered passing such information to the police would be instantly executed as an informer and probably tortured beforehand as well. A special telephone service to RUC stations was established and the special telephone numbers publicized so information could be passed on to the police discreetly, without the informer having to visit a RUC station. This did not seem to work either: there was too much fear abroad.

To obtain the views of all political leaders in Northern Ireland, Whitelaw called a conference at Darlington, England, from 25–27 September. The Social Democratic and Labor Party did not attend, as it first demanded that internment be ended; neither did the Democratic Unionist Party, led by Ian Paisley, because Whitelaw refused to institute an official enquiry into the killing of two Protestants during a gun-battle between Protestant militants and British soldiers on 7 September. Only three parties out of seven were represented at the Darlington Conference. Brian Faulkner led the Unionist Party delegation, Phelim O'Neill that of the Alliance Party, and the Northern Ireland Labor Party was represented by its only former Stormont MP, Vivian Simpson. The Darlington Conference was just talk. Eventually, on 30 October, a British Green Paper entitled "The Future of Northern Ireland" was published. (In British parliamentary jargon, a Green Paper outlines government thinking and is for discussion, while a White Paper is a statement of government policy.)

In September 1972 William Craig, leader of the Vanguard Unionist Progressive Party, formed an alliance with the UDA; and the following month, the UDA made its first major attacks on British troops. One of the UDA leaders was awaiting trial on charges of trying to buy one million dollars' worth of arms in America. In mid-October the Tartan Gangs rampaged through the streets of Belfast for three day and three nights, clashing with British soldiers. Many thought that this was the first sign of the long-awaited but almost daily predicted Protestant backlash.

Although now prominently on the Garda's "Wanted" list, Sean MacStiofean had appeared openly in October at Liberty Hall, Dublin, at the annual Provisional Sinn Fein convention, where he received a standing ovation from over one thousand delegates present. That month an article in the British *Sunday Times* referred to the "Englishness of Sean MacStiofean," which hurt his feelings considerably. After this he forbade Provos to give any more interviews to British journalists or to help them in any way. According to MacStiofean, the Provos found the Swedish press most sympathetic towards their cause and German and Continental reporters were also favorable, but he said that "London-based ones were British-biased."* At first he found the Radio Telfis Eireann (RTE) to be fairly receptive, but its attitude became cooler and then hostile as Prime Minister Lynch exerted pressure to prevent it giving favorable publicity to the IRA.

On 19 November 1972 MacStiofean was arrested in Dublin and charged with being a member of an unlawful organization. He was brought before the court that day. In the same court, a news editor of the RTE was sentenced to imprisonment for refusing to answer questions relating to an interview he had had with MacStiofean before he was arrested. Part of the RTE tape recording was played to the court and accepted as evidence against MacStiofean, who was sentenced to six months' imprisonment.

MacStiofean at once began a hunger strike. On the 26th eight Provos disguised as priests and hospital orderlies attempted to snatch him from the hospital in which he was detained. Shots were exchanged between the Provos and the policemen guarding MacStiofean. One policeman and two other people were injured, while four of the would-be rescuers were arrested. MacStiofean was taken to Curragh Internment Camp, where he eventually broke his hunger strike on 16 January 1973, after fifty-nine

Memoirs of a Revolutionary

days, allegedly on instructions from the Provo Council. On completion of his sentence he was released into obscurity, being quietly pushed out from the Provisional IRA leadership. David O'Connell became the Provo chief of staff in his place. MacStiofean had lost face with the IRA by breaking his fast—he was a failed martyr.

Prime Minister Lynch turned on the RTE, which the government owned and controlled, and on 24 November terminated the appointments of the nine-man RTE Authority and appointed a completely new board. His reason was that the RTE had been giving publicity to the IRA. The Kevin Street office of the Provisional Sinn Fein—in reality the office also of the Provisional IRA—was raided by the Dublin police and the premises sealed up.

A bill was passing through the Dail to more widely define membership of the IRA and to make certain changes in the laws of evidence in relation to illegal organizations. While this bill was being debated on 1 December, two explosions in Dublin killed two people and injured 127. This was an occasion when action by the provisional IRA was counterproductive: it caused the Fine Gael Party to withdraw amendments that would have killed the bill. It passed on 3 December.

On 29 December Rory O'Brady was arrested, and on the 31st so was Martin McGuiness, both in the Irish Republic. Prime Minister Lynch was making inroads into the top Provisional IRA leadership. The year of 1972 concluded as the worst year for terrorism in Northern Ireland. Seventeen RUC members, 129 British soldiers and UDR members, and 322 civilians were killed due to terrorist activity; and 466 RUC members, 707 British soldiers and UDR members, and 3,998 civilians were injured.

13 The Provo Bombing Campaign in England

*"Niedermayer's buried in the swampy bog area
just outside Andersonstown."*
　　　　　—Peter McMullen, deserter from the IRA

URING THE OPENING weeks of 1973, terrorist violence, mainly by the Provisional IRA in Northern Ireland, continued at the same high rate. It included the now all too familiar car bomb attacks, sectarian killings, punishments, and torture. During the course of the year, according to RUC figures, 249 people were killed, 2,651 were injured, and there were 967 explosions—not quite as bad as 1972, but not all that much better. There were only six recorded cases of tarring and feathering, a decline perhaps due to the odium it brought upon the terrorists and the general sympathy it evoked for the victim. For the first time the RUC began recording kneecapping; there were seventy-four recorded cases in 1973.

One of the most violent days of the year was that of February, when William Craig, leader of the Vanguard Unionist Progressive Party, called a mass one-day strike to protest the abolition of the Stormont government. Belfast came to an absolute standstill as Protestant gangs of militants went on a rampage through the streets, smashing windows in Catholic houses and premises. A Catholic church was broken into, and shots were fired at a Catholic funeral cortege that had an Irish Republic tricolor flag on the coffin. That day five people were killed and nine injured.

On 1 February there was a changeover of GOC's in Northern Ireland: General Tuzo departed and was replaced by Gen. Frank King. General Tuzo had desperately wanted a military victory, believed in a show of force, and was looking for an enemy to fight; insurgent warfare with a secretary of state breathing down his neck was not to his liking. He also ensured that the army continued to have supremacy over the RUC. His replacement, General King, stated that his aims were to concentrate upon Belfast rather than the rural areas, somewhat reversing Tuzo's initially declared policy, and to destroy the structure of the IRA at brigade and battalion level.

On 22 February the Community Relations Commission published a report stating that in the first three and a half years of the insurgency (from August 1969 to January 1973) between 8,000 and 15,000 families — amounting in all to probably over 60,000 people — had been forced to flee their homes because of religious and political intimidation. The Catholics had been forced out from the Protestant-dominated housing estates in the east and the north of Belfast, as had the Protestants living on the edges of the large Catholic areas in the west of the city.

Voting for what became known as the "Border Poll" took place on 8 March in Northern Ireland but was boycotted by the SDLP and the IRA. There were many incidents at the polling booths, but despite intimidation fifty-four percent of the electorate voted. The alternatives on the voting slip were plainly set out: "Do you want Northern Ireland to be joined to the Republic of Ireland outside the United Kingdon?" or "Do you want to remain part of the United Kingdom?" The results were a victory for the "unionists," as 591,820 voted to remain part of the U.K. and only 6,463 voted to join the Irish Republic.

The majority of people in Britain were scarcely aware of the Border Poll being held, as it received little media coverage, but the Provos meant to bring it sharply to their attention. In London on the same day, the 8th, a car bomb explosion outside the Law Courts killed one person and injured 147 others. Two other car bombs were discovered in time and defused. The cars were all stolen in Northern Ireland, driven to London on previous days, laden with their bombs, and put into position early in the morning. The British Special Branch moved swiftly and successfully and arrested ten suspects, some of whom were taken from an Aer Lingus aircraft that had been deliberately held back at Heathrow Airport. One who eluded arrest and returned safely to the Irish Republic was David O'Connell, the Provo chief of staff, who had been directing this operation personally in England. The suspects were eventually brought before the court at Winchester in October, at what became known as the "Winchester Trial." Nine of them were convicted and imprisoned.

The Official IRA still maintained its truce with the British army and so was able to husband its men and weapons, although some of its more militant members ignored it. The leadership of the Officials insisted that fighting simply divided the working classes, but a group of dissidents continued with acts of terrorism. One such exploit took place on 23 March. Four off-duty British soldiers in an off-limits area were enticed into an apartment by some girls. Then two gunmen entered and shot the soldiers, killing three and wounding the fourth.

The Provos' Middle East contacts were beginning to bear fruit, or so they thought, when they came to grief. On 28 March 1973 a small ship registered in Cyprus, the SS *Claudia*, was intercepted by three ships of the Irish navy when making a rendezvous with an Irish fishing launch off Helvick Head, Co Waterford, to transship a consignment of arms for the Provos. On board were Joe Cahill and five other Provos, all of whom were arrested and sentenced to imprisonment in May by the Dublin Special Criminal Court. Combined Western intelligence agencies had tracked the *Claudia* all the way from the Mediterranean Sea: the Provos never had a chance.

The arms seized by the Irish authorities included 240 automatic rifles, 25 submachine guns, 245 revolvers, 100 antitank and antipersonnel mines, and 14,000 rounds of ammunition. These arms, which had been loaded onto the *Claudia* in Libyan waters off Tripoli, amounted in weight to about four tons. The Provos had been promised one hundred tons. Not for the first or last time, the Provos found their Middle East arms suppliers to be unreliable and the men who pulled their strings, the Russians, to be malicious and mischievous. The Soviet government would have contact with and give aid to recognized "movements of liberation" only, and the IRA was not on that list; but the Soviet secret service, the KGB, had been in the habit of secretly doling out small amounts of arms to struggling terrorist organizations with a liberation aim just to keep them from going under.

On 28 February 1973, there was a general election in the Irish Republic and Prime Minister Lynch, leader of the Fianna Fail Party, went to the country in the hope of improving his slender majority in the Dail. He was disappointed and had to resign to make way for a coalition government of the Fine Gael Party, led by Liam Cosgrave, who became prime minister, and the Irish Labor Party, led by Conor Cruise O'Brien. The IRA did not have much hope that pressure against it would slacken, as the Fine Gael was traditionally hostile to the IRA.

In March and April the Provos were faced with the problem of missing and misappropriated funds. Some weeks were spent in argument, enquiry, recrimination, and punishment. Expenses were becoming heavy: not only did arms have to be bought, but the full-time volunteers had to be paid, and the families of those in detention and those who had been killed had to be provided for. The single men were given only a "small amount of drinking money," but the married volunteers had to be paid up to £15 a week.* Fund-raising for the IRA and its families was getting well under way in America, and separate organizations were busy collecting dollars and sending them to Ireland. Two of the main ones were the Irish Republican Clubs and the National Assistance for Irish Freedom, both of which supported the Official IRA. The Provisional IRA relied mainly on the Irish Northern Aid Committee (Noraid) for funds from America, but its supply of cash tended to fluctuate, especially during 1973–74. The Provisionals during that period raised most of their money from bank and other robberies, although by the end of 1973 Noraid claimed that it had raised over one million dollars for them since 1969.

Another Provo problem just as serious, if not more so, was a sudden shortage of manpower. This was caused by arrests, internment, and casualties in action, but mainly by lack of suitable volunteers coming forward, owing to the wave of unpopularity rippling through the Catholic communities because of excessive IRA terrorism. The strength of individual Provo units shrank. For example, the battalion in the Ardoyne district had to suspend its activities completely because it had so few men. As able-bodied, would-be recruits hesitated to come forward, the age limit had to be lowered to accept teenagers who were less well disciplined and less steady in action.

On 19 June sixteen Provos were arrested, including Gerry Adams, commanding officer of the Belfast Brigade, and most of the top Provo leadership in Northern Ireland. Seamus Twomey was sent to the province to revitalize the Provo movement in Belfast; he at once reorganized the old four-battalion Belfast Brigade into a three-battalion one with smaller companies. The old IRA term "ASU" (Active Service Unit) was reintroduced. Twomey's policy, which he sold to the Provo Council, was to opt out of gun-battles with the British army, owing to the shortage of experienced gunmen, and to concentrate instead on its considerable bombing capability, but to go for "soft targets" such as unguarded installations and selected individuals.

The positioning of car bombs had become more difficult owing to the countermeasures introduced by the security forces — banning vehicular traffic from town centers and not allowing parking unless one person remained in the car all the time. Motivated by sheer survival instinct, the general public had also become more vigilant and quickly reported suspicious circumstances to the RUC. This caused the Provos to introduce their "proxy bomb" attacks. A Provo team would stop a vehicle,

*According to MacStiofean

take a hostage from it, load a bomb into it, and then force the innocent driver to take it to the target and leave it there. By using this tactic, the Provo bombers and bomb carriers had more successes and ran far less risk of detection.

Successes notwithstanding, the Provos ran short of both bomb makers and bomb carriers. The RUC reckoned that by July 1973 over sixty Provos had been killed by premature explosions of their own bombs. This tended to dampen enthusiasm for volunteering for such tasks. However, the remaining bomb makers were gaining a high degree of expertise and were soon able to progress to two small incendiary devices with a sophisticated detonating mechanism. The smallest was about the size of a cigarette packet; the other, being slightly larger, was built into a tape cassette box. Both blazed fiercely initially and were very effective in furniture showrooms and clothing stores. They could be carried by women and positioned unobtrusively in the target premises. This partly solved the Provo problem of bomb carriers.

Meanwhile, on the Protestant side of the terrorist fence, two new militant groups appeared in the spring of 1973, both of which engaged in sectarian killing, property damage, and protection rackets. One was the Ulster Freedom Fighters (UFF) and the other the Red Hand Commando. The RUC claimed that seventy-five percent of the UFF and the Red Hand Commando were dockland criminals involved primarily in crime and extortion but also motivated by sectarian malice. The RUC incidentally put the Ulster Volunteer Force, now led by Kenneth Gibson, in much the same category. These two new organizations fought against each other at times for territory like gangland groups, and both clashed with the Ulster Defense Association. The chairman of the UDA, Andrew Tyrie, issued a statement saying that the UDA had no connection with the UFF. When the body of Tommy Herron, vice chairman of the UDA, was found on 16 September in a ditch outside Belfast, shot through the head, the extreme militant groups were the prime suspects. Later in the year, on 12 November, William Whitelaw banned both the UFF and the Red Hand Commando.

The first "one-person, one-vote" election conducted on the single transferable vote method of proportional representation was held in Northern Ireland on 30 May 1973 for the newly constituted "26 district councils," which had a total of 526 seats. Despite the loud Provo call for a boycott, there was a nearly seventy percent poll. The results, declared on 2 June, were that the Unionists had gained 210 seats, the SDLP 82, the Alliance Party 63, and Loyalists (the democratic Unionist Party, the Vanguard Unionist Progressive Party, and the Independent Unionists) 68 seats. There had been fifteen political parties or groupings competing in the elections, of which the Republican Clubs, the legal front for the Official IRA in Northern Ireland, gained seven seats. This was a notable departure from the IRA's traditional policy of abstentionism. Only in Derry did the election result in real power sharing, and Derry had its first Catholic local authority ever.

After the Darlington Conference, the Border Poll, a British White Paper issued in March 1973, and the district elections, the British government followed up in July with the Northern Ireland Constitutional Act, which replaced the former Stormont government with an assembly and an "executive" to represent the Catholic as well as Protestant opinion. In short, this was the British idea of power sharing. The act confirmed the status of Northern Ireland as being part of the U.K. for as long as the majority of its citizens wished. Defense and foreign affairs remained the responsibility of the Westminster government, which also reserved for itself for the time being law and order and the appointment of law and senior police officers. Both Ian Paisley's Democratic Unionist Party and William Craig's Vanguard Unionist Progressive Party opposed this reform.

The next election held on 28 June was for the new Northern Ireland Assembly of seventy-eight seats. The Unionists gained twenty-two seats, the SDLP nineteen, the Alliance Party eight, the remainder going to the Loyalists, with one to the Northern Ireland Labor Party. This gave a pro-Constitution majority of twenty-one seats. The first session of the assembly was on 31 July; then talks were begun with Whitelaw on the composition of the proposed executive. On 21 November it was announced it was to consist of eleven members: six Unionists led by Brian Faulkner, four SDLP members led by Gerry Fitt, and one Alliance Party member. Two days after being nominated for the Northern Ireland Executive, Austin Currie was luckily away when shots were fired at his home in Donoughmore, Co Tyrone. His wife and family were there but were not injured. About a year previously, Mrs. Currie had been attacked in her home by Protestant extremists who beat her up and left her unconscious after scratching the initials "UVF" on her chest with a knife.

On 11 September 1973 James Flanagan was appointed chief constable of the RUC in place of Graham Shillington, who retired. Flanagan was the first Catholic to hold this position. The RUC was still about ninety percent Protestant, and although precise figures tended to be obscured by the authorities, there certainly was a small percentage of determined and dedicated Catholics serving in the RUC, some in its higher ranks, who were rigidly and coldly ostracized by their own community. When they attended Mass on Sundays at their local churches, they had the whole pew to themselves, and sometimes even the whole of one side of the church, as no one would sit or kneel near them.

The Provos, meanwhile, had not been inactive. On 9 August, the second anniversary of internment, a large explosion at the unguarded army housing estate at the British barracks at Omagh injured twelve women and four children. In all there were 4,500 wives and children with the British army in Northern Ireland. Seamus Twomey had warned families of British soldiers and civilians working for the British army that they were "legitimate targets." This Omagh incident was the first time the Provos had deliberately hit at families.

On 16 August the Provos made another "first" on a soft target: they held up the Dublin-to-Belfast freight train just inside the Northern Ireland border. They ordered the train crew off at gunpoint and placed on board two large milk churns containing explosive. Discovered in time, the "train bomb" was then left standing in open country surrounded by a cordon of soldiers. Considered too dangerous to try to defuse, the train bombs were detonated by an army marksman with rifle shots.

The Provos now began a campaign of bombing in England, which was preceded and then accompanied by a letter bomb campaign. Within twelve months there were over 130 explosions in England. It began on 10 August 1973 when a number of letter bombs were delivered to persons at the Ministry of Defense, military clubs, and Number Ten Downing Street. On the 24th two people were injured when a letter bomb exploded at the London Stock Exchange, and the next day a Bank of England employee lost a hand in a letter bomb explosion. On the 27th a secretary at the British embassy in Washington had her hand blown off; other letter bombs were delivered to British embassies in Lisbon, Kinshasa, and Brussels, but all were detected in time.

On 19 August a statement issued by the Republican Publicity Bureau in Dublin said that fires had been caused by the Provisional IRA Active Service Units operating in Britain, and that others would follow. This was true. That day a petrol bomb blew out the windows of the Officers' Club at the garrison town of Aldershot, and two cigarette-packet type incendiary devices caused fires in large London stores. During the rest of August similar incendiary devices were discovered in other London stores, and explosive devices were even found in an underground railway station.

During August and September the Provo explosions spread to the Midlands—Birmingham, Solihull, Sutton Coldfield, and Manchester. They were meant to coincide with the much publicized and long drawn out Winchester Trial of the ten people accused of being implicated in the London Law Courts explosion.

The police made a breakthrough on 1 October when the surveillance and burglar protection equipment installed in some business premises in London filmed a man placing what proved to be a bomb on the doorstep. He was a deserter from the Irish Guards (a British regiment) who, with his female companion, was responsible for probably most, if not all, of the explosions in this wave of the Provo bombing campaign in England. Both had fled by the time the police arrived at their lodgings to arrest them. There were only two more explosions in London, after which this phase of the Provo bombing campaign drew to a close. The bomber, or bombers, were never caught.

Meanwhile, Seamus Twomey had been arrested in the Irish Republic and lodged in Mountjoy Prison, Dublin. On 31 August, in another spectacular "first," the Provisional IRA hijacked a helicopter and snatched Twomey and Kevin Mallon from the prison exercise yard. Twomey was flown back into IRA circulation again as leader of the Provos in Northern Ireland.

A tripartite conference at Sunningdale, Surrey, from 6–9 December 1973 was attended by representatives of Britain, Northern Ireland, and the Irish Republic. The U.K. delegation was led by Prime Minister Heath and that of the Irish Republic by Prime Minister Liam Cosgrave, while the Northern Ireland delegation consisted of all eleven members of its new executive. Agreement was reached on establishing a Council of Ireland, to consist of thirty members from both the Dail and the Northern Ireland Assembly.

In December 1973 Francis Pym, MP, succeeded William Whitelaw as the secretary of state for Northern Ireland. On 20 December Pym released sixty-five internees from Maze Prison, including two Protestants. This still left about 600 men in some form of detention. Whitelaw had a smooth, pleasant manner and always did his homework, but he was unable to bring about a comprehensive solution acceptable to both communities. He did have some success, however, in encouraging the splintering of the once all-powerful Unionist Party which the Catholic community was so afraid might regain its dominant role in the province. William Whitelaw's best legacy was perhaps the power-sharing district councils.

Late on the night of 27 December, Herr Thomas Niedermayer, the managing director of a major electrical company in Northern Ireland, was kidnapped from his home by two men. Niedermayer, who had lived in Belfast for twelve years, was also the honorary West German consul. On 7 January 1974 a ransom demand for £250,000 (over half a million dollars) was received. Niedermayer's remains were eventually discovered on 13 March 1980, buried in an unofficial garbage dump at Dunmurry, about two miles from his home.

The one account that might ultimately prove to be reliable was given by Peter McMullen, who claimed that Niedermayer died of a heart attack. He said that the plan was for a special strike force of the Belfast Brigade to pick up Niedermayer and hold him hostage for the release of the two Price sisters, who had just been jailed for their part in the London Law Courts explosion at the Winchester Trial. Niedermayer was taken to an apartment where he put up a struggle and, having a history of heart trouble, died of a heart attack. "He's buried in the swampy bog area just outside Andersonstown." McMullen said the "IRA never said anything about him...because they were too embarrassed."* Perhaps McMullen's account is as valid as any other, although he was slightly wrong about the location of the burial site.

The first phase of the Provo bombing campaign in England had ended in October 1973, and the second phase began suddenly on 17 December when a "book bomb" injured a senior British military officer in London. Another book bomb the same day was detected in time and defused. Following this was a series of car bombs and letter bombs. Then came a series of explosions in hotels, clubs, cinemas, and pubs. In January the explosions were mainly in London at the homes of senior military officers, but there were also some incendiary devices that caused fires in shops. On the 22nd a "Bible bomb" was sent to the senior Roman Catholic chaplain of the British army. On the 30th a prosecuting attorney for the Crown who had previously prosecuted four Northern Ireland Protestants for trying to buy arms was injured by a letter bomb. On 1 February Reginald Maudling, the home secretary, was slightly injured by a book bomb; and on the 12th an explosion injured ten people at the National Defense College at Latimer, in Wiltshire.

The worst incident in February occurred when a bomb exploded on an army coach carrying personnel on leave near Batley, Yorkshire, on the Pennine Chain. It killed twelve people: eight soldiers and an army family of four. Another eight people were injured. On 19 February a young Englishwoman, Judith Ward, was charged with causing this explosion; she was eventually convicted and imprisoned.

Judith Ward was somewhat typical of the few Englishmen and women who adopted the Irish Republican cause, joined the IRA, and developed into dedicated and dangerous terrorists. She first went to Ireland as

*Boston Globe

a girl to work at stables near Dundalk, where she became converted to the IRA cause and methods and joined the Provisional IRA. She joined the Women's Royal Army Corps in 1971 to obtain information, especially about the layout of barracks and army routine generally, and left the following year. At her trial it was alleged she gave the essential information that enabled the Official IRA to cause the explosion at the Parachute Regiment's Officers' Mess (February 1972), although it was not made clear what exactly her cross-contact with the Officials was; it was also alleged she helped similarly in the Latimer explosion. At her trial, she was alleged to have planned the exploit and, with Keirnan McMorrow, to have actually placed the bomb in the army coach.

After a five-week lull there was an explosion in Manchester on 23 March; then on the 26th three bombs exploded at Claro Barracks, Rippon, Yorkshire. The IRA deserter Peter McMullen was alleged to have been involved in this exploit. This marked the end of that phase of the Provo bombing campaign in England.

In Northern Ireland the Provos were continuing with the Twomey plan of hitting soft targets, such as communication, industrial, and economic ones, and selected personnel, such as part-time UDR men. The object was to regain terrorist capability. In February 1974 the volume of incidents dropped in Belfast, as the Provos had to spend most of their time recruiting, training new recruits, and raising money. A dispute again arose within the Provo leadership between the "political Provos in Dublin" and the "militant Provos in Belfast." Chief of Staff David O'Connell was inclined to favor political action, although he could not resist overseeing the London Law Courts explosion; Twomey, the other strong character, was a militant with little social conscience.

On 3 January the Ulster Unionist Council rejected the Sunningdale proposals for an "All Ireland Settlement" by 427 votes to 374. On the 7th Brian Faulkner resigned as leader of the splintering Unionist Party; he was succeeded on the 22nd by Harry West. On the 16th Faulkner had travelled to Dublin to meet Prime Minister Cosgrave, who had convinced him there would be no Irish government pressure used to try to change the status of Northern Ireland. Faulkner was a Unionist Protestant who realized that reforms were essential and furthermore that some compromise should be made, but he had not been able to carry his party with him. He also did not fully appreciate that on relinquishing his office as leader he lost most of his political leverage. He failed to secure the nomination for a Unionist constituency for the Westminster Parliament and in some ways was considered to be a brash outsider trying to seize power from the old "Unionist aristocracy."

On 23 January 1974 there were scenes of disorder and violence in the Stormont Assembly chamber in protest against the formation of the executive. Ian Paisley and seventeen others had to be forcibly ejected. The Official Ulster Unionists, the Democratic Unionist Party, and the Vanguard Unionist Progressive Party all withdrew from the Northern Ireland Assembly.

14 Power Sharing

*"Were this to fail . . . then there would be little hope
that we could once again reconstruct a political initiative."*
—Prime Minister Harold Wilson, 18 April 1974

IN BRITAIN'S GENERAL election on 28 February 1974,
the Tory government of Edward Heath was ousted and
replaced by Labor, with Harold Wilson back in power as
prime minister. The non-Catholic population of Northern Ireland was
not very pleased, as they suspected Wilson of having undue sympathy
toward the idea of a united Ireland and a lack of sympathy toward the
idea of the province remaining part of the United Kingdom. On the day
of the election there were a number of explosions in the province—ten
within one hour in Belfast.

Of the twelve Northern Ireland MPs elected or reelected to Westminster, eleven opposed the Sunningdale Agreement; the only MP in favor
of the Sunningdale suggestion was Gerry Fitt of the Catholic SDLP. Brian
Faulkner had been unable to obtain a nomination to stand, and Bernadette Devlin did not run for reelection. Merlyn Rees, MP, was appointed
secretary for Northern Ireland. To smooth the way for an eventual Council of Ireland, Prime Minister Cosgrave said in the Dail Eireann on 13
March that he recognized Northern Ireland was part of the U.K. until a
majority of the people wanted it otherwise.

On 4 April Merlyn Rees said at Westminster that the Labor government supported the Sunningdale Agreement and the Northern Ireland
Executive. He said there would be a phased release of all detainees, and
that a committee would be set up to review the working of the emergency
legislation. Rees also spoke of the need to restore law and order, saying,
"What we are aiming for is the minimum number of troops actually in
Northern Ireland, which the needs of the situation require, together with
the maximum degree of flexibility, and speed in response to any change
in the situation." He added that responsibility for law and order was that
of the RUC, which did not please the army in Northern Ireland, now accustomed to playing the dominant role, or the hard-line Unionists who
wanted military action to be taken against the terrorists. It did give encouragement to the RUC and its Catholic chief constable, Mr. Flanagan.

Rees removed the Ulster Volunteer Force and the Provisional Sinn Fein from the proscribed list, which meant that the Provisional IRA now had a legal political front in Northern Ireland, as did, of course, the Official IRA with its Republicans Clubs. The Sinn Fein reopened its office at 170 Falls Road, a run-down two-story terrace house in which it had squatted the previous year.

On his 18 April visit to Northern Ireland, Prime Minister Harold Wilson expressed his support for the Sunningdale Agreement and hope for the eventual appearance of a Council of Ireland, which non-Catholics considered to be the halfway house to a united Ireland. Referring to the Northern Ireland Executive, he said at a press conference that, "Were this initiative to fail, or were any of us prepared to let it be destroyed, or to founder for whatever reason, then there would be little hope that we could once again reconstruct a political initiative." At this stage neither Wilson nor Rees seemed to fully understand the depth of non-Catholic feeling on this issue.

The Northern Ireland Assembly had come into being on 1 January 1974, in spite of the solid opposition from Unionists to the idea that representatives of Catholic communities should have seats in the executive as a right. This opposition mounted, and on 26 April both the UDA and the UVF called for the abolition of the Northern Ireland Executive and an end to the Council of Ireland idea. On 14 May the Ulster Workers' Council of trade unionists called a general strike in the province. The next day the power station workers responded to the call, and electric power was severely reduced; the shipyard workers also joined the strike, and "flying columns" of Protestant strike organizers toured Belfast and other towns, intimidating workers to down tools and join the strike. Uniformed UDA members blocked the terminal ferry at Larne Harbor; the Loyalist political parties added their support, as did the UDA and the UVF.

On the 16th the strike was intensified, and bars and clubs were forcibly closed on orders of the fifteen-man coordinating strike committee, which was virtually controlling the life of the province. By the 17th there was hardly any transport on the roads, and the dockers refused to unload ships. The declared aim of the Ulster Workers' Council (UWC) was to bring Northern Ireland to a complete standstill by the 19th; that day only one power station remained working.

At last Merlyn Rees reluctantly declared a state of emergency. The next day another 500 soldiers were flown to Northern Ireland, bringing the total in the province to over 16,000. Many of the main roads were blocked by barricades, and many Protestant communities barricaded themselves within their own areas. On the 21st two very much publicized "back to work" marches, one led by the general secretary of the British Trades Union Congress, failed miserably. Troops cleared the barricades from the main roads on the 22nd, no resistance being offered by the uniformed UDA personnel manning them. On the 26th soldiers took over two oil storage depots and a number of petrol filling stations.

On 27 May the coordinating strike committee of the UWC declared that new strike sanctions would be imposed and that the army would have to be responsible for guaranteeing practically all the essential services. The next day Merlyn Rees refused to meet the UWC leaders, which caused Brian Faulkner to resign his post as chief executive; and the Unionist leaders told Rees that they were not prepared to take any further part in power sharing in the assembly. The general strike had killed the idea, and Prime Minister Wilson could no longer have any doubts about the views on this issue held by the majority of non-Catholics in the province. On the 29th the Northern Ireland Executive was prorogued for four months. In the Irish Republic Prime Minister Cosgrave bemoaned the fact that the Northern Ireland Executive had been deliberately "wrecked by misrepresentation and violence."

Two new political parties were formed: one on 22 June 1974, the Volunteer Political Party, which was to be the political arm of the Ulster Volunteer Force; and the other on 4 September by Brian Faulkner, which he called the Unionist Party of Northern Ireland, its aim being to keep the province in the U.K. and to regain control of the RUC. The Unionist parties called for the Westminster representation in Northern Ireland to be increased from twelve to twenty-two seats, to give it parity with Britain in this respect. The same day, 4 September, an SDLP spokesman said that "if the Northern Ireland majority refused to accept power-sharing, and an 'Irish Dimension,' the British Government should revoke the guarantees given in the Government of Ireland Act 1920, the Ireland Act 1949, and the Northern Ireland Constitutional Act 1973," since all had to do with linking Northern Ireland to the United Kingdon. On the 9th a British Green Paper was published which gave a financial breakdown showing that one-third of all Northern Ireland expenditures was borne by the U.K. Presumably the object was to emphasize Northern Ireland's dependence on Britain.

Merlyn Rees showed what some MPs considered to be over-liberal tendencies towards the terrorists, a trait that exasperated the army. This trend probably began at Newry on 20 August 1974 when electricity for the street lighting was cut off due to a fault in an overhead cable. This suited the British troops, who had been in the habit of switching the street lights on or off for tactical reasons, as army patrols could be silhouetted at night and become easy targets for gunmen lurking in the shadows or the darkness. Electricity maintenance men refused to repair the cable or do any outside work because of alleged army interference. This did not suit the Provos, who said that unless the street lighting was restored, maintenance men would become "legitimate targets." A strike ensued and for twelve days Newry was without electricity until Rees stepped in, pushed the army aside, and allowed control of the electricity supply to be returned to the Electricity Board. The assumed British army dominance over the civil authorities was waning: at Newry it had lost out to both Rees and the Provos.

Violence continued on much the same pattern as in the two previous years—sectarian assassinations, car bomb and proxy bomb explosions, and the killing of British soldiers and policemen. During 1974, 216 people were killed and 2,398 injured due to terrorist activity; there were 3,200 shooting incidents and 685 explosions. Of the many incidents, mention can be made of just a few that hit the headlines.

One was the killing of Billy Fox, whose body was found near the border town of Clones, Co Monaghan, on 12 March. Fox, a Protestant, was unusual in that he was a member of the Irish Fine Gael Party and had been elected to the Irish Senate the previous year. The nearby house of a Protestant farmer had been set on fire the previous night by a group of armed men; Senator Fox, who had been with the farmer at the time, was initially reported missing. The Provos denied responsibility; it was claimed by the UFF, who stated it was unfortunate that Fox was a Protestant, but that he was suspected of having contact with the IRA. However, on the 24th, five men were charged with Fox's murder at the Dublin Special Criminal Court, and all five were also accused of being members of the IRA. This was an example of the false claims that some terrorist groups made from time to time.

After the dramatic Twomey and Mallon helicopter escape, about one hundred political prisoners were transferred from Mountjoy Prison, Dublin, to either Portlaoise Prison or Curragh Internment Camp. On 18 August nineteen Provos overpowered their prison officers at Portlaoise Prison, blew gaps in the inner and outer walls with high explosives that had been smuggled in to them, and escaped. Among the nineteen were Kevin Mallon, who had been recaptured after his helicopter escape, and Michael and Sean Kinsalla, who were being held for the murder of Billy Fox.

In Northern Ireland there were disturbances in the four main prisons: Maze, Crumlin Road, Armagh Women's Prison, and Magilligan Camp.

They began on 15 October 1974 when a small group of internees in Maze Prison seized some prison officers and caused damage. Troops were called in and had to use CS gas to restore order. The next day, as rumors spread that prisoners had been killed by soldiers in Maze Prison the governor and some of his prison officers at Armagh Women's Prison were taken as hostages; and there were riots in Crumlin Road Prison and Magilligan Camp. Troops again had to use CS gas before the prisoners and internees were calmed down and the hostages released. On 6 November, an internee named as Hugh Gerard Coney was shot dead by a sentry as he and thirty-two others took part in a mass breakout through a tunnel they had dug from Maze Prison. Three prisoners escaped, but the others were quickly rounded up near the prison.

During the summer of 1974 the RUC arrested several leaders of the Provo Belfast Brigade. An informer was obviously at work, and when Billy McKee again took over as the commanding officer, he started a search for the traitor. Eventually he decided it must be Eamonn Molloy, the quartermaster of the Belfast Brigade, who was responsible for organizing safe-houses, among other duties, and had the essential information at the moments of the arrests. Molloy himself had been arrested with one batch of Provos, but without any outside Provo help at all had escaped from the Castlereag RUC Interrogation Center, which was notoriously secure.

McKee arrested Molloy, and although Molloy escaped, he was quickly recaptured and taken off to Dublin to face a Provo court-martial. Molloy was found guilty of being an informer and shot. Because of Molloy's responsible position as quartermaster of the Belfast Brigade, his personal popularity, and his good IRA record, the Provo Council gave it out that Molloy had been sent on an extended trip to America to avoid causing a leadership confidence crisis in the brigade and the Provisional IRA generally. Later both the Garda and the RUC, to whom Molloy was simply just another missing person, insisted that he was not their informer and that his death was either a Provo mistake, a personality clash that went too far, or a vengeance killing. The Provo answer was that the police could hardly be expected to confirm the identity of their informers.

Terrorist incidents in March included car bombs twice damaging Belfast's Grand Central Hotel, which had been taken over for a British army headquarters; and a gunman firing on a British army patrol from the porch of a Catholic church. In April a schoolmaster was shot dead in front of his pupils in Derrylin, and an unsuccessful attempt was made in Armagh with a car bomb to kill a judge who had earlier sentenced an

IRA girl to imprisonment. In May an explosion in a Catholic bar in Belfast killed five people and injured others. In June a car bomb on the outskirts of Belfast killed thirteen people. It was the continuing story of death, injury, destruction, and misery.

At a press conference in Belfast on 3 September, Merlyn Rees announced plans for the expansion of the local security forces and emphasized that theirs must be the responsibility for maintaining law and order in the province. The recruiting target for the RUC was to be raised from 4,500 to 6,500, and from 375 to 750 for policewomen, who had been introduced into the RUC on recommendations of the Hunt Report. The part-time RUC Reserve was to be increased from 2,000 to 4,000 men and from 250 to 1,500 women, while the quota of full-time reservists employed with the RUC was raised to 1,000 policemen and 400 policewomen.

The Transport Information Unit of unarmed civilian searchers, which had been established earlier in the year for duty at the gates of the now fully cordoned shopping center in Belfast, was to be expanded to carry out similar tasks in Derry and other towns and was to be renamed "search wardens." Other measures included the establishment of a series of centers throughout the province, to be local focal points for policing, staffed mainly by RUC reservists. The Ulster Defense Regiment was not forgotten: a recruiting effort was to be made to increase its existing strength, then about 7,500, to the permitted upper limit of 10,000. Rees emphasized that "army flexibility" must be maintained. The following month it was announced that 1,000 British troops would be withdrawn from west Belfast and South Armagh.

On 18 September at the Baldonnel military airfield, in the Irish Republic, a cross-border security conference was held between Irish Minister of Justice Patrick Cooney and Merlyn Rees, each minister being accompanied by his senior police officer. They discussed the implementation of the Anglo-Irish Law Enforcement Commission—which had stemmed from the Sunningdale Conference of December 1973—in a rather negative way.

While not neglecting its terrorism in Northern Ireland, the Provisional IRA again concentrated on an intermittent bombing campaign in England, where it still seemed to have considerable resources. During the spring and summer the incidents were widely dispersed and ceased altogether on 2 August when eight men were arrested. There were no more explosions for over two months and the British police over-optimistically thought the IRA network in England had been broken up. There was, however, a rash of letter bombs, all posted from Derry, one being discovered in Middlesex on 7 August, and several others on 6 September, all addressed to civil servants, mainly in the London area.

The bombing lull was violently broken on 5 October with an explosion in a pub frequented by soldiers and members of the Women's Royal Army Corps in Guildford, Surrey. Two soldiers and two WRAC members were killed, all aged seventeen or eighteen years, and fifty were injured. A second bomb exploded a few minutes later in an adjacent pub that was being evacuated; another seven people were injured. These explosions coincided with the Judith Ward trial. Other explosions followed in London, and on 7 November a nail bomb exploded in a pub opposite Woolwich Barracks, near London, killing two people and injuring thirty-four. There were also widely scattered explosions in Birmingham and the Midlands. James McDaid, posthumously described as a lieutenant in the Provisional IRA, was killed on 14 November by a premature explosion in Coventry. His body had to be flown back to Northern Ireland by way of Dublin as the Protestant workers at Belfast airport refused to handle it.

In an interview filmed by a British television company, shown on 17 November 1974, Provo Chief of Staff David O'Connell said that the campaign of violence in England would be stepped up until the British government announced its intention to withdraw from Northern Ireland. He said that the campaign would be directed against "economic, military, political and judicial targets" that would include railway stations and places where the military visit, obviously meaning pubs. O'Connell admitted the Provo responsibility for the army coach explosion in Yorkshire in February, for which Judith Ward had been charged.

Four days later O'Connell's threat came true. Explosions in two pubs in the center of Birmingham—the Mulberry Bush and the Tavern in the Town—killed 21 people and injured another 182. A third bomb was discovered about two miles away and was defused in time. There were no soldiers among the casualties, the victims being mainly young people, of whom several were Irish. Birmingham, like other Midland complexes, had a large Irish community. Six suspects were arrested on the 24th, five of whom were just about to board the ferry to Ireland at Heysham.

This incident aroused considerable anti-Irish feeling in Britain, particularly in Birmingham and the Midlands. A petrol bomb was thrown at a Catholic church used by the Irish; a fire was started at an Irish Community Center; fighting broke out between English and Irish workers at some factories; and there were demonstrations in several cities against Irish workers in Britain, with placards saying, "Irish Go Home." Great efforts were made by the police, civic leaders, politicians, and personalities to ease the tension between the two communities, and ugly incidents were avoided.

On 22 November the Officials openly blamed the Provos for the Birmingham Bombing, and Tomas MacGiolla, president of the Official Sinn Fein, called it a "sick joke." In an interview printed in a Dublin Newspaper on 1 December, David O'Connell declared that no member of the Provisional IRA had been involved in any way; but according to the British police all the evidence pointed to the Provos.

Shortly after the Birmingham Bombing, a girl claimed responsibility by telephone for the "Red Flag 74," which she said was a student organization of about five hundred members. This claim was disbelieved by the police. The Red Flag 74 existed as a tiny breakaway group from the International Marxist Party and probably had less than forty members in London and a few others in the provinces. It had made several claims— of responsibility for some of the terrorist incidents in England, that its members had trained with the IRA in Ireland, and that the IRA had given it explosives—but all were treated with skepticism by the British police.

After the Birmingham Bombing, on 29 November 1974, the Prevention of Terrorism (Temporary Provisions) Act was passed at Westminster. This proscribed the IRA in Britain, gave the police wide powers to arrest and detain suspects, and empowered the home secretary to expel, or exclude suspects from Britain. The police were able to detain suspects for forty-eight hours without making a charge, and up to five days with the home secretary's permission. A number of arrests were made and several expulsion orders were immediately issued by the home secretary.

On 10 December 1974 there was an impromptu meeting at Feakle, Co Clare, between a group of senior non-Catholic churchmen and representatives of the Provisional Sinn Fein and the Provisional IRA to try to find a way to bring about a cease-fire. The three principal Provos were David O'Connell, Seamus Twomey, and Kevin Mallon, who all left hurriedly when the Garda were reported to be arriving. On the 20th, through its Republican Publicity Bureau in Dublin, the Provo Council issued a long statement saying that it would observe a cease-fire from midnight on the 22nd to midnight on 2 January. Rees made a noncommittal acceptance, and the cease-fire came into effect over the Christmas and New Year period.

On 31 December Rees released twenty internees and allowed another fifty a three-day parole, but he did not respond as O'Connell had hoped he would. Perhaps Rees thought he had got the Provos on the run. Despite his disappointment that Rees would not answer his demand that the

British government set a date for its withdrawal from Northern Ireland, O'Connell persuaded the Provo Council to agree to observe the cease-fire for a further fourteen days. During the cease-fire there had been a number of terrorist incidents, including yet another explosion at the Europa Hotel on 29 December. On 8 January 1975 Kevin Mallon, commanding officer of the Provo Border Units, was arrested in Dublin.

The Provos made constant complaints that the security forces were continuing their arrests, searches, and photography during the cease-fire, and were not releasing many from internment. When John Green, described as the "Staff Captain, commanding the North Armagh units" of the Provos, was found shot dead at a farm in Co Monaghan on 8 January, the Provos claimed he had been killed by a SAS assassination squad. Green had escaped from Maze Prison in 1974, dressed as a priest. On the 13th, James Moyne, a Provo held in Maze Prison, died of a heart condition, but the Provos alleged he had been refused medical treatment.

Despite the fact that some members of the Provo Council felt that Merlyn Rees was contemptuously ignoring them, they decided to extend the cease-fire without a limitation date. It was announced on 9 February from the Republican Publicity Bureau that an indeterminate cease-fire would begin the next day at 6:00 P.M. To supervise this cease-fire, Rees said he would set up incident centers, to be manned twenty-four hours a day and linked by communication directly to his own office at Stormont. They were to be in west Belfast, Armagh, Dungannon, Enniskillen, Derry, and Newry. The Provisional Sinn Fein set up incident centers at the same places and installed a "hot line" telephone in its office on Falls Road. The Provisional Sinn Fein also said it would have a complaints desk at each center and would organize an "anti-rumor service." Despite incidents, some serious, the cease-fire creakingly held for the remainder of 1975, during which there were bouts of internecine fighting between the main terrorist groups, Catholic and Protestant, involving a considerable number of sectarian murders.

On 8 December 1974 the Irish Republican Socialist Party (IRSP) was formed in Dublin. Its founder-members, who included Seamus Costello, a Dublin left-wing lawyer, and Bernadette Devlin McAliskey (she had married), were mainly discontented members of the Official IRA who wanted both violent action and a move further to the left in political thought. The IRSP had taken arms from Officials' dumps, and this caused open friction and some fighting between them. During February 1975 fighting between the Officials and the IRSP occurred in Belfast around the pubs, bars, and clubs frequented by the respective sides; at least two people were killed and several injured. Gunmen who had defected from the Officials to the IRSP were beyond the control of their new leaders, and at the beginning of March the situation was such that the IRSP leadership in Belfast temporarily disbanded itself in the hope of isolating and eliminating the wayward gunmen.

Eventually, on 15 March, a cease-fire was arranged in Dublin between the Officials and the IRSP by Senator Michael Mullen, general secretary of the Irish Transport General Workers Union. However, the lull did not last long, and more fighting broke out between them. On 28 April Liam McMillan, commanding officer of the Officials in Belfast, was shot dead in the Falls Road area. A spokesman of the Republican Clubs said that McMillan's name had been on the IRSP's "death list."

There was also Protestant extremist friction and internecine underground warfare. On 16 March, after the killing of two UDA men in a north Belfast bar, there was fighting between the UDA and the UVF. There was also fighting between the Catholic and Protestant terrorist groups.

The black feature of 1975 was the spate of sectarian killings. RUC figures issued later indicated that between February and September 149 civilians were killed, mainly by sectarian assassination. Sectarian vengeance squads were at work, and the RUC reported that there were 189 cases of kneecapping and twenty-two of tarring and feathering during the year. On 26 June the RUC announced the formation of a special murder squad of about thirty-six detectives, to be known as "A" Squad, to track down those responsible for the sectarian killings. This was in addition to the 150-strong Special Patrol Group that was already operating in difficult areas.

On 13 March two Provos were killed by the security forces, and this caused the first real breach of the cease-fire. When a bomb exploded in the center of Belfast on 2 April, the Republican Publicity Bureau stated that it was a warning to British troops that "further violations of the cease-fire would not be tolerated." The next major breach took place on 17 July when an explosion at Forkill, near Crossmaglen, killed four soldiers. The Provos claimed this was in retaliation for general harassment and the killing by British troops of two Catholics. The 2d Crossmaglen Battalion of the Provos claimed responsibility. On 31 July in an explosion and shooting incident near Newry, three members of an Irish pop group, the Maimi Showband, died and another was injured. In the same incident a premature explosion killed two members of the UVF.

On 1 August Gen. David House took over as GOC Northern Ireland. His predecessor, General King, had been the symbol of the dominance of the military over the RUC and had come into office when this attitude was at its height. He had suddenly to adjust to the new thinking and the insistence of Merlyn Rees that control of operations against terrorists should be given over to the RUC. On arrival General House was briefed that this changeover must be made.

However, it was obvious the RUC was as yet neither conditioned nor in any position to take a leading role in the fight against terrorism, especially in certain parts of the province. The conditions in South Armagh were particularly ugly, causing Rees, on 2 September, to authorize more British troops and more Special Patrol Group and RUC policemen to be moved into that area. On the 5th he urged the people of Northern Ireland to help the security forces, but those in South Armagh and other hard-line Catholic Republican areas were long deaf to such appeals. The lapsed policy of closing more unapproved roads by cratering or spiking was resumed.

On 2 October 1975 the Protestant UVF carried out a spate of sectarian bombings and shootings in both Belfast and Co Antrim, killing twelve people and injuring over forty. The UVF spokesman said this had been done because the military authorities were taking no action against IRA terrorists. This caused the UVF to again be proscribed.

The cease-fire between the Provos and the British army still held, although precariously, and there were occasional breaches and incidents. The cease-fire notwithstanding, it was a violent year: 245 people were killed and 1,648 injured due to terrorist activity. On the credit side for the security forces, 1,197 people were charged with "terrorist offenses" and brought before the courts; 226 were charged with murder or attempted murder.

Since April 1975 Merlyn Rees had been slowly phasing out internment without trial, and he finally brought it to an end on 5 December. Since its introdution on 9 August 1971, 1,981 people had been interned, of whom 107 were Loyalists. Rees said, "As from today no one is held under a Detention Order. The rule of law will be imposed impartially and firmly through the Courts." He clearly underrated the difficulties of persuading witnesses to come forward and give evidence. Rees also said that those sentenced for terrorist offenses committed after March 1976 would not be granted special category status, which had been introduced by William Whitelaw in June 1972. It had been severely criticized in the Gardiner Report, published on 19 January 1975.

The year of 1975 was notable for the emergence of the Irish National Liberation Army (INLA). This consisted basically of breakaway members of the Official IRA, who had for some time ignored its cease-fire ruling and continued terrorist operations on their own. They teamed up with the IRSP when it was formed, which became the political front for the INLA. The political aims of both were to bring about the withdrawal of British rule from Northern Ireland through armed warfare and to unite it with the south. The next step was to withdraw the Irish Republic from the European Economic Community and to install a socialist regime in Dublin.

The INLA was initially small, probably having less than thirty members, but it began to expand by recruiting many who were rejected by or discharged from either the Official or the Provisional IRA. Although its leadership was dedicated and determined, the INLA in its early days lacked the expertise of the Provos; but as the leadership of the Provos was tending to move further to the left, there was some liaison between the two groups. The hostility of the INLA was mainly directed against the Officials. The INLA headquarters was in Dublin, but it developed a small presence in Belfast and Derry.

One event of the year of note occurred in the Irish Republic on 3 October when Tiede Herrema, the Dutch managing director of an industrial concern, was kidnapped by Provos while driving to his factory in Limerick. The Provos demanded in exchange for his safe return the release of three people held in Irish jails. They were Bridget Rose Dugdale, an English supporter of the Provos who had hijacked the helicopter that bombed Strabane RUC station in January 1974; Kevin Mallon, who had again been recaptured in January 1975; and James Hyland, a Provo leader who had been arrested with rockets, guns, and ammunition in his possession.

The Irish government rejected this demand, and the Garda began an intensive search for the kidnapped man, who was eventually located in a house at Monasterevan, Co Kildare, where he was held hostage by two Provos, Eddie Gallagher and Marion Coyle. On 21 October the house was beseiged by the Garda, who played a waiting game that was a test of nerve and endurance for the captors. Eventually, on 7 November, Gallagher and Coyle surrendered and Herrema was released unharmed. Gallagher had escaped from Portlaoise Prison in August 1974. A Provo spokesman stated that he had been expelled from the Provisional IRA before the Herrema kidnapping for failing to hand over the proceeds of a bank robbery in the Irish Republic to the Provo headquarters.

One other event of note occurred on 27 November 1975 when Ross McWhirter, a publisher and writer, was shot dead on the doorstep of his house in London. The Provos claimed responsibility. In September McWhirter had begun a "Stop the Bombers" campaign in England aimed against the IRA terrorists. He started a fortnightly periodical, *Majority*, to finance a media campaign against them, which included a coupon for people to fill in to enable them to pass on information about the IRA to the police.

McWhirter's platform was that the public must be more vigilant, that all citizens of the Irish Republic and Britain should carry identity cards, that a fund should be established to reward those who provided information leading to the arrest of terrorists, and that the death penalty should be reintroduced. There is no doubt that his campaign was damaging the IRA's reputation and fund-raising in America. McWhirter estimated that in the pevious five years well over one million dollars had been collected by Noraid, the major part of which went to the Provisional IRA. It also caused the U.S. authorities to take tighter measures to prevent arms being smuggled from America into Ireland. The RUC said that until September 1975, 1,581 arms of different types seized from terrorists or discovered in searches in Northern Ireland had been identified as being of U.S. origin. In 1975 the U.S. Justice Department indicted eighteen people for gunrunning to Ireland.

Although the cease-fire held in Northern Ireland, the Provos continued their bombing campaign in England on a much reduced scale. On 27 and 28 January 1975 there were eight explosions in the London area, in which six people were injured. Then on 12 February Frank Stagg, a Provo imprisoned for conspiring to attack targets in Coventry, died in an English jail after a sixty-one-day hunger strike. Stagg had demanded to be transferred to a prison in Northern Ireland but was refused because his home was in the Irish Republic. Stagg's death triggered off a spate of bombing in England during February and March.

Then there was a pause until the bombing campaign recommenced on 27 August, when an explosion in a pub at Caterham, Surrey, injured thirty-three people, including several soldiers. Then followed more explosions in London. On 6 September one at the London Hilton Hotel killed two people and injured sixty-three. On 9 October one at a London bus-stop killed one person and injured thirteen; on the 23rd an explosion outside the house of a prominent MP killed a passerby who was a leading cancer specialist; on the 29th an explosion in a restaurant killed one person and injured twenty. Another on 12 November killed one and injured fifteen; and yet another similar explosion on the 18th killed two and injured nineteen. On 9 November a bomb outside the home of Edward Heath, the former prime minister, was detected and defused in time. During this period the police discovered at least three Provo bomb factories in England. The police admitted they received considerable help and information from the large Irish communities in Britain who disapproved of and wanted no part in IRA terrorism.

On 6 December 1975 four Provo gunmen being chased by the police through the streets of London entered a flat occupied by a middle-aged couple on Balcombe Street. The couple was held hostage while the Provos kept the police at bay. By this time considerable expertise in what could be called "terrorist siege situations" had been gained by security forces in several countries. The technique of the British police was to surround the building, make and keep contact with the terrorists, and turn the situation into a long drawn-out test of nerves and patience rather than to burst in shooting and risk harming hostages. The IRA terrorists held out for six days and then surrendered, the hostages being unharmed. The Balcombe Street Siege, as it became known, was an example of the success of these tactics. Only one terrorist incident marred the month of December in London: on the 20th an explosion in a pub frequented by Republican Irish injured five people. On the 22nd responsibility was claimed by the UDA.

15 Bandit Country

*"Violence cannot resolve Northern Ireland's problems,
it only increases them and solves nothing."*
—President Jimmy Carter, 30 August 1977

S ECTARIAN ASSASSINATION CAME to a head in
South Armagh, an area known to British troops as Bandit Country, when on 5 January 1976 five Catholics
were murdered by gunmen. The following day, ten Protestant textile
workers returning home in a minibus were ambushed and killed at Kingsmills, near Bessbrook, by the South Armagh Action Force, a Provisional
IRA execution squad. The British government reacted with heavy measures; on the 6th the British army's Spearhead Battalion was sent over.
The Spearhead Battalion was the unit always on rotation standby ready
to move immediately to wherever required. The following day it was announced that SAS troops would be deployed in Bandit Country.

Prime Minister Harold Wilson spoke on the 12th at Westminster of
the situation in South Armagh, explaining that it was now designated a
special emergency area and that, in addition to the Spearhead Battalion
and SAS troops, extra police, including members of the Special Patrol
Group and the new antiassassination "A" Squad, were being drafted in.
He said there would be extensive use of personal identity checks, more
checkpoints for vehicles and people, more house searches, and the continued use of the existing powers to arrest and question suspects.

At this time also the British army in Northern Ireland introduced a
new information-intelligence system based on automatic data processing; details of terrorists could be fed into a central computer to give the
advantage of instant recall. The bank of information was not confined to
convicted terrorists, but widened to include suspects and many who were
not even suspects. This system had amazingly good results but the army
generally played it down and handled it carefully and delicately in case it
became a civil liberties issue. The popular British objection to such a system was the possibility that the information would be used for political
purposes or, in the wrong hands, for blackmail or criminal purposes.

Although in theory the cease-fire between the British army and the

Provisional IRA was still tenuously holding, breaches of it were occurring in increasing number and ferocity until it simply disintegrated without any announcement being made by either side. Provo terrorist activity against the British army was resumed, and on 31 March three soldiers were killed in South Armagh when their Landrover went over a land-mine detonated by remote control.

After ceasing to sit on 7 November 1975, when it had presented to Merlyn Rees proposals drawn up by the United Ulster Unionist Coalition, the Northern Ireland Constitutional Convention reconvened on 3 February 1976; but after a period of fruitless discussion, it was finally and formally dissolved on 5 March. It had failed to come to any agreement on a system of government for the province that included power sharing.

Later, on 18 August 1976, Brian Faulkner, who had been the chief executive of the convention, resigned his leadership of the Unionist Party of Northern Ireland and withdrew from active political life. He was a disappointed man who somehow felt that circumstances had combined and conspired to deprive him of the highest political office in the province and a seat in the Westminster Parliament. Without any political constitutional position he lacked political clout. Mrs. Anne Dixon was elected leader of the Unionist Party of Northern Ireland in his place. In March of the following year, Faulkner was killed in a hunting accident.

Terrorism continued throughout 1976. A total of 297 people were killed (50 more than the preceding year) and 2,904 injured (over 1,200 more than the previous year) due to terrorist acts. It was also a year of sectarian savagery and kangaroo punishments, there being ninety-eight instances of kneecapping and eighteen of tarring and feathering recorded by the RUC. The Provos extended their assassination campaign to include prison officers because of alleged harsh treatment of IRA men in detention. The first was killed on 19 April outside his house in Co Tyrone, and the next was assassinated on the 19th in Belfast.

On 10 August 1976 a car hijacked by IRA gunmen ran out of control after the driver was shot and fatally wounded by pursuing troops. It mounted a sidewalk ouside a Catholic school in Andersonstown, hitting a woman and her four children. The woman, Mrs. Ann Maguire, and one child were injured, but the three other children were killed. This incident led to the sudden rise of a spontaneous women's peace movement, at first mainly of Catholic women in Belfast. It was initially led by Mrs. Betty Williams and Miss Mairead Corrigan, the latter an aunt of the Maguire children.

This peace movement held mass rallies in various parts of Belfast on three successive Saturdays. On the 14th the rally was at Andersonstown, where an estimated crowd of 10,000 gathered, mainly Catholics. On the 21st the rally in central Belfast attracted over 20,000 people, this time with a greater proportion of Protestants. On the 28th there was a demonstration march of about 25,000 people, both Catholic and Protestant, in west Belfast, which went through both the Catholic Falls Road and the Protestant Shankill areas. This was the first time since 1969 that Catholics had dared march through the Shankill district, and it was the first time that Catholics and Protestants had marched together since the hunger marches in 1932.

This mass spontaneous peace movement was soon joined by a journalist, Cairan McKeown, who became the secretary and organizer. An executive committee was formed, and on 21 August it issued a Declaration of the Peace People to be read out at all meetings and rallies. This called for the "right to live and love and build a just, peaceful society" and asked people to dedicate themselves to "building that peaceful society in which tragedies we have known are a bad memory, and a continuing warning." The peace movement continued to attract mass support; in September meetings and rallies were held in Liverpool, Glasgow, and several parts of the province, including Derry. The success of the movement was so great that it caught world attention and approval; in October 1976 both Betty Williams and Mairead Corrigan were jointly awarded the Nobel Peace Prize.

Donations flooded in to the Community of Peace People, a name the movement adopted at its first annual conference at Enniskillen on 1–3 April 1977. The terrorists, who had no wish for peace in Northern Ireland until their political objectives had been obtained, moved into action against the Peace People, using intimidation to persuade Catholic communities to withhold support from them. They also used strong-arm methods of disrupting meetings and harassing officials and representatives of the Peace People, who began appearing in numbers to demonstrate wherever and whenever there were terrorist incidents; but they were always careful to do nothing wrong in front of reporters or television cameras. Terrorist pressure against supporters of the Peace People was indirect and backstage.

During the first twenty months' existence of the Community of Peace People, over £250,000 was donated. There were soon internal differences over how it should be spent. Also Cairan McKeown was showing marked support for the Republican cause and was taking an active interest in alleged ill treatment of Catholic prisoners in the Maze Prison. The fast momentum of the movement began to slow down, but the Community of

Peace People remained a prominent organization and continued to receive considerable overseas publicity for its cause.

One of the tasks of the Anglo-Irish Law Enforcement Commission was to find a solution to the objection by Irish courts to extraditing Irish citizens to stand trial for terrorist offenses. The commission proposed that accused persons be tried wherever they were—that is, in either the Irish Republic, Britain, or Northern Ireland—regardless of where the alleged crimes had been committed. Accordingly, the Westminster Parliament approved the Prevention of Terrorism (Temporary Provisions) Act of 1976, which came into effect on 25 March. In brief, it enabled certain terrorist offenses committed in either the Irish Republic or Northern Ireland, including murder, manslaughter, kidnapping, hijacking, robbery, and conspiracy to cause explosions, to be tried in Britain or Northern Ireland. Sufficient evidence, of course, had to be produced to gain a conviction, which was to become something of a handicap.

The comparable Irish legislation did not go through quite so smoothly, although a need for it was illustrated when figures produced showed that since January 1974, 31 people had been killed and 189 injured in the Irish Republic as the result of explosions, some of this in reprisal by terrorists from Northern Ireland. There had been eighty-one armed bank robberies, fifty-six armed post office raids, and a number of other robberies, most of which had a political motive.

The necessary reciprocal legislation, known as the Criminal Law Jurisdiction Act of 1976, was approved in the Dail and was to come into effect on 6 May. Irish President Cearbhall O'Dalaigh signed the bill into law, but he was not completely satisfied with its purpose and so referred the act to the Irish Supreme Court for a decision. There had been considerable opposition to this legislation in the Irish Republic, especially from the Fianna Fail Party and hard-line Republicans. However, the Irish Supreme Court upheld the validity of the act, which came into effect on 24 September 1976. This decision caused President O'Dalaigh to resign on 22 October; he was replaced by Patrick Hillery, who after being a Fianna Fail minister for external affairs from 1969 to 1972 had been appointed president of the Commission of the European Communities after the Irish Republic had joined the EEC.

While the Irish Supreme Court was examining the validity of the Criminal Law Jurisdiction Act, a terrorist exploit occurred in the Irish Republic which perhaps helped influence its final decision. It was the murder of Christopher Ewart-Biggs, the British ambassador, on 21 July. He was traveling from his home near Dublin when his car went over a land-mine that was detonated by remote control. He was killed instantly, as was his secretary, while the driver and another British official in the car were injured. No terrorist organization claimed responsibility, but the finger of suspicion pointed towards the INLA. The Irish minister of justice offered a reward of £20,000 but there were no takers. On 13 February 1977 Mrs. Jane Ewart-Biggs, wife of the murdered ambassador, established a branch of the Community of Peace People in Britain.

Meanwhile, all was not well between the British army and the RUC in Northern Ireland. Since 1975 the "Ulsterization program" of bringing the RUC to the fore and pushing the army into the background in a secondary security supporting role had hung fire. Ever since 1970, when Prime Minister O'Neill handed this responsibility over to the GOC (in return, it was openly alleged, for the promise of more British troops), the army had become accustomed to being in charge of all security operations in the province and was reluctant to step aside, realizing that the RUC was not really ready to take over this primary role.

On 1 May 1976 Kenneth Newman, the senior deputy chief constable of the RUC, was appointed chief constable in place of Sir James Flanagan, who retired. Newman was an English policeman who as a senior officer in the Metropolitan Police Force had been recommended to the RUC for his expertise. He was, of course, strongly imbued with the English principle of the primacy of civil authority over the military, and what he saw in Northern Ireland he did not like; so he set to work to rectify the matter. He saw that the morale of the RUC had to be raised, and that this should be done by giving it modern equipment, good training, and leadership, and by letting it be seen that the RUC was in charge of security matters. He saw that this would take time, as the army had to be persuaded to step back into the shadows. As a prelude the RUC produced a policy document, entitled "The Way Ahead," that proclaimed the primacy of the civil police; this was circulated to top security personnel, government officials, politicians, and security services leaders.

On 10 September 1976 Merlyn Rees was appointed British home secretary and thankfully left his post in Northern Ireland. Like William Whitelaw before him, and probably Francis Pym too, Rees barely concealed his low opinion of Northern Ireland politicians; but unlike Whitelaw, he had far more liberal views and seemed to bend over backwards to put them into effect, much to the discomfort of the security forces at times, who considered themselves to be in a war situation. Rees tended to be indecisive, always putting off decisions and seeking a consensus of opinion before he moved. He also encouraged his junior officials to enter into dialogues with the Provisional Sinn Fein and the leaders of the UDA to find out what they were thinking, and some of these meetings had tended to be compromising.

Rees was replaced as secretary of state for Northern Ireland by Roy Mason, MP, a more solid character who had obviously not volunteered for the position. Mason had a reputation for toughness and looked the part, but he turned out to be a stonewaller who seemed to have no intention of producing the much called for initiative. Mason seemed to concentrate upon keeping events on as even a course as possible until he was moved to another political appointment or until a general election. He quickly stopped all contact by members of his staff with the militant groups and the Provisional Sinn Fein.

Mason firmly backed Kenneth Newman, the chief constable of the RUC. On 12 January 1977 Newman and the GOC signed a joint directive that virtually stripped the GOC of his overriding powers in security matters and handed them over to the RUC. One overt sign was that the weekly joint military–police conferences were moved from the army headquarters at Lisburn to the RUC headquarters in Belfast. Newman, a shrewd operator, had taken his first step to outflank the GOC.

While the police were in favor of skillful, patient, enlightened detective work, the army still wanted more vigorous and aggressive action and had, for example, deplored the ending of internment without trial. The police were now openly to have a presence on the streets, and army patrols were to be phased out; and the police were to move up to the front in riots and disturbances, while the army was to wait in the background and intervene only if asked to do so by the RUC. The British army was to be less obvious and ostentatious; for example, the roadblocks and checkpoints manned for years by soldiers were to be either handed over to the RUC or discontinued. As a sop the army was given a more or less free hand in undercover activities, which were to be mainly surveillance ones in the rural border areas. The army was not to be allowed to infiltrate communities and would operate in Belfast and the towns of the province only when asked to do so by the RUC. The British army was not very pleased.

By this time there was some contact by radio and telephone between the RUC and the Garda across the border; but each tended to be suspicious of the other, which, together with political restraints and reservations, prevented it from becoming really effective. The army had no direct communication across the border but wanted to be able to make contact with the Irish army and to cooperate in apprehending terrorists. Mason would not allow this as he did not want the army to become too independent. In any case it was a nonstarter as the Irish prime minister would not allow it either: he also wanted to avoid giving the military too much rope.

The IRA did not like the change of emphasis within the security forces. Its members always prided themselves on being an army that was fighting the might of the British army; they saw themselves as soldiers fighting soldiers. The Provos knew the police would treat them as criminals and not as soldiers, and so they would lose prestige and dignity. However, the Provo leadership saw this move as a prelude to the evacuation of the British army from the province and so was heartened and encouraged to continue the struggle it thought it now had a much better chance of winning.

Despite the agreement between the GOC and the chief constable, relations between the army and the RUC hardly improved, causing Enoch Powell, MP for South Down, to state in Westminster on 23 February that evidence indicated "both the army and the RUC, and also the RUC and the UDR, are more out of touch with each other than is tolerable." This was quite true. Mason made the soft reply that "intelligence gathered by the army has been of great value in bringing terrorists before the courts," and added that the withdrawal of the army from Northern Ireland was "a recipe for civil war." MP Airey Neave, the opposition spokesman on Northern Ireland who favored stronger measures against the terrorists, said, "The government needs a strategic plan to bring organized terrorism under control during 1977, and to destroy the hopes of success of the IRA." Neither Rees nor Mason seemed to have a strategic plan of this nature, and both seemed to go from day to day hoping for the best.

On 2 May 1977 the United Unionist Action Council (UUAC), a consortium of ten Loyalist organizations instigated and led largely by Ian Paisley, called a general strike. The object was to bring life in the province to an absolute standstill in an effort to persuade the British government to cancel direct rule. The UUAC was the umbrella organization that included Ian Paisley's Democratic Unionist Party, the UDA, and the Ulster Workers' Council, the latter having organized the successful strike in 1974.

The strike was by no means universal: despite intimidation by Protestant extremists, many workers ignored the call to join it. The RUC recorded 1,830 instances of intimidation, and eventually 115 people were convicted of this offense. The UDR was called out for full-time duty, and the British army Spearhead Battalion was again sent to Northern Ireland from Britain, giving the security forces an overall total of about 31,000 mobilized personnel. Despite energetic speeches by Paisley and others, support for the strike waned; on 13 May it was cancelled. The newly invigorated, better equipped and trained RUC had been pushed to the front in the strike riots and disturbances and had performed well; the military had been kept in the background. Coupled with Roy Mason's stonewalling, the RUC was as responsible for the collapse of the strike as any other factor.

The failure of the strike brought about the dissolution of the United Ulster Unionist Coalition, led by James Molyneaux, which had been formed for the 1974 strike. A quarrel arose between Molyneaux and Paisley over the cause of the failure, Molyneaux alleging that Paisley was too rabble-rousing. It was generally considered that the strike's failure was a prestige blow to Paisley and that popular support for him was waning.

On 8 June Roy Mason announced further security measures, one of which was to increase the size of the RUC by an additional 1,200 personnel to bring it up to the 6,500 mark. He said the Criminal Investigation Department had been reorganized and that the RUC now had a Headquarters Crime Squad and three regional ones, all intermeshed. The formation of the Headquarters Criminal Intelligence Section meant an increase of about 150 detectives so there could be a criminal intelligence unit in each police region. Their task was to study the style and methods of the leading terrorists. Computerized automatic data processing was now in use with the RUC, which meant that vital information could be instantly recalled.

Technical services were to be improved and the RUC, for example, was to have its own forensic science laboratory. The Special Patrol Group was to be equipped with the reinforced Landrover, protected with some armor-plating against high-velocity bullets, and better personal weapons that would include American M-1 carbines and magnum revolvers. Mason insisted that the police would continue to have the central role and that the RUC reserve was to become more involved in security operations. Comfort and confidence were given later (in August 1977) by President Jimmy Carter's statement that it was the U.S. intention "to cooperate with legally established governments in their efforts to control terrorism." The secretary for Northern Ireland stated that liaison between the RUC and the army had improved, that the role of the army now was to concentrate on the collection of intelligence, that SAS-type activities were to be increased, and that additional SAS soldiers were to be sent to Northern Ireland. The UDR was to be increased by another 700 men.

One of these SAS-type operations had already gone wrong. On 14 May 1977 Capt. Robert Nairac of the Grenadier Guards, serving with his regiment in Northern Ireland, was kidnapped outside a pub in Drumintree, South Armagh, taken over the border three miles away into the Irish Republic, and killed. His body has not yet been found. On the 16th the South Armagh Brigade of the Provisional IRA admitted responsibility and stated that it had arrested Nairac and then executed him after an interrogation in which he had admitted he was an SAS man.

Officially, Captain Nairac, who was on his fourth tour of duty in Northern Ireland, was the liaison officer for his unit with HQ, 3d Infantry Brigade, and as such always operated in plain clothes in an unmarked car. He was not a member of the SAS Regiment as was (and still is, in some quarters) widely alleged. Each British major unit serving in Northern Ireland had a small number of soldiers trained in SAS surveillance techniques who operated in the unit locality to try to identify and locate Provo leaders. Nairac was one of them.

On 28 May five men in South Armagh were arrested and charged with Nairac's murder; eventually, In December 1977, they were convicted. Cross-border legislation was invoked, and a Garda officer went to Belfast to give evidence at the trial. The liaison was only partial: the Special Criminal Court in Dublin, which in November 1977 had tried and convicted a sixth man in the Provo murder team, who had been arrested in the Irish Republic, would not release certain material evidence. This was the first and only instance of the British Prevention of Terrorism (Temporary Provisions) Act and the Irish Criminal Law Jurisdiction Act being jointly invoked. It demonstrated that they could be made workable.

On 1 December 1977 Gen. Sir David House handed over his duties as "GOC and Director of Military Operations in Northern Ireland" to Gen. Tim Creasy, who became simply "GOC Northern Ireland." Like his predecessors, General House must be faulted for failing to sponsor better relations between the army and the RUC. In fact, all ranks of the RUC should be congratulated for their fortitude in the face of years of off-hand, casual treatment, especially from middle-grade and junior officers.

The economy and business life in Northern Ireland had been almost shattered by terrorist activity and was running at a very low ebb. On 1 August Roy Mason announced a £950 million plan to stimulate economic and industrial competitiveness, which included writing off a huge debt. He also announced the establishment of a new Northern Ireland Economic Council to succeed the one set up in 1964 but disbanded in October

1976. A new Northern Ireland Development Agency had replaced the old Northern Ireland Finance Corporation on 1 April 1976.

To boost the morale of the people of the province and to show that they were not forgotten by the people in Britain, Queen Elizabeth II and Prince Phillip visited Northern Ireland on 10–11 August 1977. Despite terrorist threats, the occasion passed without incident. However, several days later a large explosive device was discovered in a room where the queen had made a speech. It had failed to explode and the Provos had missed out on what would have been the terrorist exploit of the age. The queen had a lucky escape.

Two new political parties were formed in the province in October 1977. One, formed on the 7th, was the Irish Independence Party, a republican group under the joint chairmanship of Frank McManus and Fergus McAteer. McManus had been the Unity Party MP at Westminster from 1970 to 1974. The object of this new party was to bring about a withdrawal of the British presence from the province by nonviolent means; it called upon the Irish government to make a clear demand for British disengagement.

The other, which had a somewhat confusingly similar title, was formed on the 14th and called the Ulster Independence Party. It advocated an independent Northern Ireland with power sharing at all levels. Its leader was Eric Robinson, a Belfast architect who was believed to have the support of John McKeague, a prominent advocate of Northern Ireland independence. Support for this new party was also given by the Ulster Loyalist Central Coordinating Committee, an umbrella organization for a number of Protestant militant groups.

In the Irish Republic, a general election on 16 June 1977 returned Jack Lynch and his Fianna Fail Party to power, replacing the coalition Fine Gael–Labor government. The Fianna Fail won 84 seats (out of 144), Fine Gael 43, and Labor 17. Jack Lynch again became prime minister. His minister for health and welfare was Charles Haughey, who had been dismissed from the Cabinet in May 1970 over the arms-running affair. Lynch continued his campaign to obtain a united Ireland by nonviolent means and sought American help to pressure the British government into making a declaration of intent to withdraw from Northern Ireland.

On 30 August 1977 President Carter made a speech on the Northern Ireland problem that encouraged Prime Minister Lynch to press the issue. President Carter called for a peaceful solution and said that the U.S. would join with others to explore projects to stimulate employment once a settlement was reached. He said, "Violence cannot resolve Northern Ireland's problems, it only increases them and solves nothing." He asked all Americans to refrain from supporting, with financial or other aid, organizations whose involvement delayed the day when the people in Northern Ireland could work and live in harmony, free from fear. He added that the U.S. government would see how additional job-creating investment could be encouraged. Both Prime Minister Lynch and Prime Minister James Callaghan (who had replaced Harold Wilson) welcomed Carter's statement. Lynch and Callaghan met in London on 28 September; this was the first meeting of the prime ministers of the Irish Republic and Britain since that of Liam Cosgrave and Harold Wilson in March 1976. Lynch pushed his demand for a date for British withdrawal, and he did not return to Ireland entirely disappointed.

On 5 October Seamus Costello, founder-member and chairman of the Irish Republican Socialist Party, was shot dead in his car in Dublin. Both the Provos and the Officials denied responsibility, while Protestant extreme militants hinted, not very convincingly, that they might have been involved.

Also in 1977, the Official Sinn Fein Party made an addition to its title and called itself "The Sinn Fein—The Workers Party." Its president, Tomas MacGiolla, stated that this would indicate the left-wing traditions of Irish republicans.

In Northern Ireland on 15 December 1977, troops and police raided the premises of the Provisional Sinn Fein at Lurgan, where its printing plant was situated and where both the *Republican News* and *An Phoblacht* were printed. About 20,000 copies of the *Republican News* were seized. At the same time the Provisional Sinn Fein office on Falls Road, Belfast, was also raided; its telex machine, books, pamphlets, and other documents were seized and taken away. Roy Mason resisted considerable pressure from Unionist sources to proscribe the Provisional Sinn Fein, which was the barely disguised legal front for the terrorists. The army also would have liked it closed down and banned, but the RUC rather favored the idea of keeping open this source of information.

As the amount of money received by the IRA from America dwindled, especially after President Carter's speech, the Provisional IRA and the Irish National Liberation Army concentrated on funding by robberies in the Irish Republic. They still carried out the occasional armed robbery in Northern Ireland, but they were handicapped by the deployed security forces, road checks, and SAS activities. In the Irish Republic they were much less restricted and their activities worried the authorities considerably. Garda figures released at the end of September 1977 showed that from October 1975, when the terrorist organizations took to armed robbery in the Irish Republic in a big way, there had been 440 armed robberies, of which 262 were in the Dublin area and 62 were from banks. In the first nine months of 1977 there had been 215 armed robberies, as compared with 185 for the whole of 1976. The amount stolen in total was £1,388,825 (almost $3 million) of which £381,722 was from banks. The Garda claimed that 108 cases had been solved and £121,522 recovered.

A partial cause of the falling off of U.S. support were several convictions for smuggling arms or explosives from America to Ireland. In April 1977 a Belfast Provo leader, John Higgins, was imprisoned for trying to purchase 1,000 U.S. M-1 carbines and 60,000 rounds of ammunition from a British mercenary recruiter. During 1977 Gerry Adams, one of the senior Provo leaders, established an arms supply route from the Middle East by way of Cyprus, the shipping point often being Lebanon. This lessened the dependence of the Provo Council on its Dublin-based GHQ establishment and made it virtually independent of it. After the brief contact between Colonel Gaddafi of Libya and the Provos, which ended with the SS *Claudia* affair, this source of arms had dried up. However, the decline in the volume of arms received from America caused further efforts to reopen Middle East channels.

During the last three or four months of 1977, Soviet arms trickled into Ireland, the first real evidence being Soviet-made grenades that were used in attacks on British soldiers. These were the first commercially manufactured grenades possessed by the terrorists since the insurrection began. Previously, the only Soviet arms had been a few Kalishnikov AK-47 automatic rifles. On 2 December the Belgian police seized about five tons of illegal arms hidden in an electrical transformer at Antwerp docks. From Cyprus, consigned to Dublin, the shipment contained twenty-nine Kalishnikov AK-47s, twenty-nine French MAT submachine guns, twenty-nine machine pistols, two bren guns, mines, and assorted ammunition. It was obvious that the Provos were being armed from Middle East sources.

Generally speaking the first ten months of 1977 were much quieter as regards terrorist incidents, after which there was a sharp resurgence. The assassination targets were generally confined to soldiers, UDR and RUC members, and prison officers, but law officers were not excluded. On 4 March the assistant crown prosecutor, a Catholic, was shot dead in a Catholic-owned bar at Coalisland; and on the 24th, while lecturing at the Ulster Polytechnique, near Belfast, Lord MacDermott, a former chief justice of Northern Ireland, was one of the nine people injured by an explosion.

There was an increase in bombs detonated by remote control, some of which were extremely large, one containing 8,000 pounds of explosive. Generally, the explosive used was a compound of commercial materials. On 20 January the new Cooperative Store in Belfast, which had just been rebuilt after being destroyed by fire in May 1972 and was waiting to be officially reopened, was badly damaged by a large explosion. On 23 September three of Belfast's four main cinemas were damaged by explosions. There was a marked decrease in casualties, with only 112 people being killed and 944 injured due to terrorist activity. Terrorist incidents also diminished, there being only 1,081 shooting incidents and 336 explosions. However, there were 126 kneecappings, an increase over the previous year.

Sectarian killings and violence continued, and there were outbreaks of fighting between the Provos and the Officials. On 20 April a car bomb explosion at a Catholic funeral killed one person and injured several in the Ardoyne area in Belfast. Just previously, on the 10th, there had been a renewal of the feud between the Officials and the Provos, when a man and a boy were shot. This died down after a few days, only to flare up again on 27 July when four men were killed and others wounded.

Prison officers remained targets. On 22 June one was killed outside Crumlin Road Prison, and then another was shot dead in a bar at Ballymoney, Co Antrim. UDR members also remained targets: on 13 September a lieutenant was shot dead on his way to work, and on 9 October the first woman UDR member was killed, being shot in her caravan in Bandit Country. Despite this assassination program, September was the first month since June 1971 in which no civilian in Northern Ireland died as the result of terrorism.

In round figures the toll of death, injury, and destruction in Northern Ireland in 1977 was only about half that of the previous year. Also, owing to the improved capability of the RUC and to the British army's better surveillance techniques, many terrorist leaders had been captured, which considerably reduced the effectiveness of the Provos. The best capture of the year was that of Provo Chief of Staff Seamus Twomey on 3 December at Dun Laoghaire, in the Irish Republic. There was an air of triumphant and satisfied euphoria in Roy Mason's circle, described later somewhat aptly by Ian Paisley, who said, "He kept telling us the IRA were beat—but all the time they were winning."

16 The New Provisional IRA

*"We must gear ourselves towards long-term armed struggle. . . .
We recommend re-organisation and re-motivation; the building
of a new Irish Republican Army."*
—Seamus Twomey, Provisional IRA Chief of Staff,
in his staff report of December 1977

WITHOUT DOUBT THE Garda's best capture in several years was that of Seamus Twomey, the chief of staff of the Provisional IRA, in December 1977. Among other documents and papers found when his apartment was searched was a staff report, dated December. Outlining his suggestions for reorganizing the Provos and for introducing a new structure and new methods of operating, it was designed to counter informers as much as to improve effectiveness. Twomey had written that the three-day and seven-day detention orders being applied by the security forces in Northern Ireland were "breaking the Volunteers," and that

It is the Republican Army's fault for not indoctrinating volunteers with the psychological strength to resist interrogation. . . . Coupled with the factor which is contributing to our defeat, we are burdened with an inefficient infrastructure of commands, brigades, battalions and companies. This old system, which the Brits and the Branch are familiar with, has to be changed. . . .

We must gear ourselves towards long-term armed struggle based on putting unknown men and new recruits into a new structure, a cell system. The cells must be specialised into sniping cells, intelligence cells, executions, bombings and robberies, etc. They should operate as often as possible outside their own areas, both to confuse Brit intelligence, and to expand our operational areas. Disguises should be made use of in all operations. We must recommend re-organisation and re-motivation: the building of a new Irish Republican Army.

Twomey recommended a new rank, that of Education Officer, and suggested that anti-interrogation lectures be introduced. He wrote, "The ideal outcome should be that no volunteer should be charged unless caught redhanded." He also recommended greater roles for women and girls as military activists and as leaders in sections of civil administration, propaganda, and publicity. Twomey stated that the Provisional Sinn Fein should "be radicalised under IRA direction and agitate on social and economic issues which attacked the welfare of the people." He wanted the Provisional Sinn Fein to come under an IRA organizer at all levels and thought that the "Sinn Fein should be directed to infiltrate other organisations to win support from, and sympathy to, the movement."

The proposed reorganization had been the result of careful study of the several international terrorist groups that had been obtaining universal publicity for their exploits, such as the Palestinian ones, the Baader-Meinhof Gang, and the Basque ETA. In short, the plan was to abandon the old army structure and to change over to secret cells. Twomey recommended, "The cells should consist of four people. Existing battalion and company staffs should be dissolved over a period of months, with present brigades deciding who passes into the reorganised structure." The cells were to be secret in that members knew only each other and no other members of the IRA, with only the cell leader having vertical contact with a higher echelon.

Throughout Catholic areas there would also be "resident cells" that remained in one locality and were responsible for providing safe-houses, local information, and cover and assistance to "active cells" that would move into an area, commit some terrorist act, and then quickly move out again. This changeover had been discussed by the Provo Council during the latter part of 1977 and was put into effect during the first ten months of 1978.

After Twomey's arrest, Gerry Adams was appointed chief of staff in his place. He headed a Provo Council whose members were practically all from Northern Ireland. They realized that the old irregular, hit-or-miss warfare methods of terrorism were outdated, and they were impressed, as Twomey had been, with the spectacular exploits of current international terrorism. The Provo Council members included Ivor Bell, Martin McGuiness, and Brian Keenan. Rory O'Brady and David O'Connell now concentrated on political aspects and on running the Provisional Sinn Fein from Dublin. Gerry Adams was arrested in February 1978 in Northern Ireland but was released again in September on the technicality that being a member of the Sinn Fein did not automatically mean he was a member of the illegal IRA.

As a cover for the reorganization, the Provos kept terrorism at as high a tempo as possible. On 13 January 1978, for example, the Guildhall at Derry was severely damaged by an explosion. It had only recently been reopened after being gutted by fire in 1972. The Provos claimed responsibility and added that since the 1st of the month they had organized forty-six bombing and shooting incidents. On the 19th at a bus depot in Belfast, a Provo incendiary attack destroyed twenty-three buses and damaged others.

Early in January 1978 the Provos had received their first big shipment of arms from the Middle East, the fruits of new contacts with terrorist groups in that region. It included six U.S. M-60 machine guns,* Soviet automatic weapons, grenades, mines, and over 1,000 pounds of plastic, high-blast explosive, the latter being their first of this modern type. The M-60 was capable of firing over 550 rounds per minute; on 19 January in Derry, the Provos brought this prestige weapon into action for the first time and wounded three policemen with a burst of fire at an RUC Landrover. On the 29th, the anniversary of Bloody Sunday, the Provos put an M-60 on display to the press. On 1 February the Provos again used one of their M-60 machine guns against a British army patrol in Belfast, firing over forty rounds and killing one soldier. In the massive house-to-house search that followed the killing, the RUC discovered and seized a cache that included its first M-60 machine gun, which was put on display to the media. Later an M-60 machine gun was seized by the Garda in Co Donegal; and much later, in December 1978, three British soldiers were killed by fire from an M-60 machine gun in Crossmaglen.

The Provos achieved another "first" on 23 January 1978 at Forkill when they fired two twenty-five-pound mortar bombs from a hijacked truck over the roofs of houses into the military compound. Sleeping quarters and washrooms were damaged and eight British soldiers injured. Later that day three RUC men were injured while examining the abandoned truck, which was booby-trapped.

The Provos had yet another "first" on 17 February when they used their newly manufactured blast-incendiary devices to produce a fireball sixty feet in diameter that gutted the Le Mon House Restaurant at Comber, Co Down, killing twelve people and injuring thirty. In terms of the number of deaths in one incident, this was the worst so far. The blast-incendiary device was a crude napalm one that suddenly gave off great

*On 20 March 1978 the Pentagon stated that ninety-five M-60 machine guns had been stolen from the U.S. Army during the previous six years, and only forty-eight had been recovered. There was a ready black market for them in Mexico, which was also being tapped by Middle East terrorist groups.

heat on explosion; blazing fluid was violently ejected and stuck to people and objects while still fiercely burning. In this incident the blast-incendiary devices were in three cans containing a mixture of chemicals and petrol, which had been hung on a metal grill outside the restaurant and exploded by remote control. On the 20th a similar Provo attack on the bus depot at Derry destroyed eighteen buses and damaged another nineteen.

A macabre incident took place on 3 March in Belfast during the Queens University students' carnival "Rag Day" procession: gunmen posing as students, wearing carnival masks and fancy dress, killed a British soldier and a woman member of the Search Unit.

During the process of change from an army structure to terrorist secret cells, the Provos continued their blanket bombing of commercial premises during the first four months of 1978, exploding as many bombs and devices against as many buildings as possible. By May, however, terrorist incidents were waning to such an extent that, for the first time since 1972, the authorities stopped manning the checkpoints and road-blocks protecting the center of Derry. As new Provo cells were formed, trained, and came into action, they turned their attention to more carefully selected targets with the intention of disrupting communications as much as possible. The targets included bridges, vehicles of both the police and the army, government communication centers and other communication installations. It was a changeover from economic bombing to political bombing.

Against the background of the declining volume of terrorism, Secretary for Northern Ireland Roy Mason made an over-optimistic speech in which he alleged that although terrorists could still indulge in indiscriminate acts, public opinion had turned against them. He said the IRA was operating in isolation and was hated and shunned by the vast majority of people in Northern Ireland, who totally rejected their philosophy and tactics. This was undoubtedly true of the non-Catholic community, which was the majority, and may have been true to some degree in the Catholic community; but Mason was either deliberately ignoring, overlooking, or minimizing too naively the grip of intimidation the IRA had on the people in the Catholic areas. He must have had some knowledge of the Twomey staff report, as he said that the IRA had regrouped and that a hardcore of callous activists were prepared to continue with violence; but he added there would be no amnesty and all those convicted would serve their sentences. Mason was not in favor of the reintroduction of capital punishment. He added that 1977 had been a good year for RUC recruiting, and that a seventh British resident unit would arrive in Northern Ireland for an eighteen-month tour of duty.

Meanwhile, the attitude of Prime Minister Lynch—as expressed in a Radio Telfis Eireann interview on 8 January—was worrying the non-Catholic element in Northern Ireland. He had openly called for the British government to make a declaration of eventual withdrawal from Northern Ireland. He said that Prime Minister Callaghan had given him "a firm understanding" in September 1977 that "unless there was power sharing, there would be no devolved government." That day, the 8th, Harry West, leader of the Official Unionist Party, stated he would withdraw from the talks on interim devolution until the British government had clarified its position on power sharing.

On 25 February the Vanguard Unionist Progressive Party was formally dissolved when its leader, William Craig, who was its sole Westminster MP, rejoined the Official Unionist Party, thus increasing this party's Westminster representation to seven MPs. On 19 April Prime Minister Callaghan said that the number of Westminster seats for Northern Ireland would be increased from twelve to seventeen as soon as legislation could be pushed through. Unionists everywhere were deeply concerned by the splintering of the once powerful and united Unionist Party. Talks between Craig and West had been in progress for sometime and this return to the fold was considered to be a hopeful sign of a reunification and powerful rejuvenation for Unionists.

On 2 May 1978 Amnesty International issued a report by one of its research missions that had been sent to Northern Ireland to investigate allegations of maltreatment of suspects by the security forces. The research mission had visited the province between 28 November and 6 December 1977 to examine seventy-eight cases of people who had been arrested; it interviewed representatives of organizations and individuals in Belfast, Derry, and Dungannon. The authorities gave it only limited cooperation. The report stated that the rights of suspects had been eroded and that the machinery for investigating complaints against the police was not adequate; and it made certain allegations against RUC detectives and a few against the British army, but almost completely exonerated the uniformed branch of the RUC. It recommended a public enquiry.

Roy Mason replied on 8 June, pointing out that as the Amnesty International team had not seen any official papers, its report could represent only incomplete evidence. He said the independent Police Complaints Board for Northern Ireland had been operating since 1 September 1977 and was able to send reports direct to the secretary for Northern Ireland. Later, on the 16th, Mason announced there would be a committee of enquiry headed by Judge Bennett, an English Crown Court judge.

There was a weariness in Britain of the Northern Ireland problem, which seemed to be never ending. A distinct feeling was beginning to be expressed more loudly that it would be better to pull out altogether and "let them fight it out among themselves." On 18 August the *Daily Mirror*, one of Britain's popular mass circulation newspapers, came out with the banner headline of "Ulster: Bring Home the Troops" and an editorial recommending this course. Commissioned by the RTE and published in September, a Gallup Poll taken in England, Scotland, and Wales showed that fifty-five percent were in favor of a British withdrawal from Northern Ireland, and that only twenty-eight percent thought that British troops should remain until a political settlement was reached.

Meanwhile, the results of a sample poll taken in the Irish Republic were given on BBC TV on 8 May. They indicated that over forty percent wanted the British government to announce a date for its withdrawal from Northern Ireland; another thirty-six percent thought the British should withdraw without fixing a date; and only sixteen percent thought the withdrawal of British troops would not be helpful. Just over half the sample poll said that a unified Ireland was the best long-term solution, while thirty percent were in favor of a form of federation. Strangely, about seventy percent wanted a referendum in Northern Ireland itself — which, had they thought for a moment, would have produced a Unionist answer.

The Fine Gael Party came up with another idea at its annual conference on 22 May 1978. Its leader, Garret Fitzgerald, proposed a scheme for a federation or a confederation of Northern Ireland with the Irish Republic; resources on both sides of the border could be pooled in sectors where both could gain by such common action.

On 8 May the Republican Publicity Bureau in Dublin issued a long statement from the Provisional IRA leadership, saying that it would continue its campaign of violence. It stated, "We are determined to carry on the fight until our demands are met, even if it takes another ten years." It said there was no point in appealing for peace to the British government, the SDLP, or the Northern Ireland peace movement, but that it could come only from the republican movement, which "had the weapons to win a war of destruction. This message of war is vital to the eventual achievement of peace."

There seemed to be a belief in British military circles in Northern Ireland that even though the Catholic communities would not allow the RUC to patrol the streets in their areas, they would, or could, be persuaded to accept smartly uniformed British military policemen instead as a trusted symbol of law and order. This belief probably stemmed from the first months of the British military presence in the province when, fearing dire retribution from the RUC and the B-Specials, the Catholic population welcomed British soldiers with open arms and cups of tea. British military policemen manned checkpoints on the streets and carried out other duties, such as dealing with arrested suspects, that normally would have been regarded as a civil police task. Their few attempts to patrol the streets like ordinary policemen had been disastrous—the IRA had seen to that—but the idea persisted. If there is one task harder than driving new ideas into set military minds, it is that of driving old ones out.

The strength of the British Royal Corps of Military Police in the province had been rapidly increased, and two regiments were specially formed, the first in 1972 to police the country areas and to help units operating in Derry and Co Armagh. The second was formed two years later to operate in Belfast and was stationed in Blairs Yard, in the Protestant Short Strand area on the edge of Protestant dockland, to police a small Catholic "enclave ghetto" where some 2,000 people lived. Emphasis was now decidedly on the supremacy of the RUC over the army, and so, disillusioned and disappointed, the concept was abandoned in January 1978. These two regiments of military policemen withdrew to the Belfast airport area near Aldergrove, where one was disbanded and the other reduced in strength.

The general impression gained in Britain was that the Irish Catholic Church was exerting none of its authority to help curb terrorism, and that some of the younger priests were openly in sympathy with the IRA and its path of violence. The example of Father Fell, arrested in England for being actively involved in IRA activity at the height of the Provo bombing campaign there, colored this view. On the other hand the Catholic community complained that the non-Catholic clergy in Northern Ireland were actively encouraging violence, and particularly pointed its finger at the Rev. Ian Paisley, alleging he made inflammatory speeches. So far only one member of the clergy of any denomination had in any way become a casualty to terrorism—that is, until 17 June 1978.

On that day an RUC vehicle was ambushed by Provos at Bessbrook in South Armagh; one policeman was killed and another kidnapped. In retaliation, Protestants kidnapped a Catholic priest, Father Hugh Murphy, and held him hostage for the safe return of the missing policeman. This could have been the flash point of an outbreak of bitter sectarian warfare, but it was averted when the priest was released some twelve hours later. The body of the missing RUC man was found the following day; later, the Provos claimed they had executed him after interrogation, but a postmortem examination showed that he had died almost immediately from wounds received in the ambush. At the time the UFF was blamed for kidnapping the priest, but eventually (in April 1980) two RUC policemen were convicted of the offense.

Meanwhile the SAS was experimenting with an extension of its undercover surveillance role—the stakeout. When information was received that terrorists were about to carry out an exploit, such as positioning a bomb, a bank robbery, or a revenge killing, SAS soldiers would lie in a hideout, watching and waiting for the terrorists to appear, and then engage them in a shoot-out. On 9 March Roy Mason had said at Westminster that there were no restrictions on the use of SAS men apart from the fact they must not act beyond the law.

One of the first SAS stakeouts occurred on 21 June 1978 when information was received that the Provos intended to launch a bomb attack on the premises of the post office's Ballysillan transport workshop and engineering center in north Belfast. SAS men shot and killed three Provos in the act of placing an explosive device, but in the shooting an innocent passerby was also killed.

The next SAS stakeout that resulted in a fatality was on 11 July 1978 at Dunley, Co Antrim, when sixteen-year-old John Boyle was killed at night by two SAS soldiers as he was approaching an arms cache in a disused graveyard. The boy had discovered the cache the previous day and passed on the information to the RUC, who expected two known terrorists to approach the cache that night to pick up the arms. Out of curiosity, the boy again visited the cache in darkness, not knowing of the presence of the SAS men, who said they thought the figure they saw was that of a terrorist about to fire at them. The British army admitted the boy was an innocent victim.

Another SAS stakeout fatality occurred in the evening darkness of 30 September in Co Tyrone when James Taylor and two companions were returning from a wild fowl shoot to their car, which they had left in a narrow deserted lane. The SAS men said they thought they were in a terrorist situation facing men with guns, and Taylor was shot and killed. The British army admitted he was an innocent victim, but excused its soldiers as the three hunters were carrying shotguns.

The impact of SAS activities on the Provisional IRA can be judged from an interview with an unidentified member of the Provo Council that was printed in the *Republican News* on the 14th of the previous month. He said, "The fact of the matter is that it is increasingly difficult to operate with impunity, especially in the Belfast area, which is thick with undercover British operatives. There are soldiers staked out in hiding places throughout the city and the suburbs. This makes operations much more difficult than was thought conceivable a few years ago." This, of course, referred not only to the SAS but also to the soldiers in each unit trained in SAS-type surveillance tactics. Many of these soldiers moved about in civilian vehicles devoid of any military markings or identifying insignia. On 19 September the Provos issued a warning that they considered all unmarked cars leaving or entering military premises to be legitimate targets. This caused some alarm, as wives of British military personnel used their own private cars to take their children to school, for shopping, and for social purposes.

Considerable controversy was aroused by the SAS killings, especially that of the boy, Boyle. The SDLP in particular complained that the SAS men were too trigger-happy, and roused the Catholic community to protest against this "shoot to kill" policy. Roy Mason gave in to public pressure; the two SAS men were arraigned before a Belfast court in June 1979 and charged with Boyle's murder. On the first day of the hearing, in an effort to protect the SAS men's identity and so avoid retribution by Provo execution squads, the two accused soldiers appeared in the dock with several other soldiers, none of whom spoke in answer to requests for identification, or to plead to the charge. The next day, the two accused were referred to only as "Defendant A" and "Defendant B." Legal protests were made that the British army was placing itself above the law, and Roy Mason had to step in to order that the SAS men openly identify themselves and answer the charges in the normal manner. They were named as Sgt. Alan Bohun and Cpl. Ronald Temperley.

During the course of the trial, differences between the army and the RUC were revealed. The RUC had refused to give full details of the illegal arms cache to the army, offering only to brief the two SAS men; in a huff, the army had refused to allow this. The case against both defendants was dismissed, the court saying that the two SAS men had thought their lives were in danger and so had shot in self-defense.

Apprehension and dislike of the SAS caused many smears and allegations of misconduct to be made against its soldiers. For example, on 18 March 1979 allegations were made by a part-time police surgeon that SAS men had raped his wife during a house search a few days previously, and that the SAS soldiers concerned had been quickly sent out of Northern Ireland. The previous week the same surgeon had made allegations of RUC brutality against IRA suspects. The commander of the SAS Regiment, Colonel B. Franks, stated that no SAS soldiers were in Belfast on the relevant date.

In June 1977 the Geneva Convention on the Human Laws of War

recognized guerrillas as legitimate combatants even if they were in civilian clothes, provided their weapons were carried openly before and after any attack. Under these new rules a guerrilla was entitled to follow a daytime occupation and become a gunman by night, and if captured could claim Geneva prisoner of war status and receive the same treatment as any conventional soldier captured in battle. Britain had abstained from voting at Geneva on this particular issue, and the Irish government had given it no support.

If this Geneva ruling had been applied to the IRA in Northern Ireland, all prisoners would automatically have become prisoners of war entitled to be treated as such under the Geneva rules; and when hostilities ended, all would be released regardless of any sentences passed on any of them for criminal terrorist acts. The snag was that any such guerrilla fighter had to be recognized by the United Nations as belonging to a legitimate national liberation army, and the Provisional IRA had not yet been recognized as such by the U.N. Therefore this clause did not apply to Northern Ireland, although republican lawyers advised the IRA that it had a case. The Provos had begun to seek that necessary U.N. recognition; one of their methods was to make frequent television appearances with their arms and in uniform to advertise their political cause and demonstrate their military capability.

When Secretary for Northern Ireland Merlyn Rees phased out the special category status for IRA prisoners in 1975, it was laid down that men convicted of terrorist crimes on or after 1 March 1976 would be treated as ordinary prisoners. One of the first cases was Keirnan Nugent, who was sentenced to a term of imprisonment in September 1976 for hijacking a vehicle on 12 March. Nugent had transgressed the IRA code by recognizing the court and pleading guilty. However, he regained Provo favor by refusing to wear prison clothes. In March 1978 he began the "dirty strike," wherein prisoners seeking political status refused to use the lavatories and instead befouled their own cells.

Prisoners who did this were all put into a special section of Maze Prison, known as "H Block" because of its configuration. Protesting prisoners who refused to wear prison clothing were simply given one blanket and, in the jargon of the Catholic community, were said to be "on the blanket." Owing to their filthy state, the cells had to be steam-hosed frequently. Many demonstrations and protests were organized to try to obtain political status for men in H Block who were "on the blanket." In August 1978 Archbishop O'Fiaich, who had succeeded Cardinal Conway as the Catholic Primate of All Ireland and who openly held republican sympathies, was allowed to visit H Block. He criticized the authorities, saying that conditions there were inhuman.

Certainly 1978 had been a year of immense improvement from the point of view of the security forces, and Roy Mason stood up again to boast about it. He said at Westminster on 20 February 1979 that only 81 people had been killed in Northern Ireland in 1978 due to terrorist activity, and that shooting incidents had been reduced to 843, but did admit that 455 explosions had been recorded, which was about 90 more than the previous year. He also had to admit that, from 1969 up until 31 December 1978, 117 members of the RUC and the RUC Reserve had been killed and 3,251 injured. His overall figures, however, showed a sharp decline in terrorist activity, and he gave the impression that the security forces were containing and slowly defeating terrorism in the province. If he believed this, he was closing his eyes to reality. The new Provisional IRA was at work, and a large proportion of the recorded incidents had occurred during the last two months of 1978.

The reorganized Provisional IRA had begun its winter offensive of 14 November 1978, when bombs exploded in seven cities and towns in the province. More explosions occurred during the ensuing days; on the 16th, for example, one device with an estimated 1,700 pounds of explosive packed into it exploded in Lisburn and caused damage estimated to be about £12 million. Prison officers became assassination targets for the new Provo execution cells, and on 27 November the deputy governor of Maze Prison was shot dead on his own doorstep. On the 13th of the following month, the wives of three prison officers were injured by letter bombs.

The Provos' winter offensive gained momentum and was extended to England. On 17 December there were a number of explosions and exploding incendiary devices in Bristol, Coventry, Liverpool, Manchester, and Southampton, in which several people were injured. The following day there were more explosions and fires in English cities; in London two car bombs exploded. Others were detected and defused in time. This was the first Provo bombing in England for almost two years—in fact, since January 1977, when twelve bombs, mainly incendiary devices, had exploded in the center of London. There had been a small rash of eight explosions in British military installations in Germany in August 1978, for which the INLA, having links with terrorist groups on the Continent, was blamed. Almost reluctantly, the Provos observed an unofficial Christmas cease-fire from 24–26 December, after which they recommenced terrorist activity with vigor.

If Roy Mason was not expecting the Provos' winter offensive, the security forces in Northern Ireland were. This was confirmed in November 1978 when a copy of a British Ministry of Defense army intelligence report, headed "Northern Ireland: Terrorist Trends," was obtained by the Provos and published in full in their *Republican News*. It said, "We can expect to see an increasing professionalism and a greater exploitation of modern technology for terrorist purposes," and went on to give an assessment of the Provisional IRA's and INLA's state of training, quality of leadership, new organization of secret cells, weapons, arms sources, and finances; and it admitted that information about terrorist plans was suddenly drying up.

Meanwhile the Community of Peace People had run into criticism and controversy and was being accused of having republican sympathies. During the first week in November, it began campaigning against the renewal (after its statutory five-year life) of the Northern Ireland (Emergency Provisions) Act of 1973, which authorized the Diplock Courts that sat without a jury, and allowed the RUC to hold suspects in custody for up to seven days. Mairead Corrigan went to London to lobby British MPs, emphasizing the human rights aspect. On 18 January 1979 the European Court of Human Rights in Strasbourg, to which the British government had been taken by the Irish government in 1971 for its "deep interrogation" practices, ruled that the incidents complained of "did not constitute torture, but did amount to inhuman and degrading treatment."

The next blow against the RUC came on 16 March 1979 with the publication of the Bennett Report by the Committee of Enquiry into Police Procedure and Practice in Northern Ireland. It noted there was "abundant evidence of a co-ordinated and extensive campaign to discredit the police." The main finding of the report was that there was a "class of cases where injuries recorded in the medical evidence were not self-inflicted, but sustained during detention." The report made a number of recommendations: one was that a prisoner should have the right of access to a lawyer after forty-eight hours in custody, and another controversial one was that closed-circuit television should be used when prisoners were interrogated. Roy Mason stated that the government accepted the recommendations of the Bennett Report.

One other matter that had been deeply embarrassing the British government for sometime was that of British soldiers deserting from Northern Ireland and being granted refuge in Sweden. The first half-dozen British deserters had fled to Sweden in 1972, and another twenty followed in 1973. They all sought political asylum, but instead the Swedish government granted them residential permits on humanitarian grounds. Subsequently the British government unsuccessfully prosecuted a number of declared pacifists for attempting to incite British soldiers to desert rather than be sent to Northern Ireland, and for telling them how to desert and how to reach Sweden. Most of the British deserters trickled back home shamefacedly over the years to punishment and obscurity.

On 30 March 1979 MP Airey Neave, the Tory opposition spokesman for Northern Ireland, was killed by a car bomb while driving his car up the ramp from the underground garage at Westminster. The INLA claimed responsibility and its unnamed chief of staff said that a timing device had been affixed to Neave's car the previous evening when it was parked on the street outside his London apartment. The reason given for the assassination was that Neave had consistently advocated tougher measures against the IRA and greater use of the SAS in Northern Ireland.

The car bomb was of the dual trigger, mercury-tilt type, used for the first time in England. It had been used twice before in Northern Ireland, once against a UDR member and once against a prison officer. This type of car bomb had been used by the Basque ETA, the Italian Red Brigades, and by Middle East terrorist groups; the Dublin-based INLA had developed contacts with these groups and obtained the technology from them. About the size of a small cassette tape recorder, the device had been attached under the car beneath the driver's seat with a couple of magnets. The explosive charge was about one pound in weight. A timing device about the size of a wristwatch primed the bomb. Mercury would flow down a tube to complete the circuit and detonate the explosive matter if the car braked too hard, accelerated too hard or went up a slope such as the garage ramp at Westminster. The British army intelligence report was correct in its assessment that the terrorists would exploit modern technology.

17 The Tenth Year

*"The more British soldiers who go back home in coffins
the sooner it will be over."*
—Spokesman for Noraid, New York, 6 August 1979

I N THE GENERAL election in Britain on 3 May 1979 the
Conservative Party won a clear majority of forty-four
seats at Westminster and so formed a government. Mrs.
Margaret Thatcher became the first female prime minister in British history. In Northern Ireland the Unionists retained ten Westminster seats;
the other two were held by Gerry Fitt of the SDLP and an independent.

MP Humphrey Atkins was appointed secretary for Northern Ireland,
and Roy Mason thankfully bowed out of a job for which he had no liking
at all and in which he appeared consistently to be simply playing for time.
Mason had been under the illusion, or at least gave that impression, that
the IRA terrorists were being defeated; he seemed genuinely surprised by
the increasing volume of terrorism during the first four months of the
year. In the Queen's Speech (that is, the policy statement of the new government) it was stated that the Tory aim was "to restore to the people of
Northern Ireland more control over their own affairs." Atkins, new to
the Northern Ireland situation, said he was going to spend some time
consulting personalities and discussing problems.

Jack Lynch was quick off the mark and on 10 May visited Mrs. Thatcher in London. He came away disappointed, as it is believed the British
prime minister had firmly told him that Northern Ireland was to remain
part of the United Kingdom, and that she was not interested in an "Irish
Dimension."

During 1979 a number of terrorist exploits occurred on the continent
of Europe for which it was suspected the Irish National Liberation Army
was responsible, with the help of local terrorist cells. The INLA was proscribed in both Britain and Northern Ireland. Many Irish building
workers, some with IRA and terrorist police records, were attracted to
work on the Continent because of the high wages offered and the decline
in this type of work in Britain.

One of the first of such exploits took place on 22 March at the Hague,
in Holland. British Ambassador Sir Richard Sykes and a Dutch employee

were killed by automatic fire. On the same day in Belgium, a banker was shot and killed—mistaken, it is thought, for the British ambassador to NATO. The next exploit, on 25 June at Casteau, Belgium, was an unsuccessful assassination attempt made on U.S. Gen. Alexander Haig, the NATO Supreme Commander. A land-mine placed in a culvert was detonated by remote control a fraction of a second after his car had passed over it. It was almost a carbon copy of the murder of the British Ambassador near Dublin in 1976. It was thought that the INLA mistook General Haig for a British general. On 6 July an explosion wrecked the British consulate at Antwerp, Belgium; and on the 10th there were two explosions at a British barracks at Dortmund, Germany. On 28 August there was an explosion in the center of Brussels under an open-air platform upon which a British army band was scheduled to give a performance. Some sixteen people were injured. The band was late in arriving, so many of its members escaped death or injury. The INLA claimed responsibility for all these incidents.

Since the first appearance of British troops on 12 August 1969 on the streets of Derry, the days, weeks, months, and years had relentlessly gone by against a background of continuing terrorism. One of the most notorious crimes of the century occurred on 27 August 1979. It was the murder of Lord Mountbatten, a member of the British royal family who had a distinguished naval and military career, especially in World War II, and who had been the last British viceroy of India. As he did fairly frequently, he and his family had been visiting a small castle he owned at Mullaghmore, Co Donegal. An explosive device was affixed to the small fishing boat he often used. Lord Mountbatten and his party boarded it, and when it was moving out of the small harbor into Mullaghmore Bay, it was exploded by remote control. Lord Mountbatten, his grandson, Nicholas Knatchbull, and the local boat hand, Paul Maxwell, were killed, and others seriously injured.

Two men, Thomas MacMahon and Francis McGirl, had been arrested two hours before the explosion occurred, at the small town of Granard, Co Longford, some fifty miles distant from Mullaghmore, by the Garda, who suspected the vehicle they were using was stolen. They were both eventually charged with being accomplices in the Mountbatten murder and appeared before the Special Criminal Court in Dublin in November. MacMahon was convicted on technical evidence and sentenced to imprisonment, but McGirl was acquitted. On 2 December two UDA men were brought before the same court, accused of attempting to murder McGirl. No organization claimed responsibility for the Mountbatten murder.

Another major terrorist exploit occurred on the same day, 27 August, at Warren Point, Co Down, a small, almost disused port that many years before had been a direct steamer link with America, and through which thousands of the ancestors of today's Irish Americans must have passed. Nearby is a two-mile stretch of canal waterway that demarcates the boundary; the area is referred to locally as "Narrow Water" or the "Two-Mile." On both sides, it was rarely patrolled by either the Irish or Northern Ireland security forces. On this day, a British army convoy consisting of a Landrover and two trucks carrying soldiers of the Parachute Regiment moved along the roadway by the canal, when a large bomb, hidden in a stationary cart loaded with hay, exploded, blasting the last truck as it passed, killing six soldiers and wounding two others. Emergency procedures were put into operation and within minutes the British army "Quick Reaction Squad" arrived by helicopter.

As the casualties were being dealt with, another explosion occurred from a bomb hidden in a small nearby stone gatehouse, causing more casualties and slightly damaging the helicopter, which managed to take off with wounded men on board. Both bombs had been pre-positioned by the Provos, who then retired back across the canal into the Irish Republic and exploded them by remote control. Eighteen British soldiers were killed in this incident, including the commanding officer, bring their total number of dead for the ten years in Northern Ireland up to 319. Responsibility was claimed by the South Armagh Battalion of the Mid-Ulster Brigade.

Provo protection rackets and other forms of extortion practiced on the Catholic community were fairly well known, but for some considerable time there had been allegations that the Provos were extracting money from the Northern Ireland Housing Executive, which had been formed in 1971 to assume responsibility for all houses and apartments owned by the (then) sixty-one local councils and for their building programs. It was also alleged that the British Labor government had known of this and had allowed it to continue as part of its deal with the Provos to secure the cease-fire in May 1974.

A committee of enquiry was set up, and on 5 July 1979 the Rowland Report was published on this matter. It stated there was no evidence of collusion by the British government for a cease-fire with the Provisional IRA in 1974, but that the loss of $1,600,000 was the result of bad planning. It stated that the Provos had imposed protection rackets on the contractors and their employees, and that money was diverted in this way. It quoted one contractor who had to pay one million dollars to "an illegal organization in the south," and said that some workers had been forced to hand over a proportion of their wages. The Rowland Report stated that the Northern Ireland government knew this was happening but had taken no action. On 5 October 1979 it was stated that debts owed to the Northern Ireland Housing Executive for withheld rent, rates, and heating charges amounted to over $18 million.

Money was still being sent from America to the IRA despite open disapproval and condemnation by President Carter and several prominent Irish Americans. There were two main U.S. fund-raising organizations: the Irish National Caucus, which had over fifty chapters across the U.S. and was run by Father Sean McManus; and the Irish Northern Aid Committee (Noraid) run by Michael Flannery. Both the caucus and Noraid supported the Provisional IRA, but there were periodic differences between the two organizations.

The Irish National Caucus was not licensed to send money out of America but for years had used the *"Queen Elizabeth II* run," sending people over to Ireland on that passenger ship, each with $5,000, the maximum a person was then legally allowed to take out from the U.S. in cash. Perhaps much more was smuggled out by other means on the same ship. Being registered as a charity, Noraid could and did send money openly for the dependents of IRA volunteers; but there were suspicions that a large proportion of it went to the Provos and was used to buy weapons.

On 6 August 1979, in an interview printed in the *Herald Tribune*, a spokesman for Noraid stated that his organization did not provide funds for the IRA to buy weapons, but that funds raised for IRA dependents freed the IRA soldiers from financial worries, and made them better fighters. He also added, "The more British soldiers who go back home in coffins the sooner it will be over." After the Mountbatten murder, U.S. funds for the IRA declined significantly.

The Irish embassy in Washington stated that Irish fund-raising in the U.S. was providing twenty-five percent of the money the Provisional IRA expended on weapons. The intelligence services of both the Irish Republic and Britain put the yearly cost of IRA purchases of arms from all sources at about two million dollars. When Prime Minister Lynch visited America in November 1979, he openly criticized Americans who gave financial support that ended up in the hands of Irish terrorists. He estimated that financial aid from America to the IRA exceeded $350,000 annually.

On his release in August 1979 from Maze Prison, Keirnan Nugent, the Provo prisoner who started the "dirty strike" in H Block, went to the U.S. on a fund-raising tour, intending to visit sixteen cities; but he was immediately arrested in New York for entering the country without a valid visa. Both Irish American fund-raising groups admitted that British diplomatic pressure was a great handicap. Later, when British Prime Minister Thatcher visited President Carter in December, David O'Connell, the Provisional Sinn Fein leader, also slipped into America to speak at Irish American gatherings against Thatcher's policy for Northern Ireland. This caused considerable embarrassment to the American administration, as O'Connell had no valid visa but had somehow gained entry easily.

As funds from the U.S. gradually decreased, the IRA had to look elsewhere for money. It obtained much of it by a series of bank, post office, and other robberies, mainly in the Irish Republic. Armed robberies were now comparatively rare in Northern Ireland owing to the extensive security surveillance and operations, and also because of the shadow of SAS stakeouts. On 18 August the president of the Association of Garda Inspectors and Sergeants, meeting in Dublin, called for the expulsion of gunmen from the Irish Republic, which he said would be a "better effective measure" than extradition, as extradition could be fought in the courts and dragged on almost indefinitely. He pointed out that gunmen had stolen six million dollars in four years, and that only five percent of the money had been recovered.

To bank and post office robberies was added kidnapping for ransom. In at least three instances during 1979, members of families of bank managers were kidnapped for this purpose. One was the wife of the manager of a bank in Drogheda, who was ransomed for $12,000. The Garda complained of initial hesitation in reporting such cases, and that banks had instructed their local managers to report the circumstances to their own head offices, which in turn informed the Garda. In Limerick on 5 August a man suspected of giving information to the Garda about a bank robbery had tar poured over him. In Northern Ireland on the 28th November, in Co Tyrone, a bank manager handed over a large sum of money, having been hoaxed that his wife had been kidnapped.

A new dimension was added to IRA fund-raising, or so it was suspected: that of drug trafficking. On 25 August 1979 the Garda in the Irish Republic seized a truck loaded with drugs, mainly cannabis, valued at over two million dollars on the street market, which had been smuggled into the country from Ecuador. The Garda arrested three men, but a fourth escaped. The arrested leader was James McCann, a Provo who had escaped from Crumlin Road Prison in 1971, and since had successfully and successively resisted extradition while in Canada and France. The drugs were to be sold on the Continent and the money used to buy weapons. This was the first known occasion the Provos had dabbled in drug trafficking. While in detention, McCann was attacked by other Provo prisoners, as it was alleged he had gone independent in his fund-raising and was not handing over the proceeds of his crimes to the Provisional IRA.

At the end of 1979 the Provos were estimated by the RUC to possess about 5,000 weapons of various sorts, including radio-controlled bombs and large mortars, although their strength was not much above 500, and that of the INLA only between 40 and 50. The Provos were making and bringing into action more frequently their "Mark Ten Mortar," which weighed about 100 pounds and fired a 40-pound bomb up to a distance of about 400 yards. Basically it was a commercial metal gas cylinder fired electronically by remote control and was mainly used in the Bandit Country of South Armagh.

The bulk of the IRA arms was now believed to come from European sources, and some also from the Middle East, with a trickle still arriving from America. One attempt to ship in almost a million dollars' worth of American arms, hidden in sealed containers, was foiled on 2 November, when police seized the shipment in a ship in Dublin docks. There were 156 assorted weapons, including two M-60 machine guns, fourteen armalite rifles, and some 30,000 rounds of ammunition, some armor-piercing. Information had been passed to the Garda, and the police watched the ship for two days before pouncing, but no one showed up to collect the arms. The ship, still unnamed, was allowed to sail away. This incident caused some embarrassment to the U.S. administration as it occurred only a few days before Prime Minister Lynch was due to visit President Carter.

The RUC ordered from America 6,000 magnum .357 revolvers and 500 M-1 .233 rifles, regarded as being the best weapons with which to combat terrorism. About 3,000 magnum revolvers had already been delivered to the RUC when the transaction was highlighted by extremists in the Irish American organizations. Feeling against this deal was aroused until, on 3 August, the matter was raised in Congress by Mario Biaggi. The U.S. State Department announced it would review this particular arms sale. No further arms reached the RUC from America. This embittered the non-Catholic community in Northern Ireland, which pointed out that while American arms were smuggled in quantity into Ireland for use by terrorists, a purchase of arms for a legally and properly constituted police force was banned. It accused the U.S. administration of applying double standards.

In a speech at Westminster on 3 July, Humphrey Atkins confirmed much of what had been contained in the British Ministry of Defense intelligence document, "Northern Ireland: Terrorist Trends," that had been leaked to the media. He said British security forces in Northern Ireland were now facing a more professional enemy, one "organised on a system of self-contained, close-knit cells which make it difficult to gather information." He also confirmed that although terrorism had diminished during the previous two years, "during that period the Provisional IRA were re-grouping, re-training, re-equipping themselves, and re-thinking their future tactics." He added that interrogation was a vital weapon in the armory of the security forces.

The Provos in Northern Ireland, operating mostly in small cells, had given up attending mass anniversary rallies, and all low-level Provo contact with the press was absolutely forbidden. The Provo leadership was leaning farther to the left politically, and so its contact with the INLA increased. In an interview with *Time* Magazine,* Provo Chief of Staff Gerry Adams said that the IRA was not Marxist, as was usually alleged, but that "the working class majority from Ulster, Protestants and Catholics, don't simply want to be absorbed into a decadent state. The Republic has got severe economic problems, high unemployment and all the ills of an unjust society whose wealth is controlled by a very small group. Obviously that Government has got to come down, and they know it." Adams also added, "There have never been close links between the Republican movement and the Palestine Liberation Organization, the Basques, or any other revolutionary group." But he did not say there had been none at all.

The year of 1979 was a bad one for terrorist activity in Northern Ireland. A few incidents can be mentioned to give an idea of the trends. On 5 April two British soldiers were shot dead in Belfast by a female Provo sniper who was arrested and charged with their murders; this indicated that women were playing an active role in the IRA. Loyalists were also involved in terrorism; on 4 July in Belfast, there were twenty-five bomb alerts, twenty-three of which were deliberate hoaxes to disrupt life in the city. The reason given was to highlight allegations that non-Catholic prisoners in Maze Prison were being brutalized and ill-treated by detectives during questioning.

On 9 September Gerry Adams spoke through the *Republican News* threatening "many more blows against prestige targets." He had already said, "We are opposed to big business, to multi-nationals and to the maintenance of a privileged class. We are opposed to all forms, and all manifestations, of imperialism and capitalism."

Terrorist attention was directed toward prison officers. On 19 September an assistant prison governor was shot dead, the gunman firing

*Of 19 November 1979

from a car. He was the sixteenth prison officer to be killed in Northern Ireland since special category status had been withdrawn from political prisoners. On 17 December another prison officer was killed. On 7 October the South Armagh Action Force, which had been reactivated, had killed a non-Catholic and threatened counteraction in a local sectarian murder campaign that was in progress in Bandit Country.

On 8 October in Belfast, an SAS man had been killed and another wounded. They were in plain clothes in an unmarked car. Provo snipers in a house overlooking the entrance to an army camp had waited for eight hours for them to emerge. On 26 November there was a province-wide spate of bombing in which twenty explosions injured thirteen people. This was a protest against a conference suggested by Humphrey Atkins. On 16 December, five British soldiers were killed (the first since the Warren Point incident in August), four in Dungannon when a land-mine exploded under their Landrover; and the fifth in an explosion in a derelict farmhouse in the village of Tullydonnel, in Bandit Country. Due to mistaken identity, two more British soldiers on an ambush patrol were killed by their comrades on the last day of the year, also in Tullydonnel.

On 17 December a letter bomb exploded in the post office sorting office at Dover, England. This was the first of about twelve, all posted from Belgium to personalities in England. Only two exploded, the others being detected and defused in time. The British Special Branch made a number of arrests and this activity died away. On the other side of the fence, the Provos admitted that during the ten year period they had lost 118 men killed.*

The Provos still carried out punishments of their own members and members of the public, ranging from execution and kneecapping to dropping concrete blocks on hands or feet. On 2 September a woman who had handed a gun to a man who robbed a Catholic social club was beaten up and shot in both forearms and one ankle. On 15 November a sixteen-year-old boy in Andersonstown had both his arms and legs shattered by bullets for "anti-social behavior after repeated warnings"; what exactly his offense had been was not specified. After many years of dealing with kneecap wounds, surgeons were in many cases able to restore victims almost to normality. Accordingly, IRA punishment squads began to shoot their victims in the ankle or elbow instead of the kneecap.

During 1979 Secretary for Northern Ireland Humphrey Atkins had come down heavily on the side of the RUC; the army was no longer allowed to search houses without RUC consent. The British army had not

*Sunday Press, 16 December 1979

taken too kindly to being pushed aside to take second place in the security field. The army noted that new, modern equipment was being given to the RUC, and the GOC had mentioned on several occasions that he was not happy at seeing policemen doing jobs that he called "soldier's work," such as patrolling the streets in armored vehicles and manning roadblocks. Vested interest seemed to be at stake, and the army seemed to be in no hurry to return to barracks.

After the Warren Point incident, senior army officers in conference complained they were fighting with one hand tied behind their backs and urged that more vigorous measures be taken against terrorists. They favored the reintroduction of internment without trial, complaining that too much time had to be spent watching known terrorists; but this was not politically acceptable at Westminster. The army versus the RUC controversy was erupting again.

Under Chief Constable Newman, the RUC had developed into an efficient and well equipped police force and had gained considerable confidence. On 31 August it was announced that its strength, then given as 5,797 men and 639 women, was to be increased by another 1,000 to enable it to cope with the greater work load it was taking on. The RUC Reserve was quoted as having 3,839 men and 702 women. The RUC, which now had a budget of about $200 million annually, still contained only about nine percent Catholics, most of whom were in senior ranks. It was also announced that Sir Kenneth Newman was to be promoted to the rank of inspector of constabulary and was to take up the appointment of commandant of the British Police Staff College in January 1980. Newman had served in the RUC for six years, three of them as deputy chief constable. His greatest contribution to the RUC, apart from revitalizing it, probably was to assert its supremacy over the military in Northern Ireland; while his failure, if indeed it was a failure, was that he had not been able to break down completely the barrier of suspicion between the RUC and the Catholic community. Newman was succeeded by his deputy, Jack Hermon, who had served for thirty years in the RUC.

The British army complained of shortage of resources—in spite of some modern equipment for its counterinsurgency role that included the Anglo-French Lynx helicopter which could carry eight soldiers at 160 mph and climb to 1,200 feet within a minute—muddled priorities, and the lack of a firm plan to fight terrorism socially and economically. The RUC continued to press for freedom from political and military control, and criticized the army, especially the SAS stakeout "shoot to kill" policy. At the annual republican parade in Belfast on 12 August, a few masked men in IRA garb and carrying guns were briefly displayed; with them was an unmasked woman wearing a black IRA beret, who posed for press photographers, clutching a huge .45 revolver in her small hand. The RUC men monitoring the procession made no arrests despite this illegal public IRA demonstration, for which they were criticized by the army as well as by the non-Catholic population. Later the woman was identified, arrested, and charged.

It had become obvious that some sort of "supremo" should be appointed to command both the army and the RUC, so as to enforce cooperation between them. The army had hoped for a senior general who might be expected to sympathize with the military view, while the RUC hoped for some extremely senior police officer who might be sympathetic to their view. On 7 October Sir Maurice Oldfield, the former head of the British MI-6 (Intelligence), a very shadowy figure who had retired the previous year, was appointed "Co-ordinator of Security in Northern Ireland." His job was obviously to persuade the army and the police to work together harmoniously, and perhaps also to improve and coordinate intelligence gathering and assessment, but he was not given any executive powers. Oldfield took up residence in Stormont Assembly building, and little has been heard of him since.

One of the biggest problems facing the British security forces in Northern Ireland was the open border across which terrorists could move freely to sanctuary in the Irish Republic. The RUC complained that there were at least one hundred men in the Irish Republic who were wanted for murder and terrorist offenses committed in the province, but that Irish courts would not allow any of them to be extradited. On 12 July 1979 the RUC stated that the legal machinery set up in 1976 to enable terrorists to be tried in either Northern Ireland, Britain, or the Irish Republic had been used only once—in the case of Captain Nairac. There was no single example of a terrorist being tried in the Irish Republic for an offense committed in Northern Ireland. On 1 September the RUC stated that it had made seventy-five applications for the extradition of suspects but all had been rejected. The Irish courts naturally demanded evidence, but whatever was produced always seemed insufficient.

Meanwhile the rest of the world was fascinated and frightened by Ireland's and other international terrorist activity and perplexed as to how to combat this new form of warfare against established society. The ideal solution would be to ensure conviction and punishment of terrorists no matter where they were found, either by way of extradition to the country in which they had committed crimes, or by the country where they were arrested. If all the nations in the world agreed to this, terrorists would be deprived of sanctuary. Alas, the political aspect obtrudes, as one man's terrorist is another man's freedom fighter; attempts made in the United Nations and elswhere to obtain agreement on this principle seemed doomed to failure for this reason.

European countries did succeed to some extent: the Suppression of Terrorism Convention was signed in Strasbourg in January 1977 by seventeen of the nineteen member states of the Council of Europe. Its purpose was to declare acts of terrorism to be extraditable offenses. This convention was ratified by Britain in March 1978, but the Irish Republic was one of the only two states not to sign it (the other was Malta). Its excuse was that its 1937 constitution would not allow a national to be extradited for a political offense, and also that the convention would restrict the independence of Irish courts in such cases. A further excuse was that to comply with the spirit of the Suppression of Terrorism Convention, the Irish constitution would have to be amended by a national referendum, which would fail if put to the Irish people.

The Irish Republic had joined the European Economic Community at the same time as Britain in 1973, and the EEC countries were deeply concerned about terrorists escaping justice after committing offenses in countries other than their own. Talks between members of the EEC took place, and on 10 October 1978 the Irish government agreed to sign an EEC Convention on Terrorism that would oblige it either to extradite, or try in the Irish Republic, any nationals accused of terrorist offenses in other EEC countries. This was based on the pattern of the bilateral legislation of the Irish Criminal Law Jurisdiction Act and the British Prevention of Terrorism (Temporary Provisions) Act, both of 1976. There was hesitation, however, and it was not until 4 December 1979 that the EEC Convention on Terrorism was actually signed in Dublin on behalf of the Irish government. It remains to be seen how effective it will be and what degree of sincerity is applied to implementing its provisions.

The border was a considerable handicap to British security forces in Northern Ireland because so much of it lay open, thus allowing terrorists to cross from the Irish Republic, commit crimes, and then withdraw again into their sanctuary. The British army wanted the right to cross it "in hot pursuit," while the RUC wanted to be able to cross it to question suspects in Garda custody. On 1 September 1979 the chief constable of the RUC complained of the presence of small, active IRA units at various towns just on the Irish side of the border, such as Dundalk, Letterkenny, Clontibret, Monaghan, and Castleblaney. He said his own intelligence revealed that many wanted terrorists were in those locations, but that because they were in the Irish Republic, the RUC was unable to question or arrest them or to keep them under surveillance. His unspoken complaint must have been that the Irish authorities were either unable or unwilling to do anything about this frustrating situation.

Prime Minister Lynch was quick to reply. The following day, the 2nd, he flatly ruled out any thoughts of "hot pursuit" for the British army, or of RUC detectives questioning suspects in the Irish Republic. He said that one-third of his police force (total strength about 8,000) and one-third of the Irish army (total strength about 12,500) was in the border area. He then shot his barb at the British government and asked why he should be expected to put more Irish troops right up against the actual border when the British had pulled back their troops to distances of between five and ten miles, thus leaving that strip a "hiatus of ineffectiveness." This was true, and many places adjacent to the border were not patrolled on foot by British security forces, especially in Bandit Country of South Armagh. Nor were roads in them regularly patrolled in vehicles; the only surveillance was by helicopter. Warren Point had been an example. Helicopters were the only means of safe movement for British troops in some border areas, and by the end of the year it was noticeable that British military vehicles did not venture onto roads near the border unless the reason was an urgent one, thus handing over sections of the terrain to the IRA terrorists.

Prime Minister Lynch said that antiterrorist measures were being taken in the Irish Republic. In January 1979 he had set up a Garda antiterrorist task force of about forty police officers who had undergone several months' special training and could be called together to deal with exceptional incidents, such as kidnapping, hijacking, and hostage situations. Like the 600 members of the Irish Special Branch, all members of this task force were armed. The superintendent in charge had been trained in antiterrorist methods in West Germany and had also visited other EEC special antiterrorist police groups. This precaution had been prompted not by British demands, but by fear that prominent Irish personalities, perhaps MPs, might be kidnapped and held hostage in an attempt to secure the release of IRA men in Irish prisons. On 20 December 1979 the Irish government announced that it was to equip its army with ground-to-air missiles, motivated no doubt by the thought that terrorists might hijack aircraft and helicopters and use them to attack government or other buildings.

Terrorists sought to harness the media to their cause as much as they could. Security forces in Northern Ireland and in Britain criticized the media for giving this publicity and furthering the terrorist cause. Some of the smaller terrorist groups sought to appear on television to demonstrate they were a viable, armed force. Invariably these interviews had to be covert, which drew even more criticism. There was considerable unease, for example, in Britain and in the non-Catholic community in Northern Ireland when on 19 July the BBC TV showed a "back-to-the camera" interview with an alleged INLA leader, given in Dublin. Another was held on 26 August in Belfast by an organization whose title did not become clear. The leaders interviewed wore masks, refused to be named, and stated that their organization had been restructured on the secret-cell system with members being drawn from the Red Hand Commando, the UDA, and the UVF. They said they had a "death list" of members of the Provos and the INLA. A fortnight later, on 2 September, determined not to be upstaged, the proscribed Ulster Freedom Fighters also held a secret press conference in Belfast, to which selected journalists and press photographers were invited. Ten masked men were interviewed and photographed, but again no names were mentioned.

By this time the RUC and the British government had become extremely sensitive to press conferences and briefings given by terrorist organizations in their midst, and to the criticism that they were unable to prevent them or to arrest the terrorists being interviewed. On 4 September Pierre Salinger, a former Washington White House press officer, was arrested briefly in Belfast, while working with an ABC TV film crew. The RUC, which quickly released Salinger, said their information was that the Provos were about to stage a weapon display for the ABC TV. Despite Provo denials, this was most probably the purpose of the invitation to Salinger.

A minor storm of protest suddenly blew up in Britain against the BBC TV when it was revealed (in November) by an Irish reporter who had been working on another story that on 19 October the IRA had taken over the small village of Carrickmore, Co Tyrone, and had invited a BBC TV film crew to come and see the IRA operating openly in Northern Ireland. The film crew concerned denied that it was "a put up job" and claimed that it had gone there in response to an invitation that "something of interest" could be seen, not knowing precisely what it might be. It was said that the team only filmed a few Provos drilling and manning a roadblock. Accounts of what was actually seen, what was actually filmed, and the circumstances of the IRA invitation were conflicting, to say the least. The film was not shown on BBC TV, and British Prime Minister Margaret Thatcher stated later at Westminster that the "BBC should put its own house in order."

Prime Minister Lynch had been heartened in his ambition to achieve a united Ireland by the support of four powerful American political figures who echoed and, within their means, furthered this ambition. They were Senator Edward Kennedy; Hugh Carey, governor of New York; Tip O'Neill, Speaker of the House of Representatives; and Mario Biaggi, chairman of the 130-strong ad hoc House of Representatives' Committee on Ireland. All four men, however, condemned terrorism.

Prime Minister Lynch had persistently pursued the policy officially adopted by his Fianna Fail Party in 1975 of calling for the British government to give a declaration of intent to withdraw from Northern Ireland, and for it to set a date for this to take place. When the governments of Wilson and Callaghan were in power, there seemed to be fairly good prospects of achieving this aim, as can be judged from an interview released on RTE on 20 September, with Peter Jay, Callaghan's son-in-law. Jay, who had been the British ambassador in Washington, said that a united Ireland was the "ultimately desirable solution." There can be little doubt as to what might have happened had Callaghan been returned to power in May 1979 instead of Mrs. Thatcher.

It was generally felt in Britain that Lynch could and should have done much more to curb IRA terrorism. The suspicion was that he was content to allow it to continue until the required British declaration of intent was forthcoming, when, like his predecessors in office, he would suddenly and effectively clamp down on the IRA and crush it. After the Mountbatten murder, Prime Minister Lynch suddenly changed his tack. On 3 September, the day after his curt refusal to allow British troops the facility of crossing into the Irish Republic in "hot pursuit," in an interview shown on BBC TV, he called for power sharing in Northern Ireland and stated that the Catholic community should become involved in governing the province. He also said, a couple of days later, that he would agree to more "cross-border liaison." Although there may have followed some vague, secret agreement that allowed British helicopters to use Irish Republic air space, it did not amount to anything tangible; but because he refused to explain it or discuss it, a wave of criticism rose up against him.

Three things probably caused Lynch's change of policy. The first was the repercussion overseas of the Mountbatten murder and adverse foreign comment on the fact that IRA terrorist activities took place inside the Irish Republic. The second was the sudden scarcity of information about the IRA, due to its new secret-cell structure, which made him realize that he might not be able to step in to crush the IRA when it suited his purposes, and that the IRA might eventually be able to unseat him by force and change the form of the government in the Irish Republic. The third reason was that he was beginning to lose his political nerve. It was already rumored that he would resign the premiership in 1980, when his term of office as president of the EEC Parliament terminated. Additionally, Prime Minister Thatcher had probably convinced him that Northern Ireland was to remain part of the U.K., and he noted that she would most likely be in power for at least another four years, perhaps longer. On 17 October it was officially confirmed that his party had shelved its demand for a British withdrawal from the province until there was agreement within Northern Ireland on a Catholic and non-Catholic power sharing administration.

Opinion polls taken in 1979 gave widely varying estimates of opinion on the Northern Ireland problem. The results of one taken by a government–sponsored agency in the Irish Republic before the Mountbatten murder were released on 15 October and indicated that twenty percent of the population of the Irish Republic (shown as 3.3 million) supported the activities of the IRA, while forty-two percent in all sympathized with the motives of the IRA. This result astonished the Irish government. When questioned about it, Jack Lynch stated that another poll taken by the BBC was far more accurate and showed that only two percent of the Irish people supported the IRA. The fallibilities of public opinion polls were simply accentuated in Ireland. Another poll taken in Northern Ireland, which showed that fifty percent of the Catholic population wanted to remain part of the U.K. and only thirty-nine percent wanted to join the Irish Republic, may have further depressed Lynch and helped to influence his change of policy.

In Britain, vocal sections of the community still pressed for a British withdrawal from Northern Ireland, with the slogan of "Troops Out." This issue was put to a vote at each of the autumn annual conventions of the three main British political parties, but in each case was overwhelmingly defeated. The ruling Tory Party policy was that British troops should remain in Northern Ireland until the problem was solved to its liking.

In June 1979 the first elections for the EEC Parliament were held. Of the three seats allocated to Northern Ireland, one was won by John Taylor of the Official Unionist Party (OUP), another by John Hume of the SDLP, and the third by Ian Paisley. Paisley's victory over Harry West, leader of the OUP, came as a surprise, it being thought that Paisley's political stock had slumped after the failure of the May 1977 strike. After his defeat, Harry West resigned as leader of the OUP, and James Molyneaux was elected in his place. In the Irish Republic, which had been allocated fifteen seats, Lynch's Fianna Fail Party won only five instead of the expected eight. Fine Gael won four, the Labor Party won four, and independents held the other two. This setback must have also adversely affected Lynch's ebbing political confidence.

For almost six months Secretary for Northern Ireland Humphrey Atkins had seemingly been leisurely consulting politicians and others in both Northern Ireland and Britain as to what could or should be done to implement the Conservative Party objective to restore more control over their own affairs to the people of the province. Eventually, on 25 October, he announced his long-awaited initiative: to call a four-party conference in December to discuss means to "find the highest level of agreement for the transfer of powers of government in Northern Ireland." The four parties invited to participate were the Democratic Unionist Party, the Official Unionist Party, the Alliance Party, and the SDLP.

Initially only Paisley's DUP agreed to attend. The OUP declined because it declared it had no faith in the project, and that such conferences had been tried before and had failed. The Alliance Party also had reservations, but eventually agreed to attend. The SDLP, led by Gerry Fitt, showed an interest but inquired whether the "Irish Dimension" would be on the agenda for discussion. When told it would not, the SDLP declined to attend. This brought about a crisis within the SDLP, as Gerry Fitt was in favor of attending Atkin's conference anyway. Fitt was overruled by his party and resigned as leader of the SDLP on 22 November, his place being taken by John Hume, a member of the European Parliament.

On the 22nd Humphrey Atkins presented for discussion six alternative forms of power sharing with safeguards for the Catholic minority. All had been put forward before in one form or another. The idea was to offer more powers to a new Northern Ireland assembly and to persuade the political parties in the province to accept some form of devolved government "in which both parts of the community can have confidence." The concept of a united Ireland was rejected by Atkins, as was total non-Catholic domination. As only the DUP and the Alliance Party had so far agreed to attend, however, the proposed conference had to be postponed to January 1980, by which time it was hoped that all four parties could be persuaded to take part. Prime Minister Thatcher had said that if there were no acceptable agreement among the political parties in Northern Ireland, a "solution may have to be imposed."

On 5 December 1979 Jack Lynch suddenly resigned as prime minister of the Irish Republic and leader of the Fianna Fail. His party had just unexpectedly lost two seats in bye-elections in Lynch's home area of Cork, which perhaps was the final straw. For some weeks he had been under heavy criticism for making his mysterious cross-border agreement with Britain. His government also had domestic problems, such as a sixteen percent inflation rate, unemployment, and strikes; already a postal strike was in its fourth month.

On 7 December 1979 Charles Haughey was elected leader of the Fianna Fail Party by a narrow majority and so became prime minister of the Irish Republic. The majority of ministers had voted for George Colley, but the majority of the backbenchers who had their eyes and thoughts on 1982, when a general election was due, wanted a dynamic man as leader and so voted for Haughey. For many years Haughey and Colley had competed for the leadership of the party; after the resignation of Sean Lemass in 1966, Jack Lynch had been chosen as a compromise candidate because support for both men was so closely balanced. It was held against Haughey that he had been somehow involved in the arms running affair of 1970; although acquitted, he had been dismissed from the Irish Cabinet by Prime Minister Lynch, which caused the non-Catholics in Northern Ireland some anxiety and prompted Ian Paisley to comment that "the IRA has an ally in Charles Haughey." Against this was balanced the fact that in 1961, while minister of justice, Haughey had reintroduced military tribunals to try IRA men.

Haughey, whose parents had come from Derry, was an Irishman of the new type, who had made himself a millionaire in Ireland and not overseas. He joined the Fianna Fail Party in 1948, entered the Dail Eireann in 1956, and married the daughter of Prime Minister Sean Lemass. In 1972 Haughey attended the funerals of those killed on Bloody Sunday in Derry. When the Fianna Fail returned to power in 1977, he became minister of health and social security. He was responsible for introducing the rule that artists and writers living in Ireland, even foreigners, would be exempted from income tax, which brought a certain amount of foreign currency into the country.

At his initial press conference as prime minister, Haughey stated that his policy was to achieve a united Ireland by peaceful means. He ruled out any cross-border cooperation with British security forces, saying, "I believe the responsibility for the preservation of peace and security in this State belongs to the Garda and the military." When pressed he said, "I condemn the Provisional IRA and all their activities"—something he had not said publicly before.

Terrorism had continued throughout the year of 1979, and there was official pessimism as to whether it could ever be defeated or even contained. Secretary for Northern Ireland Humphrey Atkins said, "I cannot claim, as the '70s finish, that an end to terrorism is in sight"; while John Hume, leader of the SDLP, who claims to be a moderate, said, "There is no instant solution to the Irish question, it is a long-term one."

On 13 December a Provisional IRA statement threatened a bombing campaign in England, saying, "The question is not if we would bomb London again and other big cities, but when." It added, "The IRA is planning to maintain a steady level of attacks in Ulster, with occasional publicity-catching spectaculars." The main propaganda weapon was to be the "dirty strike" to gain political status for prisoners. The National H Block Committee had been formed and held a conference in Dublin on 16

December; its stated aim was to publicize the protest, collect funds, and set up a subcommittee to mobilize support in the Irish Republic. In December 1979 there were six non-Catholic prisoners out of 380 "on the blanket" in Maze Prison.

An interview with an unnamed Provisional IRA leader published in the *Sunday Press,* a Dublin newspaper, could perhaps be taken as a further statement of future Provo policy. It said, "We have conditioned our people to think in terms of a long struggle. We don't speculate how long it will take. We did make the mistake early on of predicting armed victory in successive years." It also said, "We have suffered too much, and come through too much, to settle for anything less than full freedom. We have the determination, and resolve, and the resources, to keep going until we get the Brits out." Indications from the RUC are that the Provos are preparing for a long war of terrorism that will last between seven and ten years.

On his way to America Pope John Paul visited the Irish Republic from 29 September to October, and while there made a carefully worded call for an end to terrorist violence. The Protestant UVF offered the Provos a truce if they would respond to the pope's appeal, but there was no answer. The pope's visit to Ireland had been masterminded by Cardinal O'Fiaich, Primate of All Ireland, whose seat was in Armagh, Northern Ireland. He held strong republican views, and his utterances frequently embarrassed the Northern Ireland and British authorities. The cardinal had hoped the pope would visit Armagh, but the Rev. Ian Paisley and other non-Catholics in the province raised such loud objections that, for reasons of personal safety, this was ruled out. Although the pope's visit passed off without incident, it did not help peace, as it merely hardened existing attitudes. That he made no outright condemnation of terrorism and gave no hint that religious sanctions should be taken against terrorists disappointed many in Ireland, Catholic and non-Catholic alike.

The pope had not pleased the terrorists either. On 16 December 1979 a Provisional IRA statement made some revealing and harsh remarks about the papal visit, saying, "In all conscience we believe that we are morally right, as we are fighting a just war, and the Pope asked us to surrender. He showed bias in other ways. He did not mention H Block, yet the first thing he mentioned when he arrived in New York was that there must never be another Auschwitz." The religious plea made by the head of the Roman Catholic Church had failed and been rejected by the Irish terrorists.

18 Prospects: A United or Divided Ireland

"Wars cannot be won by military means alone these days."
—from "Northern Ireland: Terrorist Trends," British
Ministry of Defense Intelligence Report, November 1978

THE YEAR 1980 dawned with black clouds hanging heavily over Ireland as a new decade began. Will it unfold like the decade of the 1970s and bring more death, injury, and destruction? Will the bloody standoff over the Northern Ireland problem continue unresolved for another decade, to become even more violent as opposing parties become more deeply entrenched in their prejudices and more hardened in their attitudes? Initial forecasts are not hopeful. The Provisional IRA has said it is preparing for a long haul—between seven and ten years—before it anticipates final victory, while the British secretary for Northern Ireland says that he cannot see an end to terrorism in the province.

During the past decade the Provisional IRA's considerable experience in guerrilla-type urban warfare against the British security forces has resulted in the complete changeover from an army style framework, concept, and tactics to one copied from international terrorist organizations of secret cells. On the other hand, the British security forces, especially the RUC, have also gained considerable experience and have evolved new methods of combating terrorism. A sort of armed stalemate exists between the two struggling sides and may continue for a long time without one or the other gaining the upper hand.

Fresh personalities are appearing in the field, perhaps with fresh drive, fresh ideas, and hopefully with a willingness to compromise. In Britain, Prime Minister Margaret Thatcher has been in office only eight months, at this writing. In the Irish Republic, Charles Haughey has been prime minister for only three weeks. In Northern Ireland, Humphrey Atkins has been secretary for only eight months; Sir Maurice Oldfield, coordinator of security for only three months; while both Lt. Gen. Sir Richard

Lawson and John Hermon do not take up their respective appointments as GOC British Forces in Northern Ireland and chief constable of the Royal Ulster Constabulary until January 1980. It is early yet to see how this new set of leaders make out with the Northern Ireland problem.

On the other hand, the Provisional IRA seems to have retained almost intact the same leadership it has had for four or five years: hard-line men from Northern Ireland described by British Intelligence as "talented and dedicated," who feel they are historic figures fighting for the age-old goal of a united Ireland completely free of any trace of British domination or imperialism. At the moment, less is known about the small but vicious INLA. About 500 active terrorists are successfully waging urban guerrilla warfare and terrorism against nearly 30,000 members of the British security forces (being some 13,500 British troops, 5,500 members of the UDR and about 11,000 members of the RUC and the RUC Reserve), but there are no signs of the IRA terrorists being defeated or of any political compromise that might lead to a peaceful solution generally acceptable to all involved. The Official IRA seems to be moribund, but appearances may be deceptive.

It is necessary to clarify the issue of who wants what before trying to make assessments and predictions. Basic issues have become blurred and entwined with unthinking emotion; so in an attempt to separate basic issues from the emotion, I will briefly mention the various governments and factions involved as I have seen and studied them first hand, to determine what each wants and how each hopes to get it, before going on to speculate whether there is any way out of this seeming impasse.

First of all, what do the terrorists want? The Provisional IRA leaders are convinced they are the true inheritors of the Irish Republic, declared during the Easter Rising of 1916, and that the legal powers of the Second Dail of 1919 were passed to the IRA by the so-called IRA–Dail Treaty of 1938.* The Provos and the INLA want the British military forces withdrawn from Northern Ireland so they can have a free hand to achieve their aim of uniting Ireland by violent means. They want the United Nations to recognize them as a national liberation movement, which would make their cause a legitimate one in most U.N. member-countries; and

---

*IRA leaders are obsessed with both legality and becoming historic figures. It is of interest to note that records and documents of the Provisional IRA Belfast Brigade have been regularly lodged with the Belfast Public Records Office. How long they will survive intact for future historians to study is problematic, as governments and the IRA have a record of selectively destroying records that may reflect them adversely in history whenever they get the chance.

they want political status for prisoners, or better still, an amnesty for them.

Next, what do the people of Northern Ireland want? They are sharply divided into two distinct groups, the Catholics and the non-Catholics, and each wants something entirely different. The non-Catholics, who are in a two-thirds majority, want to retain their link with the British Crown and to remain part of the United Kingdom. Above all they want the British government to hold firm in its guarantee not to desert them. They do not want to become part of the Irish Republic where, as a minority, they fear they would be discriminated against. The once solidly united Ulster Unionist Party has now splintered, but the differences between the splinters are over clashing personalities and the means to be adopted, rather than a fundamental issue of continued union with Britain. There is no sign of any significant non-Catholic group with contrary views. The Democratic Unionist Party, led by Ian Paisley, and the Official Unionist Party, led by James Molyneaux, want a return of the Stormont parliament, but others may be content with direct rule for the time being.

The non-Catholics want the terrorists to be defeated quickly and the British government and security forces to take stronger measures that could include internment without trial, censorship, no media contact with terrorists, identity cards, banning the Provisional Sinn Fein, and probably sealing off the border with the Irish Republic as much as possible. They want the Irish Republic to stop giving sanctuary to terrorists and to hand over for trial the hundred or so wanted men now sheltering there. They want the British government to threaten or even to impose economic sanctions against the Irish Republic until this is complied with. They also want the American government to prevent Irish American organizations from sending arms and money to the IRA terrorists.

The other group, the Catholics, are in the one-third minority in Northern Ireland. They all seemingly want to merge into the Irish Republic, although it is suspected that, due to IRA terrorist pressure, none dare openly express any contrary views. One opinion poll taken by an Irish government–sponsored organization showed that only thirty-nine percent wanted union with the Irish Republic. They certainly want the terrorist war to end, as they are the victims of so many protection rackets, but dare not say so. They do not want the return of the Stormont government, which they think would bring back Protestant rule and Protestant discrimination, but prefer direct rule from Westminster for the time being. The SDLP, now led by John Hume, is campaigning for a united Ireland by constitutional means.

Next, what does the Irish Republic want? For many months Prime Minister Jack Lynch had said that he wanted to unite Ireland by peaceful means, and that he wanted the British government to make a declaration of intent to withdraw from Northern Ireland and to set a date for that withdrawal. He had launched his reunification program in October 1975 and then set out to internationalize the issue and to persuade the U.S. government to pressure the British government into making that declaration. He had wanted the British government also to condition, pressure, and reconcile the non-Catholic population in Northern Ireland, as he put it, to "the inevitability of Irish reunification, and to open a way for a peaceful settlement."

In September 1979 Jack Lynch suddenly changed his policy and urged the Catholic population in the province to become involved in local government as a first step to the formation of the eventual Council of Ireland, as suggested in the Sunningdale Talks of December 1973—the so-called "Irish Dimension." The reasons for his sudden change of policy were a combination of the realization of the strength, capability, and ultimate aim of the IRA; the determination of the one million Protestants in Northern Ireland not to become part of the Irish Republic; and failing political support at home. The new prime minister, Charles Haughey, has stated he will seek the reunification of Ireland by peaceful means, but it is early yet to see how he will go about it. One other suggestion, thrown up by the Fine Gael Party, is that there should be a federation or confederation between politically autonomous Northern Ireland and the Irish Republic; but this does not seem to have much support in the south, and none at all from the Protestants in the north.

Next, what do the Irish Americans want? In the U.S. there are about 20 million descendants of Irish immigrants (as against only 4.8 million in the whole of Ireland), and they have a fairly powerful lobby at Washington. They want a united Ireland under the Dublin government and simply cannot understand why the British insist upon retaining Northern Ireland as a colony against its will. The Irish Americans want their elected representatives to pressure the U.S. president to persuade the British government to hand over Northern Ireland to the Irish Republic.

The average American or Irish American may have not studied the Northern Ireland problem in depth, but instead accepted without question republican and IRA propaganda, which is often based on emotion. The British case has not been put across very well in the U.S. if at all. Questions I was frequently asked on a lecture tour of the U.S., included, "Why is the British government using aircraft and tanks to bomb and shoot the people in Northern Ireland?" and others in a similar vein. The one million Protestants in the province and their wishes were seldom mentioned, and on occasions not even known about. The ogre was the British government, and the grail was a united Ireland.

Next, what do the British want? The general impression is that the British government wants one thing and the British people another. Successive British governments have affirmed that Northern Ireland is a part of the United Kingdom and will remain so until a majority of the people in the province wish it otherwise. The British government wants to defeat the terrorists and restore peace, law, and order so that the troops can be withdrawn. It also wants an internal constitutional solution acceptable to both communities. Proportional representation was introduced at local council level in 1973 to produce coalition councils, and it is claimed that twenty-three out of the twenty-six are operating as such. It hopes this idea will expand upwards. The British government also wants to be considered as a good member of the European community and one setting a good example in observing human rights. But this is proving difficult in Northern Ireland.

That is basically what the British government wants, but what do the British people want? Go into any pub, club, or shopping center and ask them. They are either indifferent or express views that can be generally summed up as, "Let's get out and leave them to fight it out among themselves." Their interest in the Northern Ireland problem is almost negligible, and any sense of involvement even less. The British media generally supports its government's policy over this issue, presumably in the cause of a democracy of "one-man, one-vote," but certain editorials have supported, with some reservations, the "Troops Out" movement, which is becoming vocal. Sample opinion polls indicate that a majority of the British people are in favor of abandoning Northern Ireland. Already 326 British soldiers have been killed there since 1971, and the people ask "For what?" If a referendum were held in Britain on the Northern Ireland problem, the result would both startle and embarass the British government.

It has often been said there is no solution to the Northern Ireland problem. This has almost become the complacent excuse for inaction, but it is not so. Certain solutions are being pushed hard by interested parties, so perhaps it is only a matter of time, determination, skill, and luck as to which might eventually succeed. There are four obvious solutions: the IRA one, the British government one, the Irish government one, and the Northern Ireland Protestant one.

There are also five inescapable basic facts that may affect the outcome of any of these solutions. These are, firstly, there are one million

Protestants determined not to become part of the Irish Republic; second-
ly, the Provisional IRA and INLA are determined to achieve by violence
a united Ireland to their own political taste; thirdly, the Irish prime minister is determined to achieve a united Ireland by peaceful means; fourth-
ly, the British government is determined to support the non-Catholic
majority decision to remain part of the U.K.; and fifthly, most important
of all, all four are determined and convinced that their own course is the
correct one. There is no sign at the moment of any of them weakening in
their resolve, or softening or changing their rigid attitudes. One looks in
vain for any hint of a compromise.

The IRA solution is simple and violent: maintain a high level of terrorism until British troops are withdrawn from the province, and then
deal with the Protestants in Northern Ireland before turning on and top-
pling the government in Dublin. The ultimate aim of the IRA is a socialist, Cuba-like state embracing the whole of Ireland. The economy of
Northern Ireland has to be heavily supported by the already heavily
over-burdened British taxpayer. The allocation for 1978–79 for the so-
called Northern Ireland Consolidation Fund is about $1,700 million,
which together with the extra cost* incurred by the security forces means
that Northern Ireland is costing the British government at least $2,000
million annually. Other statistics can be equally depressing. During the
past ten years an average of 11,000 people annually have left Belfast; of
those remaining, about one-third are old-age pensioners. The British
government has to consider the mood of the British people. These dismal
facts give encouragement and hope to the IRA.

IRA terrorists have issued bold manifestos and uttered brave and
boastful words, claiming that they are able to continue the struggle for
another ten years if necessary, and that they have the will and the means
to do so. They hope the British government will tire first of the sterile
drain on its manpower, energy, and money. There is much to encourage
the IRA to feel this way, but its leadership has many fears.

The IRA leaders fear the loss of Irish and Irish American emotional
support for their cause. The longer the struggle continues, the more facts
will emerge and become universally known that will shred IRA propaganda and raise doubts about the purity of its cause and its methods.
Will Irish Americans really willingly help establish a Cuba-like state in
Ireland? The IRA leaders fear the drying up of funds and arms from overseas, and that the American government and the Irish Americans, now

---

*One BBC estimate is that the extra military cost in Northern Ireland for the years
1969-80 is $1,820 million.

with their experience of the Teheran hostage situation as a poignant example, may turn sharply against terrorism as a weapon, no matter how just the cause or how great the provocation.

The IRA leaders fear that the longer the struggle goes on, the more chance there is of losing grass-roots support in the Catholic communities in Northern Ireland, which they now retain only by intimidation. Any IRA setback, any signs that the IRA may be losing out to the security forces, or of a peaceful solution emerging, might start a ground swell of opposition. IRA demands might be resisted by the Catholic communities and information would once gain flow into RUC ears.

The comparative prosperity brought to the Irish Republic by its membership in the EEC has inculcated an interest in accumulating wealth and living the good life to the detriment of Irish idealism formerly nourished on poverty and repression. The IRA leaders fear that the traditional tolerance of Irish governments may evaporate under materialism; harsh measures may be reintroduced against the IRA, and wanted terrorists may be tried in number in Irish courts for offenses committed in Northern Ireland. They fear the new Irish prime minister, who might turn on them suddenly in the interest of his country, as his predecessors have done at times, to cripple and perhaps crush them, especially if his policy of reuniting Ireland seems to have a chance. Then the Irish Republic may no longer provide them with a sanctuary. Without the Irish Republic as a sanctuary and the open border, the days of the IRA terrorists in Northern Ireland would be numbered.

There may be changes of IRA leadership as leaders are arrested, resign, or are dismissed due to infighting over policies or tactics. The present Provo Council, dominated by Northern Ireland men, enforced the drastic change in structure and tactics from the old, almost open army framework and urban guerrilla warfare to secret-cell terrorism on the lines of that of the Baader-Meinhof Gang and certain Palestinian groups. There are even now signs that the Provo rank and file do not like the new system, which is rather alien to their character, traditions, and inclination. They like to to be known among their fellows that they are in some way associated with the IRA cause and are doing something about it. They like the old military framework and guerrilla-style warfare, which gave them the status and dignity of being a "soldier" in an "army" fighting a "lawful war," which the secret-cell system lacks.

There may be leadership quarrels or even open fighting between factions over recruits, money, arms, and territory. The informer may reappear to enable the RUC to decimate and behead the IRA. There are signs this may already be happening. On 2 January 1980 Gerry Adams, the Provo chief of staff, who was working openly as the vice president of the Provisional Sinn Fein, was arrested in Belfast, although he was soon released owning to lack of evidence. Adams had been betrayed by an informer, and he may be only the first of many leaders if the cell system breaks down.

The British solution is to defeat the IRA terrorists so that Northern Ireland can remain part of the United Kingdom. Then the British government would be able to pursue its policy of developing grass-roots power sharing, with the Catholic community having a voice in the form of devolved local government, in which it hopes both parts of the population would have confidence, reserving for itself eventually only the portfolios of foreign affairs, defense, security, police, prisons and the courts—in other words, almost full internal autonomy. But as long as the border remains open and the Irish Republic remains a sanctuary and a Ho Chi Minh Trail for the IRA, it is doubtful the British security forces can defeat the terrorists. They are also unable to protect the Catholic communities against the IRA intimidation and extortion.

As a practicing democracy, Britain is severely handicapped in its war against terrorism. The terrorists may use all the dirty tricks in the book, and more besides, but the British government has to be seen to fight them openly and cleanly and in a manner that will not offend democratic world opinion or give the slightest cause for criticism. The British government hesitates to introduce certain restrictions that would be a considerable help in combating the IRA, such as internment without trial and the issue of identity cards. The Bennett Report, for example, has established safeguards for suspects and prisoners under interrogation that have to be observed and that may enable many terrorists to escape conviction.

Preceding Labor governments were almost on the point of selling the Protestants in Northern Ireland down the river, but the Thatcher government has a much more positive attitude toward them. The present British Conservative government obviously hopes to lobby to change adverse foreign views on British handling of the Northern Ireland problem, especially those held in certain quarters in the U.S. Prime Minister Thatcher may succeed, but for her solution to work she will also have to persuade the prime minister of the Irish Republic, Charles Haughey, to agree to clamp down on IRA terrorists hiding in his country and to institute joint British–Irish security forces cooperation along the border to seal it off to terrorists. This will be more difficult.

Much smeared and maligned in the past, the Royal Ulster Constabulary has reemerged as a well equipped, well trained, well disciplined, and well led police force that is gradually reasserting the writ of law throughout the province. Although it still has some way to go in this respect, its future is encouraging. The RUC is looking forward to the day when the troops can return to barracks, and when solitary policemen, either Catholic or Protestant, can patrol safely on foot in both the Shankill Road area and the Ballymurphy estate.

In theory the British army in Northern Ireland is doing a temporary job, one it generally dislikes and would like to be rid of. British soldiers have conducted themselves magnificently on the whole in the face of extreme provocation in the province, but they have been there for over ten years, and the situation has begun to affect the whole army, which is a small, volunteer one committed to the NATO role. Problems that neither the British government nor its Ministry of Defense like to air in public are being raised and discussed by the media.

Senior military commanders, staffs, and advisers are divided on the value of the army being and remaining in Northern Ireland. One section wants to retain the commitment as long as possible, and even to enlarge it, as it is the only British territory (apart perhaps from Belize) where young officers and soldiers can be blooded on active service. The other section wants to end the Northern Ireland commitment immediately, or as soon as possible, as it is detrimental to the major NATO role.

The old truism is emerging that an army cannot be successfully trained for more than one type of warfare at a time, no matter how professional it might be. It may be all right in theory to say this is possible, but it is ineffective in practice. The major part of the British army combat element—that is, mainly the infantry, artillery and armored units—spends about half its time in or training for a counterinsurgency role in Northern Ireland, and the other half training for nuclear and conventional warfare in Germany. By simple deduction it can therefore be only half as well trained and efficient as if it were exclusively engaged in one or the other. Excluding the half-dozen or so resident units in Northern Ireland, to maintain the current strength of about 13,500 soldiers, at least some forty units are required in rotation each year and more when trouble is expected. Each major unit should have about 650 officers and soldiers, but most are understrength and have difficulty mustering about 500 all ranks. There are, for example, only about fifty regular infantry units in the British army; artillery, armored, and other specialist units have to be dismounted and used in an infantry role. At other times ad hoc ones have been specially formed for the purpose.

If serving in Germany, for example, as most are, each unit has to be taken from its NATO role to be given one month's special training in a counterterrorist role. It then serves four months in Northern Ireland, and afterwards the officers and soldiers have one month's leave. In short, the unit is away from its NATO role for six months. British military morale is high, but one senses the disillusionment and frustration felt by the officers and men, which is to some extent reflected in the "wastage" rate of those leaving the army by resignation or purchase or of soldiers not reengaging when their contractual period of service ends. Soldiers return again and again to Northern Ireland only to see the same hopeless situation, without any improvement or prospects of improvement. Many British army units have completed half a dozen four-month tours of duty in Northern Ireland, and one is already on its ninth.

Until recently the solution of the Irish government had been to persuade the British to evacuate Northern Ireland completely and hand it over to the Republic. If the British government did that, at the best there would be a dissident non-Catholic problem, probably of terrorist proportions, and at the worst civil war. Prime Minister Lynch suddenly realized he could cope with neither. The new Irish solution is to persuade the Catholic population to take part in the British-instigated grass-roots power sharing in local councils and to work for a Council of Ireland in some form, which could have representatives from both the Irish Republic and Northern Ireland. The eventual objective of a Council of Ireland would be to bring the two parts together and gradually eliminate all traces of British influence from the province. This, in essence, seems to be Prime Minister Haughey's peaceful solution, which may in the long term materialize.

The Catholic birthrate in Northern Ireland is higher than that of the Protestants but has until recently been offset by a higher rate of Catholic emigration. In 1969 Prime Minister Terence O'Neill was wrong when he said there were more Catholic children of school age than Protestant ones, but he would not be wrong to say that today. School children in Northern Ireland are generally segregated into separate denominational schools. According to the January 1977 figures, there were 190,058 children at "voluntary" Catholic schools, and 178,297 at "controlled" non-Catholic schools. There were a few other exceptions, but none of any significant size. If the present trend of the higher Catholic birthrate continues, as is expected in view of the present pope's ruling on birth control, by the year 2000 Catholics will form the majority block of voters. With proportional representation in force (it is proposed for the Northern Ireland Westminster seats at the next British general election) there will be an ever increasing Catholic majority that will take over control of most of the councils and their affairs and any future Stormont

Assembly. Then Catholics, being in the majority, will be able to bring into being a Council of Ireland. Patience is all that is required for this solution to materialize.

In the meantime it cannot be overlooked that it is to the advantage of the Irish government that a terrorist problem continues in Northern Ireland, as it attracts international attention, especially over such issues as human rights, which keeps the problem alive. If there were no terrorism in the province, international interest would soon fade as bombing and shooting gave way to endlessly boring conferences and political dialogue. This suspicion will always exist in many minds, as will the opinion that sterner measures against the IRA should be taken by the Irish government. Once prospects of a Council of Ireland emerge, my guess is that the Irish government will quickly step in to crush the IRA with a heavy fist. In the meantime it may only curb it, protesting weakly but unconvincingly that it is doing its best. It has to condition the Irish people and carry them with it: 1982 will be an election year in the Irish Republic, after which we may see stronger action being taken against the IRA.

Lastly, although the primary solution of the Protestants for Northern Ireland is to remain part of the U.K., they sense the mood of the British people, more accurately perhaps than the Westminster Parliament at the moment, and they fear that one day they may be abandoned by them. This fear was apprehensively real to them under the Wilson and Callaghan governments, but is less so under the Thatcher government. Should British troops and support be withdrawn, to preempt being forced into an Irish Republic, their extreme solution may be a unilateral declaration of independence from Britain, as happened with Rhodesia in 1966.

This possibility was voiced at the time of the O'Neill reforms of 1969, when William Craig, the Stormont minister for home affairs, was dismissed for openly advocating such a course. It was again raised and discussed in May 1977; and in October that year the Ulster Independence Party was formed. Support for UDI grew among non-Catholics; and many who were not extremists by any means had this thought at the back of their minds. But since the Thatcher government came to power in 1979 with the good prospect of at least five years' tenure in office, perhaps more, and is strongly committed to Northern Ireland remaining part of the U.K., support for UDI has declined. For a non-Catholic Northern Ireland to go it alone, international recognition would be required, as would financial and diplomatic support, which might be sought from EEC sources. It might have a fair chance of survival, as the population is hard-working. There would probably be a brief civil war over frontiers.

This Protestant emergency solution is an alternative that should not be completely overlooked.

What then is likely to happen? Clearly, any of the four alternative solutions could, if the circumstances were favorable, be enforced, but would mean resistance and reluctance from one or the other communities in Northern Ireland. The longer the status quo continues the less chance there is of the two communities becoming friends and living together in peace. More years of bitter civil strife would simply increase existing communal hatred and take generations to live down. The IRA terrorist aim is to ensure that peace does not happen. Despite official platitudes, at the moment fear and suspicion sharpened by ten years of virtual civil war are slowly driving the two communities farther from each other instead of closer together. If the Irish Republic solution obtains and the Protestants in the province refuse to accept mass emigration or absorption—and surely no one suggests a final Hitler-type solution because they refuse to merge into a Catholic-majority Ireland—it could result in a Basque ETA-type terrorist insurrection.

Another solution not yet seriously put forward as far as I know, but a good one in theory and a feasible one in practice, if it could be enforced, would be for Northern Ireland to become an independent state, probably within the framework of the EEC. It would be smaller than its present size, having a predominantly Protestant population of over one million, with redrawn boundaries that hived off the Catholic-majority fringe areas, such as the Bandit Country of South Armagh, and parts of Co Tyrone, Co Fermanagh, and Co Down, adjacent to the Irish Republic. It could be somewhat like Luxembourg, which comprises 999 square miles, has a population of about 340,000 people, and a boundary length of about 4,000 miles. The present size of Northern Ireland is approximately 5,462 square miles. It has a land frontier of 317 miles, a boundary that could be considerably shortened to perhaps less than 200 miles, which would be short enough to enable it to be effectively closed to terrorist infiltration.

Perhaps after a referendum some international body such as the U.N. or the EEC could impose such a solution, or perhaps some future president of the United States could successfully apply the formula used at Camp David in 1978–79 that led to the Egyptian-Israeli peace agreement. Then the island of Ireland would contain two separate, independent countries—a predominantly Catholic one with a population of over 3.5 million people, and a Protestant one with over one million—which after initial eruptions could settle down in peace, much as Spain and Portugal have done in the Iberian Peninsula, each with its own religion, traditions, and way of life.

However, if patience can be exercised, which one hopes it can, the IRA terrorism curbed, discredited, or defeated, the probability is that the British government solution for power sharing at and above grass-roots levels will be imposed on Northern Ireland; within a couple of decades that will be superceded by the Irish Republic Council of Ireland. Then by the year 2000 there could be a united Ireland.

Proclamation of the Irish Republic 24 April 1916

IRISHMEN AND IRISH WOMEN. In the name of God and of the dead generations from which she receives her old tradition of nationhood, Ireland, through us, summons her children to her flag and strikes for her freedom.

Having organised and trained her manhood through her secret revolutionary organisation, the Irish Republican Brotherhood, and through her open military organisations, the Irish Volunteers and the Irish Citizen Army, having patiently perfected her discipline, having resolutely waited for the right moment to reveal itself, she now seizes that moment, and, supported by her exiled children in America and by gallant allies in Europe, but relying in the first on her own strength, she strikes in full confidence of victory.

We declare the right of the people of Ireland to the ownership of Ireland, and to the unfettered control of Irish destinies, to be sovereign and indefeasible. The long usurpation of that right by a foreign people and government has not extinguished the right, nor can it ever be extinguished except by the destruction of the Irish people. In every generation the Irish people have asserted their right to national freedom and sovereignty; six times during the past three hundred years they have asserted it in arms. Standing on that fundamental right and again asserting it in arms in the face of the world, we hereby proclaim the Irish Republic as a Sovereign Independent State, and we pledge our lives and the lives of our comrades-in-arms to the cause of its freedom, of its welfare and of its exaltation among the nations.

The Irish Republic is entitled to, and hereby claims, the allegiance of every Irishman and Irishwoman. The Republic guarantees religious and civil liberty, equal rights and equal opportunities to all its citizens, and declares its resolve to pursue the happiness and prosperity of the whole nation and of all its parts, cherishing all the children of the nation equally, and oblivious of the differences carefully fostered by an alien government, which have divided a minority from the majority in the past.

Until our arms have brought the opportune moment for the establishment of a permanent National Government, representative of the whole people of Ireland and elected by the suffrages of all her men and women, the Provisional Government, hereby constituted, will administer the civil and military affairs of the Republic in trust for the people.

We place the cause of the Irish Republic under the protection of the Most High God, Whose blessing we invoke upon our arms, and we pray that no one who serves that cause will dishonour it by cowardice, inhumanity, or rapine. In this supreme hour the Irish nation must, by its valour and discipline and by the readiness of its children to sacrifice themselves for the common good, prove itself worthy of the august destiny to which it is called.

Signed on Behalf of the Provisional Government
THOMAS J. CLARKE,
SEAN MacDIARMADA,   THOMAS MacDONAGH,
P. H. PEARSE,   EAMONN CEANNT,
JAMES CONNOLLY,   JOSEPH PLUNKETT.

The Terms of Surrender, 1916

In order to prevent the further slaughter of Dublin citizens, and in the hope of saving the lives of our followers now surrounded and hopelessly outnumbered, the members of the Provisional Government present at Head Quarters have agreed to an unconditional surrender, and the Commandants of the various districts of the City and County will order their commands to lay down arms.

—P. H. Pearse
29 April 1916
3:45 P.M.

I agree to the conditions for the men only under my command in the Moore Street District, and for the men in Stephen's Green Command.

—Eamonn Ceannt
April 29/16

On consultation with Commandant Ceannt and other officers I have decided to agree to unconditional surrender also.

—Thomas MacDonagh

The Provisional IRA's first communique, issued by the Republican Publicity Bureau, Dublin, on 28 January 1970

Arising out of reports in a Dublin newspaper today, it has been found necessary to clarify the position of the Irish Republic Army.

In view of a decision by a majority of delegates at an unrepresentative convention of the Irish Republican Army to recognise the British, Six County and Twenty-Six County parliaments, we the minority of delegates at that convention, together with the delegates denied admission, and the representatives of the areas including Belfast which had already withdrawn allegiance from Army control, having reassembled in convention do hereby repudiate those compromising decisions and reaffirm the fundamental Republican position.

We declare our allegiance to the Thirty-Two County Irish Republic proclaimed at Easter 1916, established by the first Dail Eireann in 1919, overthrown by force of arms in 1922, and suppressed to this day by the British-imposed Six County and Twenty-Six County partitionist states.

Already a majority of Army units, individual volunteers and Republicans generally have given their allegiance to the Provisional Executive and Provisional Army Council elected by us at this convention, and have rejected the new compromising leadership, in the election of which we did not even participate.

The adoption of the compromising policy referred to is the logical outcome of an obsession in recent years with parliamentary politics, with the consequent undermining of the basic military role of the Irish Republican Army. The failure to provide the maximum defence possible of our people in Belfast and other parts of the Six Counties against the forces of British imperialism last August is ample evidence of this neglect.

We call upon the Irish people at home and in exile for increased support towards defending our people in the North and the eventual achievement of the full political, social, economic and cultural freedom of Ireland.

Bibliography

Bell, J. Bowyer. *The Secret Army.* London: Anthony Blond, 1970.

Bennet, Richard. *The Black and Tans.* London: Paperback Four Square, 1959.

Caulfield, Max. *The Easter Rebellion.* London: Frederick Muller, 1964.

Ellis, Peter Berresford. *Hell or Connaught.* London: Hamish Hamilton, 1975.

Faulkner, Brian. *Memoirs of a Statesman.* London: Weidenfeld and Nicolson, 1978.

MacStiofean, Sean. *Memoirs of a Revolutionary.* London: Gordon Cremonesi, 1975.

McGuire, Maria. *To Take Arms.* London: Macmillan, 1973.

Moss, Robert. *Urban Guerrillas.* London: Temple Smith, 1972.

Pollack, Sam. *Mutiny for the Cause.* London: Paper Back Sphere Books, 1969.

Stewart, A. T. Q. *The Ulster Crisis.* London: Faber Paperback, 1967.

Sunday Times Insight Team. *Ulster.* London: Penquin Special, 1972.

INDEX